THE
MARGARET RUDKIN
PEPPERIDGE FARM
COOKBOOK

THE
MARGARET RUDKIN
PEPPERIDGE FARM
COOKBOOK

ILLUSTRATIONS BY   *ERIK BLEGVAD*

Grosset & Dunlap
NEW YORK

TO HENRY

THE MOST PATIENT MAN IN THE WORLD

This book would never have been written without the encouragement and support during the past twenty-six years of the many wonderful people in the food business who have become my treasured good friends.

I also want to express my great appreciation and gratitude to the food editors of the newspapers and magazines who, by their constant, intelligent work with new foods and new cooking methods, have brought American cooking up to a high level of interest and variety.

To many others too numerous to list here, I am indebted for unfailing interest and encouragement.

Margaret Rudkin

FOREWORD

WHY, OH, WHY did I ever think I could write a book!

That's what I've been saying to myself for a long time.

It was always easy enough for me to talk about food and recipes and all the fun and excitement I've had in my life—especially in the past twenty-five years, with the development of the Pepperidge Farm Company.

When so many of my misguided friends kept saying "Just write it all in a book," it seemed easy enough to do, but alas! —I have learned the difference between talking and writing.

Once started, of course, I had to finish. I became nervously aware of a word in publishers' language—deadline!—and it hung over me like the sword of Damocles.

Time for the book had to be sandwiched in among my regular business hours at Pepperidge Farm, running two houses three thousand miles apart (one in Connecticut and one in Ireland), long business trips here and trips abroad.

The effort of trying to get the thing done on time changed me into a growling, snappy, unapproachable creature, and occasionally, in desperation, I locked myself in a room to get away from interruptions. Dozens of times I heard my patient husband ask plaintively "What are you doing now?" and the short answer was "Writing that book!"

When it came to testing the recipes in the chapter about the antique cookbooks, I couldn't stretch the hours in each day long enough. That's when my dear friend June Platt came to the rescue, and when I modernized those ancient mixed-up recipes into something usable for today, she was the willing victim for the cooking and tasting experiments.

She trudged with undaunted cheerfulness to out-of-the-way shops to find strange ingredients, and she and her hus-

band ate each adventurous new dish with courage and forti-
tude before I tasted the finished product.

Some of those dishes had to be cooked and eaten more than
once as we changed the recipes to suit contemporary taste
and methods of cooking.

Sometimes I arrived at her apartment for a tasting session
to hear her say, "Oh, we just love this one and we've been
tasting and tasting, but there's still a little bit left for you!"
and I had to make do with a tiny tantalizing morsel.

Well, now the book is finished with the hope that the tale
of some of my experiences with food and cooking will give
pleasure to the reader.

Some of these recipes are amusing, some elaborate and
some just plain and easy. That's a good pattern for eating
and living—something for fun, something super for special
times and something plain for the quiet days with just the
family to say "Golly, that's a good egg!" and you sort of feel
they mean you're a "good egg" too.

Few things are more rewarding to a woman than that
happy feeling she has when she knows that the food she has
prepared with love and interest brings pleasure to her family,
served in a setting more important than any glamorous restaurant—dinner at home!

CONTENTS

PART ONE

CHILDHOOD

WHEN I was a child, I lived in a brownstone private house on a quiet street, paved with cobblestones, in the section of New York now known as Tudor City, high above the present United Nations Plaza.

The old narrow house was four stories high, with a stoop —an outside stairway of stone steps—leading up to the big front door. That word *stoop* is left over from the early Dutch settlement in New York and originally meant a platform with steps at the door of a house.

The wide stone steps were used by children for playing games, and on hot summer evenings we were allowed to sit there until dark, cooling off by eating enormous ice-cream cones, which cost five cents. If we didn't have a nickel, we sucked on a piece of ice dipped in sugar. We waited for the lamplighter to come by with his long lighting stick and, with a quick touch of the flaming tip, light up the gas mantle on the lamppost at the corner.

Sometimes at dusk the gypsies came, too, in the summertime, to tell our fortunes, mend the pots and pans and scamper off with anything lying around loose.

[*3*]

Years later a part of old New York disappeared when all those private houses were torn down to make way for big apartment buildings. All the houses in the block were exactly alike. At the front of each basement was the dining room, with the kitchen behind it, opening onto a small yard. Upstairs on the parlor floor, where you entered from the big door at the top of the stoop, were the "front parlor" best room and the "back parlor" everyday room. The bedrooms were on the third and fourth floors.

But the large, brick-floored kitchen was really the heart of the house. There was an enormous coal stove set back into the chimney wall, with a six-foot hearthstone in front of it. The gray stone laundry tubs stood along the opposite wall, and on laundry days not much cooking was done because the copper clothes boiler was steaming on the stove all day, with the laundress trotting back and forth from the tubs to the boiler, fishing the boiled laundry out of the bubbling water with a long "clothes stick" which had become soft and soggy from the constant hot-water dips. Woe betide anyone who got in her way!

I always wanted to eat lunch in the kitchen on laundry day, for it was sure to be cold boiled ham, soft, floury boiled potatoes and a mug of milk. I ate very slowly because I loved to sniff the spicy, soapy, steamy air, which I was told "cleared out your tubes." More important, the steam made my red hair curly, and I thought that improved my looks.

Our cooking was always simple and delicious—no fancy stuff and sauces for us. We lived with my grandmother, and with love, happiness and pride—and the help of one devoted old housekeeper—she took care of her large family. Born in Ireland, she had come to the United States as a young bride in a very small ship when passengers usually brought extra food with them. She had been supplied by her mother with a good, nourishing blood pudding—but she never ate blood pudding again!

Her cooking was flavored with memories of her old home. It was said that her grandmother had raised the finest beef cattle in County Cork and was the only woman in Ireland who could skin a calf! My grandmother must have inherited something from hers, for she was particularly fussy about the quality of the meat she bought and had intricate discussions with the butcher about the proper way to cut a steak or roast of beef.

She preferred to do her own marketing, but occasionally she decided that I could do with a bit of training and let me go to the store for her.

I solemnly presented myself to the grocer to recite my order—"a shilling's worth of eggs [a dozen and a half eggs for 25 cents], a loaf of sugar [a 3½-pound solid cone of sugar wrapped in blue paper], rashers of bacon, a dip of milk [milk was sold from an open barrel and was dipped out into your own milk pail], a cake of 'east and a tin of treacle." A bit of the old country always lingered on in our household.

As a reward for doing the errand, I was allowed to fish out, with a sharp pointed stick, a big dill pickle from the wooden barrel in the back of the store.

My grandmother used to corn her own beef and also corned leg of lamb, which she served with a mustard sauce and mashed yellow turnips.

Her corned beef and cabbage and plain boiled potatoes made a divine dish—melting corned beef, simmered for hours with spices and herbs, and the potatoes cooked soft in madly boiling water, drained thoroughly, and then shaken in the pan over the heat until the "taters opened up and smiled at you." They were always snow white and floury, never damp and soggy.

My grandfather often did a bit of shopping on his way home, and when he stopped at the slaughterhouse on First Avenue where the United Nations Building now stands, he would bring home a treat—"the liver and the lights." That meant calves were being killed that day and he had bought a fresh calf's liver and sweetbreads. Sometimes he brought home tender little lambs' tongues, which were pickled and served with an egg sauce.

The calf's liver was left whole, larded with thin strips of salt pork, sprinkled with herbs and spices, covered with

strips of bacon and roasted, being basted often with the bacon fat and plenty of melted butter. It was heavenly served
hot with a purée of dried peas, or served cold next day with
rye bread and mustard pickles.

If you were sick in our house, you went straight to bed
with a "physic," and then came a cup of delicious beef tea
with buttered toast. The beef tea was made from top round
of beef cut into tiny cubes and was really a rich consommé.
The cooked cubes of meat came right along with the beef
tea.

Another invalid's drink was called fluffin—a handful of
oatmeal or barley boiled in a quart of milk and flavored with
nutmeg and sugar. If you were quite sick, you got a dash of
the "real thing" in it, too—the best brandy was taken out of
its hiding place for the occasion.

Soup was a great favorite in our house, for we were a
large family of children, and soup and bread and butter
could be counted on to fill us up. Most often it was the good
old stand-by, beef and vegetable soup. My mother always
hummed the recipe like a little tuneless song when she made
it or else she would forget to put something in:

> *A shin of beef and bones,*
> *Pepper, salt, and onions,*
> *Carrots and celery,*
> *Bay leaf and parsley,*
> *Leeks and potatoes,*
> *A can of tomatoes,*
> *And a handful of oatmeal to stick to your ribs.*

How much of each thing? That's simple: just enough. If
times were good, there was lots of everything and not too
much water. If times were bad, there was lots of water and
less of everything else, but it was always delicious.

The meaty shin of beef, with extra veal knuckle and marrow bones, was the main item. All the vegetables were cut up
in small pieces, and the good handful of oatmeal flakes thickened up the soup a bit. Long, slow cooking for about four
hours, and then big soup plates full of golden, fragrant liq-

uid with slices of the tender boiled beef and all the vegetables served with it. It was eating and drinking too, we were
always told.

When one of us had a birthday or deserved a reward for
good behavior, we were allowed to choose some favorite dish,
and mine was always "some of Grandma's soup."

When I was ten years old, I learned both to sew and cook.
My grandmother said no one could cook without wearing an
apron, so before I learned to cook I had to make my own
aprons. All dolled up in my frilly, starched white apron, I
started with baking-powder biscuits and then learned to
make cream sauce without any lumps. Next came chocolate
layer cake. The ten-year-old red-haired freckle-faced plump
little girl was all eyes and ears at these lessons, and the
chocolate cake was important, for it was her favorite dessert.

It was a two-egg yellow cake baked in two layers. I was
taught how to separate the eggs and beat the yellows till
really thick, not halfway, and beat the whites just right—
careful, not too dry. Then, when the flour went in, no more
beating, just careful folding. The two layers were cooled
after baking and each was split so there would be more room
for the soft, creamy chocolate filling—a sort of Irish Dobos
torte.

Now my repertoire was complete from soup to dessert,
and I looked forward to rainy days when I could wheedle my
way into the kitchen because I couldn't go outdoors to play.
On would come supper all done by me, but inevitably it was
my sole menu:

> *soup*
> *baking-powder biscuits and*
> *chocolate layer cake to end up with*

Turkey time at Thanksgiving was a great treat—not because of the turkey, to my mind, but for the stuffing. I was so
crazy about the stuffing that after the turkey was stuffed to
bursting, an extra portion was wrapped loosely in a square
of cheesecloth and tucked into the pan alongside the turkey.
The rich turkey fat sizzled round my little bundle, and when

the cheesecloth was opened up, there was a crisp golden ball with a soft, spicy, fragrant center, all for me.

Toast made over hot coals was something special. Orders were given by me every winter morning when I left for school: "Don't put any coal on the fire till after I get home" because after school the warm, happy kitchen meant homework at the kitchen table and "a bit of food to keep up a poor child's strength for study"—cups of sweet, milky tea and hot toast made over the glowing coals. I took the stove lid off and carefully inspected the fire. It mustn't have any little bluish licks of gassy flame, and the red embers had to

be just right. Out came the long toasting fork, the thick slice of bread was speared on carefully and held over the hot coals just high enough so as not to burn my fingers or the toast. Then, when the toast was golden brown, I spread it generously with sweet butter and back over the coals it went for just the right few seconds while I watched the golden liquid bubble and froth. Oh, perfection! No electric toaster can match it.

The Christmas dish was always a roast goose, and Grandma had to make several visits to the butcher to be sure we were getting a fine, plump, young "green goose." That meant this year's goose, not last year's—and no trying to put one over on Grandma. She knew what the young ones looked like: soft yellow feet and a soft yellow beak. She tweaked and pinched a dozen beaks before she decided which goose she wanted.

The goose was stuffed with a special potato stuffing— creamy mashed potatoes full of chopped onions which had been simmered in butter, dried bread crumbs, two beaten eggs and lots of sage and thyme, salt and pepper and the cooked giblets, chopped very fine.

The roasting was done in the hot oven of the coal stove. All the drafts were opened up and the oven was tested with a piece of white paper; the exact minutes necessary to brown

the paper were carefully computed. Who needed an oven thermometer? The roasting was carefully watched, for the goose fat had to be spooned off several times as it cooked out. It mustn't be allowed to burn, for it was kept to be mixed with camphorated oil and rubbed on chests when we had coughing colds.

To go with the goose, red apples were cored but not peeled. Cut into thick slices, they were fried in butter and sprinkled with sugar.

Mashed turnips, which I hated, and cabbage went with the goose, and dessert was plum pudding. The goose was served on a special large platter which was called an ashet— a word still used in Ireland for a large platter. It must come from the French word for a plate, *assiette*.

We never had anything out of season, so when things

were in season we enjoyed them every day, and it seems to me they were sweeter, more tender, more luscious and surely more appreciated than the all-year-round foods we have today. We looked forward to our seasonal treats and listened for the peculiar street cries of the sellers.

The fruit carts, gay with bright paint and flags and banners, and ringing bells or blowing whistles, came to the houses, and we knew the Rhubarb Man would come in the spring, the Strawberry Man in June and the Grape Man in September. Then what a doing there was!

In the spring we were dosed with rhubarb, sulfur and molasses, good for the blood! In June we had the Strawberry Festival; in September we had the Grape Cure for our "insides," as it was delicately explained.

We waited for the Peach Man and the Banana Man, who sold you a "hand" of bananas. In the summer the Pineapple Man came around and cut ripe, juicy pineapples into long, thin strips. The Watermelon Man would sell a big slab of juicy melon for a couple of pennies. Oranges appeared only at Christmastime in our stockings. Even today when I peel an orange on the Fourth of July, I think of Santa Claus and Christmas trees.

Another itinerant friend was the Coconut Man, who had pieces of fresh coconut for sale—hard on the teeth of a young one, but deliciously sweet and chewy, and a penny piece lasted quite a while. I seldom eat candy, but about twice a year I go on a coconut binge. Coconut bonbons and coconut kisses are my downfall.

The Strawberry Festival was put on to raise money for the Ladies' Aid Society. Everybody we knew bought tickets —twenty-five cents for children and fifty cents for grownups and you had a feast of all you could eat.

The menu was

> *fresh strawberries and cream*
> *strawberry short cake*
> *strawberry pie*
> *strawberry ice cream*
> *strawberry soup*

The "soup" was just crushed berries and sugar and water, served in a cup, and I didn't think much of it! I suspect now that the grownups had a touch of something extra in theirs because their cups seemed to be refilled pretty often.

Not until the summer of 1961, when I was in Vienna, did I ever see strawberry soup again. At the Imperial Hotel there, I found "Strawberry Soup" on the menu. It was served as a first course, icy cold, and the crushed berries and sugar had been mixed with white wine slightly thickened with fine tapioca and flavored with a spot of something else (maybe brandy—I couldn't find out), and that's why I suspect the Ladies' Aid strawberry soup for the grownups was spiked. The Viennese version, incidentally, was wonderful!

I remember May parties in Central Park on the first day of May. All the girls wore gay colored crepe-paper dresses and danced around the Maypoles, winding ribbons around the poles and each other. Somebody supplied a big picnic lunch, but not for me. I was very fussy and didn't like anything not made at home. So I carried my lunch and, no matter how many May parties and outings I went to, my lunch was always the same—ham sandwiches on thickly buttered white bread, crusts cut off, no mustard; one pear, apple or banana; one cupcake with white icing; and lemonade in a bottle, usually with a slightly leaky cork. All in a cardboard shoebox—but tied with ribbon, not string! It was a Plain Jane kind of lunch—no fancy aluminum lunchbox or Thermos bottle to be cleaned. I ate the sandwiches, drank the lemonade and threw away the bottle, threw away the shoebox (but saved the ribbon!) and didn't have to worry about carrying things home. Very practical indeed.

In the kitchen alongside the coal range we had a gas stove for summer cooking. But very often in summer when it was too hot to cook or eat much, we would have just one wonderful dish for supper.

Strawberry shortcake in a deep soup plate with a warm, crisp biscuit base, crushed sugar and berries ladled generously onto the biscuit and thick yellow cream poured on. No foolish business about whipping the cream! In those days we had to do that with a flat hand beater and it took too much elbow grease, so we just poured on the cream as it came.

Blueberries with cinnamon toast were good. White bread was toasted, lavishly buttered and sprinkled with cinnamon sugar and put in a deep dish. Half the blueberries were crushed and mixed with sugar and poured over the toast, and the rest were left whole and put on top; then another sprinkling of cinnamon sugar and heavy thick cream was poured on.

Raspberries were made into flummery—a very soft rice pudding with stewed raspberries and cream. Flummery was made with all kinds of fruit.

With these summer dishes we drank milk or cold tea, and sometimes we drank ice-cold buttermilk with tiny golden flakes of butter floating in it.

We never had very fancy rich desserts. Mostly we ate fruit—sliced bananas sprinkled with lemon juice and brown sugar, prunes and apricots cooked together, applesauce, rhubarb stewed, berries of all kinds, melons, apples, pears and peaches.

In winter we had fruits that had been put up in jars during the summer.

Cakes were rather plain, but pound cake was a specialty.

This pound cake was the real thing, made of only four ingredients—a pound of butter whipped to a light cream; a pound of fine sugar added and whipped with the butter to frothy lightness; a pound of eggs, yolks beat up first and put into the butter and sugar; then a pound of flour gently sifted in. Egg whites, beaten till stiff, were folded in last, and a few drops of brandy or whisky gave flavor to the cake.

We always had a light supper the day the pound cake was made because the cook spent all afternoon whipping the batter by hand in a large yellow bowl which could eventually be scraped by a patiently waiting child.

The oven had to be loaded several times, for a dozen cakes would be made on these occasions. Wrapped in brandy-soaked clean linen napkins, they kept well for several weeks.

The cakes had no leavening but the egg whites and the air beaten in, but they rose up into golden mounds and split open in the middle just enough to give a soft uneven surface —not like today's machine-made, flat, dark brown, square-top cake.

My grandmother had a cousin who was full of airs and graces and fancied herself as a singer. The pound cake was always on hand for her visits, and the two Victorian ladies and I would sit on the spindly gilt chairs in the front parlor, drinking endless cups of tea and enjoying the pound cake. The cousin would finally compliment the hostess on the superb cake, and only then would the hostess ask the guest to sing.

She would seat herself at the old square piano and, in a lovely contralto voice, sing Irish songs. They were always sad songs, about Kathleen Mavourneen, Mother Machree and a girl named Macushla, all of whom were pining away with broken hearts, and I would sit on my gilded chair, crying my eyes out for the lost loves of Irish lads and lassies. Because I felt so badly for the sorrows of Ireland, I would be given an extra piece of cake.

My other memory of pound cake is connected with September 3, 1939. Hitler had invaded Poland two days before. Always, when I am distressed, I have to keep very busy with my hands, and on that Sunday, upset by war news, I decided to mix a batch of pound cake. I was in the midst of it when the children ran into the kitchen to tell me there was special news on the radio, so I took my mixing bowl into the living room and continued to cream the butter and sugar while listening to the voice of the Prime Minister, Neville Chamberlain, declaring that England was at war with Germany.

Another favorite was what I called my "bread cake." A thick slice of crusty fresh bread was extravagantly buttered and spread thick with vanilla sugar. That solid cone of loaf sugar always had to be grated, and that was my job. Some was kept in a special glass with a vanilla bean, to be used just for cakes.

[*13*]

Hot gingerbread eaten with a dish of applesauce was good. The next day the leftover gingerbread was covered with a vanilla icing.

On Sundays or birthdays we had layer cakes with fancy fillings and frostings.

Milk puddings were not great favorites of mine. I always said they were too white! Rice puddings, junkets, cornstarch puddings, custards appeared in the winter.

We seldom had pies because my grandmother said she had "a heavy hand and foot for pastry."

Breakfasts were simple but filling. A good start means a good day. We never had fruit or fruit juice in the morning, but started right in on good stirabout, which was oatmeal porridge with a bit of butter melting on the hot surface and plenty of brown sugar and half cream, half milk—or cornmeal mush, or fried eggs and rashers (bacon), or pancakes and sausage cakes. Bread and butter, and jam on the side. Milk to drink in summer and weak tea in winter, but never coffee for the children. For that we had to sneak a taste from some indulgent aunt or uncle.

We never ate such a thing as a raw vegetable except sliced tomatoes—good heavens, no! You would have been considered "quite singular" if you did any such crazy thing.

I never saw a cookbook in our house, and I never saw my grandmother or my mother write anything down. So my family recipes come "out of my head"—just memories of how things tasted and looked, and that's the way I've cooked these favorites of ours all these years.

MEATS
&
OTHER
FIRST CLASS
PRODUCTS

BEEF AND VEGETABLE SOUP

(Serves 6—8)

5- to 6-pound shin of beef
large veal knuckle
marrow bones

Cover the beef and bones with 5 quarts cold water and add:

1 tablespoon salt
fresh ground pepper to taste
2 large onions, sliced
2 large carrots, sliced
2 stalks celery, leaves and all, sliced
1 bay leaf
handful of parsley, chopped
4 leeks, tops and all, sliced
2 large potatoes, sliced
1 no. 2 can tomatoes
handful of uncooked rolled oats

Bring to a boil and simmer for 4 hours.

This soup is delicious the first day and improves as it stands in the refrigerator. Always reheat all of it each time and it will keep well for 4 or 5 days.

Be sure to slice the boiled beef and put a piece in each soup plate.

COCKY LEEKY SOUP

(Serves 6)

1 boiling chicken
4 leeks, sliced
2 tablespoons chopped parsley
1 teaspoon salt
½ cup long-grain rice
2 tablespoons butter ⎫ creamed together
2 tablespoons flour ⎭
12 pitted cooked prunes

Clean the chicken and cut in pieces.

Put in a saucepan with boiling water to cover.

Add the sliced leeks, salt and chopped parsley.

Simmer about 2½ hours until the chicken is tender.

Remove the chicken from the soup.

Add the rice to the soup and cook about 20 minutes until the rice is very soft.

Thicken the soup with the flour and butter which have been creamed together.

Just before serving, add the pitted cooked prunes, cut into halves, and a few slices of the white meat of the chicken, cut into small pieces.

Use the rest of the cooked chicken for chicken salad.

OATMEAL SOUP

(Serves 4)

½ cup rolled oats
1 quart chicken broth
1 large sliced onion
1 bay leaf
salt and pepper
1 cup medium cream or milk

Put together everything except the cream or milk and simmer for at least 1 hour.

Pass the soup through a strainer, return to the heat and bring once more to a boil.

Remove from the heat and add the cup of cream or milk.

Serve very hot.

GREEN SOUP

(Serves 4)

pea pods from 2 pounds fresh peas
2 quarts boiling water
1 teaspoon salt
pepper to taste
1 small white onion, sliced
1 carrot, sliced
1 stalk celery, cut into small pieces
4 tablespoons butter
4 tablespoons flour

Wash the pea pods and place in a large enamel pan.

Add the salt, the other vegetables, and cover with the boiling water.

Cook until tender, or for about 1 hour.

Strain and save the water.

Rub the pods through a sieve, using a wooden spoon or potato masher, moistening with some of the water as needed. Discard what won't go through.

Add the remainder of the water, which should give you about 4 cups of clouded green broth.

Add pepper to taste and bring to the boiling point.

In the meantime melt the butter over low heat, stir in the flour, cook for 1 or 2 minutes without browning, then add gradually the hot broth.

Cook for 1 or 2 minutes and keep hot over boiling water until ready to serve.

SCOTCH BROTH

(Serves 6)

2 pounds mutton, neck or shoulder
1 onion
2 leeks
1 large carrot
parsley
handful of barley
2 large potatoes, cut into small pieces

Cut the meat into small pieces.

Cover with about 2 quarts hot water.

Add the seasonings and the vegetables, cut into small pieces, and the barley.

Cover and simmer for 2 hours.

Add salt and pepper to taste and serve very hot.

BEEF TEA

(Makes 2 cups)

1 pound top round steak
2 cups cold water
salt

Cut the meat into small pieces, about ½-inch cubes, and let stand in the cold water for 2 hours.

Then bring to a boil, cut the heat down to very low and just barely simmer for 2 hours.

Season to taste with salt.

Serve in a cup with the bits of meat.

ANOTHER WAY TO MAKE BEEF TEA

1 pound top round steak
2 cups cold water
salt

Cut the meat into small pieces, about ½-inch cubes.

Put the meat into a quart glass jar with a screw top.

Add the water.

Cover the jar and place on a rack in a pan of cold water with enough water to come above the quantity in the jar.

Bring the water in the pan up to simmering temperature and simmer for 2 hours.

Season to taste with salt.

TOMATO SOUP

(Serves 6)

2 cups canned tomatoes
4 cups milk
4 tablespoons butter

pepper
salt
1 teaspoon sugar

Put the tomatoes in a saucepan and chop them up into small pieces.

Add the butter, sugar, pepper and salt and bring to a boil.

Boil for about 5 minutes, then add the milk and bring again to a boil.

Serve as is, without straining.

STRAWBERRY SOUP

(Serves 6–8)

2 quarts ripe strawberries
juice of 1 lemon
3 cups water
1 cup sugar
2 tablespoons minute tapioca
1 cup sweet white wine

Clean and crush the strawberries.
Add the lemon juice.
Cover with water.
Add the sugar.
Add the tapioca.
Boil gently for 15 minutes.
Remove from heat and add the sweet white wine.
Chill thoroughly and serve very cold as a first course.

FRIED FISH IN BATTER

(Serves 3)

1 pound fillets of flounder
2 tablespoons oil (olive or corn oil)
1 tablespoon white wine
1 tablespoon lemon juice
1 small onion, sliced thin
salt
pepper

For the batter

1 cup flour
1 cup milk
1 beaten egg
salt
pepper

Cut the fish into serving pieces and lay in a flat dish.

Mix the oil, wine, lemon juice, salt and pepper.

Pour over the fish.

Lay the slices of onion on top of the fish.

Let soak for 1 hour.

Remove the fish and drain on a paper towel.

Make a batter of the flour, milk, egg, salt and pepper.

Dip the pieces of fish into the batter and cover all sides of each piece.

Fry in hot fat and drain on paper before serving.

Serve with Tartar Sauce (below).

TARTAR SAUCE

Mix 1 cup mayonnaise with ¼ cup chopped sweet pickle relish, or ¼ cup chopped dill pickles.

Serve with fish, hot or cold.

ELECTRIC BLENDER MAYONNAISE

(Serves 6–8)

2 whole eggs
2 tablespoons cider vinegar
½ teaspoon dried mustard
1 teaspoon salt
¼ teaspoon white pepper
¼ teaspoon cayenne
2 cups olive oil
1 tablespoon strained lemon juice

In the glass container of an electric blender place the eggs, cider vinegar, mustard, salt, pepper and cayenne.

Cover the container and run the motor at low speed while you count 5.

[20]

Remove the cover and continue blending at low speed while you add gradually the olive oil.

Continue blending while you count 5.

Turn off the motor and transfer the mayonnaise to a small bowl.

Stir in gradually the lemon juice, and the mayonnaise is ready to serve.

SCALLOPED FISH
(Serves 4)

Preheat oven to 400° F.

> *1 pound flaked cooked fish (cod, haddock, salmon)*
> *1½ cups thick cream sauce*
> *¼ cup grated Parmesan cheese*

Butter scallop shells and fill with the flaked fish.
Cover each scallop with Cream Sauce (p. 34).
Sprinkle with Parmesan cheese.
Bake for 20 minutes at 400° F. until browned on surface.

GRILLED OR BROILED SALMON

> *salmon steaks ½ inch thick*
> *Hollandaise sauce*
> *butter*
> *salt*
> *pepper*

Wipe and dry the salmon steaks.
Place on a flat pan with a pat of butter on each one.
Sprinkle with salt and pepper.
Broil for 5 minutes.
Turn carefully with a flat pancake turner and broil on the other side 5 minutes, placing a piece of butter on the second side when you turn it up.
Serve with Hollandaise Sauce (p. 406).

SALMON PIE

(Serves 4)

Preheat oven to 350° F.

Make a single pie-crust shell of Plain Pastry (p. 153) and place in the refrigerator to chill while preparing the filling.

Beat together 2 eggs and 1 cup milk and add 1 cup canned or cooked salmon which has been separated into pieces with a fork and all bones removed.

Pour into the pastry shell and bake in a moderate oven (350° F.) for about ½ hour.

CORNED BEEF

(Serves 6–8)

The best cut of corned beef is brisket, as there is a mixture of fat and lean. Rump has no fat, and I find it too dry.

> *5- to 6-pound piece of brisket of beef*
> *celery leaves*
> *1 large onion, sliced*
> *6 whole peppercorns*
> *6 whole allspice berries*
> *1 parsnip*

Wash the meat.

Cover with cold water.

Add all the seasonings and sliced onion.

Bring just to simmer—*do not boil!*

Simmer 4 to 5 hours.

Remove from the water and cut in thin slices.

Serve with boiled cabbage and boiled (dry) potatoes.

Use a hot Mustard Sauce with this (p. 150).

FRESH LAMBS' TONGUES WITH CAPER SAUCE

(Serves 4)

4 lambs' tongues
2 tablespoons butter
2 tablespoons flour
4 cups chicken broth
1 teaspoon vinegar
1 tablespoon capers

Soak the tongues in cold salted water for 1 hour.

Drain, cover with cold water, bring to a boil and drain again.

Put the tongues in a saucepan with enough chicken broth to cover them.

Bring to a boil, skim and simmer for 2 hours.

When tender, remove from the broth, cut off the root ends and remove the skin.

Cut into lengthwise slices.

Measure the remaining broth, and, for each cup, cream together 2 tablespoons flour with 2 tablespoons butter.

Add to the hot broth and stir over a low flame until thickened.

Add the vinegar and capers, pour over the tongue and serve.

PICKLED LAMBS' TONGUES

(Serves 4–5)

1 9-ounce jar pickled lambs' tongues
1 cup mayonnaise
1 cup sour cream
1 large white onion, chopped fine
1 hard-boiled egg, chopped fine

Remove the tongues from the jar and freshen them by running cold water over them for a few minutes.

Dry well.

To 1 cup mayonnaise, add the sour cream, the onion and the hard-boiled egg.

Place the tongues on lettuce leaves and cover with the sauce.

BOILED LEG OF MUTTON OR LAMB
WITH CAPER SAUCE

(Serves 6)

1 leg of mutton or lamb (about 6 pounds)
salt
pepper
1 onion
1 stalk celery
½ teaspoon thyme
8 peppercorns
6 tablespoons butter
6 tablespoons flour
3 tablespoons capers

Cover the meat with boiling water, bring to a boil again and skim. Add vegetables and seasonings, except capers. Cover pot tightly.

Simmer for 3 to 3½ hours.

When the meat is tender, make the sauce:

In the top of a double boiler over direct heat melt the butter.

Add the flour and cook together for 3 minutes.

Remove the pan from the heat and add gradually 3 cups of the strained broth from the boiled mutton, stirring constantly.

Return to the heat, bring to a boil and cook until thickened, about 3 minutes, stirring constantly.

Add the capers with a teaspoon of the caper liquid.

Place over hot water in the bottom of a double boiler and keep hot.

Serve with boiled potatoes.

Onion Sauce (below) is also delectable with Boiled Mutton or Lamb.

ONION SAUCE (for Boiled Leg of Lamb)

6 small white onions
1 cup milk
2 tablespoons flour
2 tablespoons butter
¼ cup cream
pepper and salt to taste

Clean and skin the onions, cover with cold water, bring to a boil for 2 minutes.

Strain the water off and cover again with boiling water.

Add salt and simmer until tender.

Drain and chop fine.

In a double boiler make a cream sauce of the butter, flour and milk.

Add the chopped onions and the cream.

Serve very hot.

BOILED HAM

Modern commercial hams do not need to be soaked; they are advertised as "tenderized." Smoked country hams, if they can be found anywhere today, need to be soaked overnight in cold water.

A ham should be well scrubbed with a brush, placed in a large pot and covered with hot water (180° F.) so that the ham is just covered. The water should not boil; it should only simmer during all the cooking.

Allow 25 minutes per pound for a ham up to 10 pounds and 20 minutes per pound for a ham from 10 to 15 pounds.

Boiled ham should always be cooled in the water in which it has been cooked; then remove it from the water and take off the outer skin.

One cup brown sugar may be added to the water in which the ham is cooked, or 2 cups cider.

You may also add to the water a sliced onion, some celery leaves, some whole cloves, a teaspoon of whole allspice.

BAKED HAM

If you wish to bake a ham after boiling it, the process for boiling is just the same. After you have removed the outer skin of the cooked ham, cover the fat surface with a mixture of:

> *1 cup brown sugar*
> *½ cup fine cracker crumbs flavored with*
> *1 teaspoon ground cloves*

Bake for 1 hour in a slow oven (300° F.).

RAISIN SAUCE FOR HAM

½ cup sugar
1 teaspoon dry mustard
¼ cup seedless raisins
1 cup red wine
1 cup water

Mix all ingredients and cook together for 20 minutes.

A glass of currant jelly added to this sauce makes a very pleasant addition to the flavor.

OXTAIL STEW

(Serves 6)

2 large oxtails
1 onion
2 cups beef broth
2 cups water
2 cups canned tomatoes
1 teaspoon salt
pepper, freshly ground
1 bay leaf
¼ cup chopped carrots
¼ cup chopped celery
1 tablespoon chopped parsley
6 potatoes boiled separately

Have the butcher cut the oxtails in pieces.

Roll them in flour and brown well in butter or shortening.

Brown the onion at the same time.

Add the beef broth and water, tomatoes and bay leaf, salt and pepper.

Simmer for 4 hours.

At the end of 3 hours add the carrots, celery and parsley.

Boil potatoes separately, drain and shake over heat until dried out.

Thicken the gravy with flour and butter, and serve all together.

[26]

LEFTOVER LOAF

Preheat oven to 350° F.

Line a well-buttered bread pan, bottom and sides, with an inch of well-seasoned mashed potatoes.

Chop together any leftover cooked vegetables and meat plus a cooked sausage or two, add some chopped onion, salt and pepper, mix together with a beaten egg and a little gravy, and fill the loaf pan.

Put mashed potatoes on top and bake in a 350° F. oven until brown.

The loaf should slip out of the pan easily if you have used enough butter.

ROAST TURKEY

Our preference was a large hen turkey, but a large young tom turkey was better when the whole family came for Thanksgiving.

Weigh the cleaned bird before stuffing it. Figure the cooking time from the table below and allow about 15 minutes to make the gravy after the turkey is done.

Wash the turkey well inside and out with cold water, dry thoroughly, rub inside with salt.

Have your stuffing ready and fill the cavities lightly. Never pack in the stuffing, as it needs room to swell a bit.

We used to sew up the bird with a big darning needle and heavy linen thread, but nowadays I use a few skewers thrust from one side of the opening to the other and crisscross thin string across the ends of the skewers. Then it is easy to pull off the string and skewers after roasting.

Tie up the legs close to the sides.

Cover the bird generously all over with soft butter, then sprinkle the butter with salt and pepper.

Place in the roasting pan breast up (no need to turn it).

The old way of roasting poultry was to start with a very hot oven and after ½ hour reduce the heat to moderate. Today's method of using a low heat all the way through seems better to me. There is more moistness to the meat and less shrinkage. Use a 300° F. oven.

[27]

Put ¼ pound butter in the pan and baste occasionally with the butter and the drippings from the bird.

When done, remove from pan to a platter and remove the skewers and string.

Keep warm.

Make gravy from the pan drippings.

Time Table for Roasting Turkey

WEIGHT (WHEN READY TO STUFF)	OVEN TEMPERATURE	TIME PER POUND
10 to 12 pounds	*300° F.*	*20 minutes*
12 to 16 pounds	*300° F.*	*18 minutes*
16 and over	*300° F.*	*17 minutes*

TURKEY GRAVY

While the turkey is cooking, cover the giblets, wing tips and neck bone with 2 quarts cold water, add 1 onion, celery and parsley and simmer for 2 hours.

Strain the broth and put aside for the gravy.

When the turkey is cooked, remove it from the pan and pour off all the fat into a small bowl. In a few minutes the fat will rise to the top and the brown drippings will settle in the bowl.

Place the roasting pan on a surface burner of your stove.

Spoon off the fat carefully from the bowl and place it in the roasting pan.

To each tablespoon of fat, add 1 tablespoon flour.

Cook the flour and fat together until well browned.

Then add the brown drippings in the bowl to the flour and fat and cook for 1 minute more.

Then add 1 cup broth for each tablespoon of fat used in the base mixture. If there is not enough broth, add canned chicken broth or water.

Add salt, pepper and a good pinch of oregano to taste.

Boil up again for 5 minutes and strain.

TURKEY GIBLET GRAVY

When you remove the cooked giblets from the broth, pick off all the meat from the neck and wing tips, put all the giblets and meat in a chopping bowl and chop fine.

Add this to the finished gravy and boil for a few minutes.

BREAD STUFFING

Making stuffing when I was a child was quite a performance. We liked a dry, crumbly, buttery stuffing, not a wet, soggy one.

Three or four days ahead, white bread was set aside to dry out.

When the big day came, the kitchen table was cleaned, a bowl of cool water was placed on one side, a large empty bowl on the other side, and in the middle were thick slices of dry bread with the crusts removed.

Each slice was dipped into the water and then squeezed out thoroughly.

Why it had to be dried out for days and then wet again was a mystery, but whoever figured it out was mighty smart because the moisture was just right.

The moist slices were crumbed by rubbing between the hands, and then salt, pepper, sage, thyme and finely chopped white onions were added and well tossed together.

Melted butter was poured on and everything tossed together lightly with a fork.

My grandmother didn't use any measuring spoon for the spices—she gauged the amounts by tasting and sniffing. But here is a good guess at the amounts used.

To a 1-pound loaf of bread use:

> *1 white onion, chopped fine*
> *1 teaspoon salt*
> *freshly ground pepper*
> *½ teaspoon sage*
> *½ teaspoon thyme*
> *¼ pound butter, melted*

Taste and sniff as you go, because you might like more sage or thyme.

SAGE AND ONION STUFFING

> *1 large white onion*
> *½ teaspoon powdered sage*
> *2 cups soft bread crumbs*
> *4 tablespoons melted butter*
> *salt and pepper to taste*

Chop the onion very fine.
Mix with the bread crumbs.
Add the powdered sage, salt and pepper, and mix well.
Add the melted butter and toss well with a fork.

POTATO STUFFING

2 cups mashed potatoes
2 cups soft bread crumbs
4 tablespoons butter, melted
1 teaspoon salt
½ teaspoon sage
½ teaspoon thyme
1 onion, chopped fine
2 beaten eggs

Mix the bread crumbs with the seasonings, beaten eggs and butter.

Add then the potatoes.

Taste and sniff as you go, adding more sage and thyme if desired.

Add the cooked chopped giblets if you like.

TURKEY LOAF

Preheat oven to 350° F.

leftover turkey
onion
salt and pepper
gravy
leftover stuffing
eggs

Remove the meat from the bones and put through the coarse blade of the grinder together with the onion.

Season to taste with salt and pepper, some leftover gravy and some leftover stuffing.

To each 2 cups of meat add 1 beaten egg.

Bake in a loaf pan in a moderate oven (350° F.) for 1 hour.

Serve with hot Turkey Gravy (p. 28) if any is left.

ROAST WHOLE CALF'S LIVER

(Serves 6)

Preheat oven to 350° F.

A young calf's liver should weigh no more than 2½ to 3 pounds.

Leave it whole and ask the butcher to lard it and also to pound out a thin sheet of salt pork to cover it with (or use thin slices of bacon as a covering).

You might also ask the butcher to slit one side of the liver with a gash about 6 inches long and about ¾ of the way through to make a pocket for stuffing.

Use any stuffing you like.

If you stuff it, tie it together before roasting to keep the stuffing in place.

Place the liver in a roasting pan.

Add 2 cups chicken broth, a bay leaf, a pinch of thyme and 4 tablespoons butter.

Roast in a medium oven (350° F.) for 1 hour, basting frequently with the liquid in the pan.

Thicken the liquid slightly with 1 tablespoon butter and 1 tablespoon flour, creamed together, and serve as a sauce with the liver.

Fluffy mashed potatoes would be good with this.

BAKED BACON

(Serves 6)

For this dish a good piece of Irish bacon is best. Irish bacon can be procured at certain specialty shops.

Preheat oven to 350° F.

5- to 6-pound piece of good Irish bacon (not too fat)
2 cups cider
1 stalk celery
parsley
bay leaf
½ teaspoon powdered cloves
½ cup bread crumbs
¼ cup brown sugar

Soak the bacon overnight in cold water.

Next morning pour off the water, cover the bacon with fresh water, add the cider, the celery, parsley and bay leaf and bring to a boil.

Cook slowly just at simmering—do not allow the water to boil.

Simmer for 2 hours.

Let the bacon cool in the water, then remove from the water and peel off the skin.

Cover the fat surface with a mixture of the brown sugar and bread crumbs.

Sprinkle with powdered cloves and bake for ½ hour in a moderate oven (350° F.).

Boiled cabbage or spinach would go well with this.

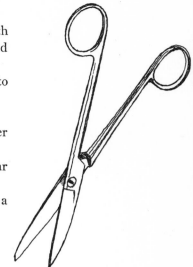

TRIPE AND ONIONS

(Serves 4)

2 pounds tripe
1 cup milk
1 cup water
1 teaspoon salt
1 large white onion, sliced
12 small white onions, whole
1 tablespoon flour
milk

Cover the tripe with cold water, bring to a boil for 2 minutes, then drain.

Cut into small squares and put in a saucepan with the milk, water and salt.

Add the sliced onion.

Simmer slowly for 2 hours.

After an hour and a half, add the small whole onions.

When done mix the flour to a thin paste with cold milk and thicken the milk gravy by slowly adding the paste as the gravy cooks.

BROILED SWEETBREADS

(Serves 4)

Sweetbreads from young calves are the only kind to be used. Do not keep sweetbreads, but use as soon as purchased.

Cover 2 pairs of sweetbreads with cold water and let stand for 1 hour. Drain and cover with cold water well salted, and to 1 quart water add 2 tablespoons lemon juice.

Simmer for 10 to 15 minutes, then drain and cool in running cold water. Remove the tubes and membranes.

Split in two and flatten under a weight for 15 minutes.

Then place in a broiling pan, rub all over with soft butter, leaving plenty on the surface, and sprinkle with salt and pepper.

Broil for 5 minutes.

Serve on a slice of fried ham, with Lemon Butter Sauce.

LEMON BUTTER SAUCE

(Makes ½ cup)

Melt ¼ pound butter over low heat, add 1½ tablespoons lemon juice and serve hot over broiled sweetbreads, fish, cooked broccoli or broiled lamb chops.

BASIC WHITE CREAM SAUCE

2 tablespoons butter
2 tablespoons flour
1 cup milk
salt and pepper

In the top of a double boiler, over direct heat, melt the butter.

Add the flour and cook for 3 minutes, stirring constantly.

Remove the pan from the heat and slowly add 1 cup milk, stirring with a wooden spoon.

Return to direct heat and bring to a boil, stirring constantly. Place the pan over boiling water in the bottom of the double boiler, add salt and pepper and cook until thick, stirring as it thickens.

Beat with an egg beater when it has thickened.

Keep covered until ready to use.

[*34*]

When cooled, this sauce will keep in a covered jar in the refrigerator for several days and can be used for many variations.

WHITE CREAM SAUCE VARIATIONS
(Each makes 1 cup)

Substitute chicken broth for milk and add a pinch of thyme

Substitute fish broth for milk and add a little lemon juice.

Beat 1 egg, add slowly half of the white sauce and add this combination to the rest of the sauce with 1 teaspoon lemon juice

Add 1 chopped hard-boiled egg to 1 cup white sauce.

Add 1 tablespoon capers and 1 teaspoon vinegar to 1 cup white sauce.

For a rich cheese sauce, add 2 tablespoons grated American or Parmesan cheese to 1 cup hot white sauce and stir until melted.

Add 2 tablespoons of any chopped fresh herb—parsley, chives, thyme, marjoram or a mixture of them.

Add a few sliced and cooked fresh mushrooms or 1 small can sliced mushrooms to 1 cup white sauce.

Slice thinly 1 large white onion and cook in butter until soft but not brown. Add the onion and the melted butter to 1 cup white sauce.

Add 2 tablespoons white wine or sherry to 1 cup white sauce.

BROWN SAUCE

1 onion
2 tablespoons butter
2 tablespoons flour
1 cup consommé or soup stock
salt and pepper
½ teaspoon liquid gravy seasoning or beef extract

In the top of a double boiler, over direct heat; cook the sliced onion in the butter until well browned.

Add the flour, stir well and cook together about 5 minutes until well browned.

Remove from direct heat and stir in the consommé a little at a time.

Return to direct heat and bring to a boil, stirring constantly.

Place over boiling water and cook for ½ hour until thick, stirring once in a while.

Add the liquid gravy seasoning or beef extract.

BREAD SAUCE

In England and Ireland this is always served with roast poultry and game birds, pheasants and grouse!

1 cup milk
1 onion, chopped
¼ teaspoon powdered nutmeg
1 bay leaf
fresh-ground pepper
salt to taste
2 slices white bread, crusts removed and bread crumbed
2 tablespoons butter
1 tablespoon cream

Simmer the onion and seasonings in the milk for 20 minutes and strain.

To the strained milk add the crumbs and butter, simmer together for 10 minutes and add the cream.

Do not boil, but keep very hot until ready to serve.

FAVORITE SAUCE (FOR BEEF DISHES)

1 onion, chopped
3 mushrooms, cleaned and sliced
2 tablespoons butter
dash of cayenne
dash of powdered allspice
2 tablespoons red wine
1 cup Brown Sauce (p. 35)

Cook the onion and sliced mushrooms in 2 tablespoons butter. Add the rest of the ingredients.

PLAIN TOMATO SAUCE

(Makes 1 cup)

1 no. 2 can tomatoes
½ teaspoon salt
¼ teaspoon pepper
1 onion, sliced
2 tablespoons flour
2 tablespoons butter

Add the seasonings and onion to the tomatoes and simmer for 10 minutes.

Force through a sieve.

Melt the butter, stir in the flour, cook for 1 minute and add gradually the tomato purée.

Cook gently for 3 minutes.

MASHED POTATOES

(Serves 4)

Boil 6 medium-size potatoes until soft.

Drain and dry out by shaking the pan over heat.

Put through a ricer and add ½ teaspoon salt.

Heat ½ cup milk to just under boiling and melt in it 2 ounces butter.

Add to the potatoes and beat well until light and fluffy.

BOILED POTATOES

Peel the potatoes, drop into boiling salted water and cook until soft—approximately ½ hour for medium-size potatoes.

Drain and return the pot to the heat for a few minutes, shaking the pot to turn the potatoes over until well dried out.

MASHED TURNIPS

(Serves 6)

Peel and slice 6 small yellow turnips, and boil in salted water until soft. Drain and mash well and add butter, pepper and salt to taste.

[37]

BAKED CELERY

(Serves 4)

1 head celery
salt and pepper
2 eggs
1 cup milk

Clean the celery and cut into 1-inch pieces, discarding the leaves.

Cover with water and boil until tender (about 15 minutes), adding salt and pepper to taste.

Remove from the water and place the celery in a pyrex pie pan.

Beat together the eggs and milk and pour over the celery.

Bake for 30 minutes in a moderate oven (350° F.).

This would be good with ham.

CABBAGE

There are two ways of cooking cabbage: in solid pieces or shredded.

Remove the tough outside leaves, cut the cabbage into quarters (or smaller pieces if it is a large cabbage) and cook in boiling salted water for 20 to 30 minutes until soft.

Or shred the cabbage very fine, drop into boiling salted water for 5 minutes, drain and season with butter, salt and pepper.

The cabbage will be crisp and delicate in flavor.

WHITE BAKED BEANS

(Serves 10–12)

We didn't like Boston beans because they were too wet and had molasses in them. Our baked beans were always white and mealy.

1 quart dried beans
½ pound salt pork
1 tablespoon salt
¼ cup sugar
1 teaspoon dry mustard
4 to 6 small white onions

Soak the beans overnight in cold water.

Next morning drain off the water, put the beans in a saucepan, cover with fresh water, bring to a boil and simmer until tender.

Test by taking a few beans on a spoon and blowing on them; if done, the skins will burst.

Drain the beans, but keep the water.

Place the beans in a shallow roasting pan, burying the whole onions here and there in the beans.

Mix the salt, sugar and mustard with enough of the bean water to just cover the beans. (If there is not enough to cover, add more water.)

Cut the salt pork in thin slices and cover the top of the beans.

Bake in a slow oven (250° F.) for 6 hours. Cover with aluminum foil for the last hour of baking.

Serve hot with ketchup, Boston brown bread and Coleslaw (p. 146) with a Boiled Dressing (p. 147).

Very good next day cold with mustard pickles.

CREAMED ASPARAGUS

(Serves 4)

2 pounds asparagus
pepper and salt
4 tablespoons butter
cream

Wash the asparagus thoroughly.

Break off the tough ends, and scrape off the scales.

Cut the asparagus into small pieces about ½ inch long.

Reserve the tips.

Drop the pieces into boiling salted water and cook for 10 minutes.

Add the tips and cook for 10 minutes more, or until all the pieces are tender.

Drain.

Heat enough cream to cover the asparagus generously.

Add the butter to the hot cream and let it melt.

Add the asparagus to the hot cream, and season to taste.

Serve in deep side dishes and eat with a spoon.

FRIED PARSNIPS
(Serves 4)

Wash and cook 1 pound parsnips in boiling water until soft, about ½ hour.

Drain and cover with cold water.

Take off the skins.

Cut into quarters and if core is fibrous, remove it.

Fry in deep fat until golden brown, or approximately 10 minutes.

STEWED TOMATOES
(Serves 6)

12 fresh tomatoes
1 onion, finely sliced
salt and pepper
½ teaspoon sugar
1 tablespoon butter
toast

Dip each tomato into boiling water for a few seconds until the skin bursts.

Slip off the skins.

Remove the stem ends.

Cut the tomatoes into quarters.

Put in a saucepan with the sliced onion, salt and pepper to taste and the sugar.

Simmer for 30 minutes, add the butter and serve in deep dishes with toast cut into small squares.

FRIED GREEN TOMATOES
(Serves 6)

6 green tomatoes
salt and pepper
melted butter

Cut the tops and bottoms off the tomatoes and slice in half crosswise.
Sprinkle with salt and pepper and dip lightly in flour.
Fry in hot butter till brown on both sides.

CANDIED SWEET POTATOES
(Serves 4)

Preheat oven to 350° F.

4 sweet potatoes
½ cup brown sugar
2 tablespoons butter
½ cup sherry

Scrub and boil the potatoes until tender, 20 to 30 minutes.
Peel and cut in slices.
Put into a buttered baking dish in layers, with a little brown sugar over each layer.
Dot each layer with butter and a little sherry.
Bake in a moderate oven (350° F.) for ½ hour.

BAKED ONIONS
(Serves 3–4)

Preheat oven to 325° F.

12 medium-size white onions
2 tablespoons melted butter
3 tablespoons tomato juice
2 tablespoons sugar
salt and pepper to taste

Peel the onions, but leave them whole.
Put them in a well-buttered baking dish.

[41]

Mix the other ingredients together and pour over the onions. Cover the baking dish with aluminum foil and bake in a moderate oven (325° F.) for 1 hour.

SCOTCH-STYLE OATMEAL

(Serves 6)

1 cup coarse oatmeal
4 cups cold water
1 teaspoon salt

Place the ingredients in the top of a double boiler.
Cover and soak in the refrigerator for at least 24 hours.
Boil over direct heat for 10 minutes.
Then place over boiling water and let cook for 2 hours.
Serve with cream and brown sugar.

CRACKED-WHEAT CEREAL

(Serves 4–6)

¾ cup cracked wheat
3 cups cold water
¾ teaspoon salt

Place ingredients in the top of a double boiler.
Cover and soak overnight in the refrigerator.
In the morning place on the stove and boil over direct heat for 10 minutes.
Place over boiling water and let cook for 1 hour, or until tender.
Serve with cream and brown sugar.

STIRABOUT

(Oatmeal Porridge)

(Serves 4)

In the top of a double boiler bring to a boil 4 cups water with 1 teaspoon salt.

[*42*]

Add to the rapidly boiling water 1 cup oatmeal flakes or rolled oats, stirring all the while.

Cook over direct heat for 3 minutes.

Then put the top of the double boiler over boiling water in the bottom part and cook covered for 1 hour, or according to directions for whatever oatmeal you are using.

CORNMEAL MUSH

(Serves 6)

3 cups water
1 cup milk
2 teaspoons salt
1 cup cornmeal
1 tablespoon sugar

Combine the water and milk and bring to a boil in the top of a double boiler over direct heat.

Mix the salt, sugar and cornmeal and add slowly to the boiling liquid, stirring constantly.

Cook and stir until thick.

Then place over hot water, cover and cook for 30 minutes.

Serve with cream and brown sugar.

FLUFFIN

Fluffin is really an oatmeal or barley gruel.

To make it add ¼ cup rolled oats or barley to 1 quart milk and simmer slowly until the oatmeal or barley is completely soft.

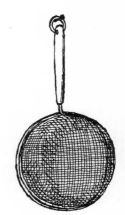

Strain through a fine strainer, pressing the oatmeal or barley through.

Return to the fire, add 1 tablespoon sugar, a little grated nutmeg and a few drops of good brandy.

This should be served as a hot drink or as a soup.

If you have cooked oatmeal porridge left over, make oatmeal muffins for lunch.

[43]

OATMEAL MUFFINS

(Makes 12)

Preheat oven to 400° F.

> *1 cup cooked oatmeal*
> *2 cups sifted flour*
> *3 tablespoons sugar*
> *4 teaspoons baking powder*
> *¾ teaspoon salt*
> *½ cup milk*
> *2 beaten eggs*
> *3 tablespoons melted butter*

Thin out the oatmeal with the milk.

Add the sugar and beaten eggs.

Sift together the flour, salt and baking powder and add to the oatmeal, mixing well.

Add the melted butter and bake in buttered muffin tins for about 25 minutes in a hot oven.

BAKING-POWDER BISCUITS

(Makes 12 biscuits)

Preheat oven to 450° F.

> *2 cups sifted flour*
> *2 teaspoons double-acting baking powder*
> *1 teaspoon salt*
> *1 teaspoon sugar*
> *4 tablespoons butter (2 ounces)*
> *¾ cup milk*

Sift together the flour, baking powder, salt and sugar.

With fingertips rub in the butter until the flour looks like coarse meal.

Add the milk and mix well to a soft dough.

Flour a board lightly, dump out the dough, pat out gently to ¾ inch thick and cut out pieces with a round biscuit cutter or cut in 2-inch squares.

Place on a well-buttered cookie sheet and bake in a very hot oven (450° F.) for about 12 minutes, or until golden brown.

[*44*]

BASIC TWO-EGG CAKE

Preheat oven to 375° F.

> *¼ pound butter*
> *1 cup sugar*
> *2 eggs, beaten*
> *½ cup milk*
> *1¾ cups sifted cake flour*
> *½ teaspoon salt*
> *2 teaspoons double-acting baking powder*
> *½ teaspoon vanilla*

Butter thoroughly 2 9-inch layer-cake pans, sprinkle with flour and shake each pan until it is evenly covered with a thin film of flour. Dump off any excess flour.

With a wooden spoon cream the butter well and gradually add the sugar.

Mix until very light and fluffy.

Add the beaten eggs and mix well.

Sift together the flour, salt and baking powder and add alternately with the milk to the butter mixture.

Beat well but only enough to mix thoroughly.

Add the vanilla.

Divide the batter between the 2 pans and bake in a 375° F. oven for 25 to 30 minutes.

Turn out onto a wire-mesh cake cooler and turn over immediately so the cake cools with the top of the layer up.

If you use an electric mixer, follow the directions closely and do not overbeat.

SOFT CHOCOLATE FILLING FOR LAYER CAKE

2 squares unsweetened chocolate
1 cup milk
6 tablespoons sugar
2 tablespoons flour
¼ teaspoon salt
1 teaspoon butter
½ teaspoon vanilla

Add the chocolate to the milk and heat in the top of a double boiler over boiling water until the chocolate is melted.

Beat well with an egg beater.

Mix together the sugar, flour and salt.

Add to the milk mixture and cook until thick (about 3 minutes), stirring constantly.

Add the butter and vanilla and cool before using on the cake.

POUND CAKE

(Makes 2 cakes)

Preheat oven to 350° F.

1 pound butter
1 pound fine granulated sugar
1 pound sifted cake flour
10 eggs
¼ teaspoon salt
1 teaspoon vanilla
¼ teaspoon mace

Cream the butter until very light and creamy.

Add the sugar a little at a time, continuing to mix, until very light.

Beat the egg yolks until thick and lemon-colored.

Add to the butter and sugar, mixing well.

Add the vanilla and mace.

Add gradually the sifted cake flour and salt and mix until smooth.

Beat the egg whites till stiff but not dry and fold into the batter.

Pour into 2 loaf pans 9 by 4 by 3 inches, well buttered and lined with buttered white paper, filling ⅔ full.

Bake in a 350° F. oven about 1¼ hours until golden brown and slightly shrunken from the sides of the pan.

CUPCAKES

(Makes 1 dozen medium-size cupcakes)

Preheat oven to 375° F.

Use the Basic Two-Egg Cake mix (p. 45) and fill buttered and floured muffin tins ⅔ full.

Bake in 375° F. oven for 20 to 25 minutes until brown and slightly shrunken from sides of the cups.

Turn out onto a wire-mesh cake cooler.

When cool, sprinkle with powdered sugar or cover with an icing.

GINGERBREAD

(Serves 6–8)

I have used this gingerbread recipe for thirty years, but I have no idea where it came from.

Preheat oven to 375° F.

> 1 cup molasses
> 1½ cups boiling water
> 1 teaspoon baking soda
> ½ cup (4 ounces) butter
> 1 cup sugar
> ½ teaspoon salt
> 1 teaspoon ginger
> 2 teaspoons cinnamon
> 1 egg
> 2½ cups sifted flour
> 1 tablespoon double-acting baking powder

Combine the molasses with the boiling water and soda.

Allow to cool and then add to the butter, which has been creamed with the sugar.

Add the salt, ginger and cinnamon.

Beat well, add the well-beaten egg and the flour, which has been sifted with the baking powder.

Have the batter very thin. If the batter is not very thin, add a little more milk so that it runs off the spoon and "ribbons." Pour into 2 well-greased pans (11 by 7 by 1½ inches) and bake in a moderately hot oven (375° F.) for about 20 minutes. Then reduce the heat to 300° F. and bake for 20 minutes more.

Baking the cake in this way gives a very crisp, candied crust with a light, delicate crumb. Milk may be substituted for water.

Serve with Applesauce (p. 53).

CREAMY RICE PUDDING
(Serves 6)

Preheat oven to 325° F.

> *1 quart milk*
> *⅓ cup rice*
> *½ teaspoon salt*
> *½ cup sugar*
> *¼ teaspoon nutmeg*
> *½ cup of white raisins*

Wash the rice well.
Put it in a sieve and let water run through it.
Butter a pyrex pudding dish.
Put all the ingredients in the dish.
Bake in a slow oven (325° F.) for 3 hours.
Stir several times during the first hour to keep the rice from settling on the bottom.

BREAD PUDDING
(Serves 6)

Preheat oven to 325° F.

> *6 slices stale bread*
> *1 quart milk*
> *½ cup sugar*
> *3 eggs, slightly beaten*

> *2 tablespoons butter*
> *½ teaspoon salt*
> *¼ teaspoon cinnamon*

Trim the crusts off the bread and cut the slices into cubes.
Place the bread in a buttered pudding dish.

Mix together the milk, sugar, salt, beaten eggs and cinnamon.

Pour over the bread.

Cut the butter into small bits and add to the mixture.

Bake 1 hour in a slow oven (325° F.).

Serve warm or cold with thick cream.

BAKED CUSTARD
(Serves 6)

Custards must be baked at very low temperature or they will curdle and be tough.

Preheat oven to 300° F.

> *3 cups milk*
> *3 eggs*
> *½ cup sugar*
> *¼ teaspoon salt*
> *nutmeg or cinnamon*

Beat the eggs slightly.

Add the milk, sugar and salt.

Pour into a buttered pudding dish or 6 individual custard cups.

Sprinkle the top lightly with nutmeg or cinnamon.

Set the container in a pan with 1 inch of hot water in it.

Bake at 300° F. for 1 hour or until a knife inserted in the custard comes out clean.

TREACLE PUDDING

(Serves 6)

For Treacle Pudding we always used corn syrup, although molasses is really treacle. You could also use maple syrup.

Preheat oven to 400° F.

> *¼ cup syrup*
> *buttered slices of white bread*
> *2 cups baked (p. 58) rhubarb or applesauce*
> *white custard cream*

In a pyrex pie pan put ¼ cup syrup.

Tip the pan back and forth so the syrup covers all the surface and rolls up a bit on the edges of the pan.

Butter some slices of white bread with the crusts removed and put on top of the syrup, buttered side down.

Cut the bread slices so they fit and cover the bottom of the pie pan.

On top of the bread put baked sweetened rhubarb or Applesauce, sweetened and flavored to your taste, and then put on a top of more buttered white bread, buttered side up.

Sprinkle the bread with more syrup.

Cook in a hot oven (400° F.) for 20 to 30 minutes, or until the top surface of the bread is golden brown.

Serve with white custard cream (p. 161).

BANANA PUDDING

(Serves 6)

> *Plenty of stale sponge cake, cut thin*
> *4 ripe bananas*
> *confectioner's-sugar*
> *2 cups plain custard (p. 54)*
> *1 cup heavy cream, whipped*

Line a deep rectangular dish with stale sponge cake.

Cover with a layer of sliced bananas.

Sprinkle with confectioner's-sugar.

Cover with more sponge cake, and more sliced bananas.

Sprinkle again with confectioner's-sugar.

Pour over the bananas a plain Boiled Custard (p. 54)
Refrigerate for about 1 hour.
When ready to serve cover the top with whipped cream.

GOOSEBERRY PUDDING
(Serves 4–6)

Preheat oven to 350° F.

> *4 slices buttered white bread*
> *2 cups Stewed Gooseberries (p. 52)*
> *3 eggs*
> *¼ cup sugar*
> *3 cups milk*

In a 2-quart casserole put the white bread, which has been
buttered and cut into small cubes.
Pour over the bread the stewed gooseberries.
Beat the eggs with a fork.
Add the sugar and milk.
Pour this egg-and-milk mixture over the bread and goose-
berries.
Bake in a moderate oven (350° F.) for 1 hour, or until the cus-
tard is firm.

BLACKBERRY TRIFLE
(Serves 6)

Line a 2-quart mold or pudding dish with slices of stale
sponge cake.
Sprinkle the cake lightly with blackberry cordial or light
rum or sherry.
Half fill the dish with crushed, sweetened blackberries.
Place another layer of stale sponge cake over the berries;
sprinkle the cake with blackberry cordial or light rum or sherry.
Fill the dish with more crushed blackberries.
Pour a Boiled Custard (p. 54) over the top.
Chill thoroughly.
When cold and ready to serve, cover the top with whipped
cream.

[*51*]

RASPBERRY FLUMMERY

(Serves 6)

¾ cup rice
1 quart milk
¼ cup sugar
1 cup cream, whipped
1 teaspoon vanilla
2 cups Stewed Raspberries (below)

In a double boiler cook the rice, sugar and milk until the rice is very soft, about 1 hour.

Pour the cooked rice into a shallow bowl and let cool.

Cover thickly with stewed, sweetened raspberries.

Cover the berries with whipped cream flavored with vanilla.

STEWED RASPBERRIES

(Serves 6)

2 cups water
1 cup granulated sugar
1 tablespoon strained lemon juice
2 pints raspberries, carefully picked over

Moisten the sugar with the water and add the lemon juice.

Bring to a boil, skim carefully and boil for 5 minutes.

Add the raspberries and boil for 1 minute.

Cool, chill and serve.

STEWED STRAWBERRIES

Same as above recipe, substituting strawberries for raspberries.

STEWED GOOSEBERRIES

1 pound gooseberries
⅔ cup granulated sugar
½ cup water

With scissors, snip off the tops and tails of the gooseberries.
Moisten the sugar with the water and bring to a boil.

Wash the gooseberries, add them to the boiling syrup and
stew until tender, or approximately 20 minutes.

GOOSEBERRY FLUMMERY or
STRAWBERRY FLUMMERY

Same as Raspberry Flummery (p. 52), but use stewed,
sweetened gooseberries or strawberries.

HOMEMADE APPLESAUCE

(Serves 8)

12 large green apples
2 cups water
1½ cups granulated sugar

Wash, peel, quarter and core the apples.
Cook them in the water until tender, or for about 15 minutes.
Remove from the fire and rub through a fine sieve.
Add the sugar and cook about 5 minutes longer.
Cool and chill before serving.

PEACH TRIFLE

(Serves 6)

Line a 2-quart mold or pudding dish with slices of stale
sponge cake.

Sprinkle the cake very lightly with Apricot Liqueur or Kirsch.

Spread the cake with a generous layer of peach jam or de-
frosted frozen peaches.

Cover with another layer of sponge cake.

Sprinkle with more Apricot Liqueur or Kirsch.

Pour a Boiled Custard (p. 54) over all.

Chill thoroughly.

When cold and ready to serve, cover the top with whipped
cream.

PLAIN BOILED CUSTARD

(Makes about 3 cups)

3 or 4 egg yolks
2 cups milk
3 tablespoons granulated sugar
½ teaspoon vanilla (or more)

Heat the milk in the top of a double boiler.
Add the sugar.
Beat the egg yolks until light, add a little of the hot milk and stir well, then add this to the remainder of the hot milk.
Place over boiling water and cook, stirring constantly, until thickened and until it coats the spoon—or for about 4 to 5 minutes.
Remove from the fire and cool, stirring occasionally.
When cold, flavor with the vanilla.

BLUEBERRY DISH

Toast 2 slices white bread for each portion.
Butter hot toast generously and spread with cinnamon sugar.
Place a slice in the bottom of an individual serving dish and pile with fresh sugared blueberries, half of which have been crushed and sweetened.
Cover the berries with heavy cream.
Cut the other slice of cinnamon toast into triangles and place around the sides of the dish.

APPLE CHARLOTTE

(Serves 6)

Preheat oven to 450° F.
Line a well-buttered 2-quart pyrex baking dish with slices of buttered white bread with crusts removed, buttered side of the bread next to the dish.
Fill the dish with 4 cups canned or fresh Applesauce (p. 53) and cover with more buttered slices of bread, buttered side up.

Bake in a 450° F. oven until bread is golden brown, or approximately 30 minutes.

Turn out onto a platter and serve warm with heavy cream.

There are two varieties of the great American favorite, strawberry shortcake—one made with crusty biscuit dough and one made with cake.

BISCUIT DOUGH STRAWBERRY SHORTCAKE
(Serves 6)

Preheat oven to 450° F.

> *1 quart ripe strawberries*
> *1 cup sugar*
> *½ pint heavy cream*
> *½ teaspoon vanilla*

Biscuit Dough
2 cups sifted flour
3 teaspoons baking powder
1 teaspoon salt
1 tablespoon sugar
4 tablespoons (2 ounces) butter
¾ cup milk

Before baking your biscuit dough, clean and hull the strawberries.

Crush the berries with the sugar and place in the refrigerator.

Whip the heavy cream, flavor with the vanilla and place in the refrigerator.

Biscuit Dough

Sift together the flour, baking powder, salt and sugar.

With fingertips rub in the butter until the flour looks like coarse meal.

Add the milk and mix to a soft dough.

Turn out onto a lightly floured board, pat out gently to ¾ inch thick and cut out pieces with a round biscuit cutter or cut in 2-inch squares.

Place on a well-buttered cookie sheet and bake in a very hot oven (450° F.) for about 12 minutes, or until golden brown.

Split the hot biscuits with a fork, butter well and spread with the cold crushed berries.

Place the top half of the biscuit on the berries and spoon more crushed berries on top.

Garnish each shortcake with plenty of whipped cream.

Serve while the biscuits are still hot and crisp.

INDIVIDUAL STRAWBERRY CAKES
(Makes 12 small cakes)

Prepare berries and cream as for Biscuit-Dough Strawberry Shortcake (above).

Make a Basic Two-Egg Cake mix (p. 45) and bake in cupcake pans.

When cooled, split each cupcake, spread with crushed berries, place the other half on top with more crushed berries and cover each one with whipped cream.

SWEET SHORTCAKE

Prepare berries and cream as for Biscuit-Dough Strawberry Shortcake (p. 55).

Make a Basic Two-Egg Cake mix (p. 45) and bake in 2 layers.

Turn out on a wire rack and cool.

Spread one layer with the crushed berries, place the other layer on top.

Spread the top layer with the remainder of the crushed berries and cover generously with the whipped cream.

SOUR-CREAM TART
(Serves 6)

Preheat oven to 425° F.

> *Plain Pastry*
> *2 eggs*
> *1 cup thick sour cream*
> *1 tablespoon sugar*
> *2 tablespoons white raisins*

Line a 9-inch pie pan with Plain Pastry (p. 153).

Sprinkle the pastry with the sugar and raisins.

Beat the eggs.

Add the sour cream to the beaten eggs and pour into the shell.

Bake in a hot oven (425° F.) for 10 minutes, then bake at 350° F. for about 30 minutes, or until brown.

STRAWBERRY PIE
(Serves 6)

Preheat oven to 450° F.

> *Plain Pastry for 2 crusts*
> *1 quart ripe strawberries*
> *½ cup sugar*
> *2 tablespoons flour*
> *¼ teaspoon salt*

Line a 9-inch pie pan with Plain Pastry.

Brush the bottom of the crust with beaten egg white.

Clean the berries, slice them in half and place on the pastry.

Mix together the sugar, flour and salt and sprinkle over the berries.

Roll out the top crust and place over the berries, sealing the edge well.

Prick the top crust and brush with egg yolk or milk.

Bake in a hot oven (450° F.) for 10 minutes, then reduce the heat to 350° for 40 minutes more.

PRUNES

(Serves 6)

Prunes can be very plain or very fancy. Either way, they should be cooked with very little sugar.

Cover a 1-pound package of tenderized prunes with boiling water.

Simmer for 20 minutes or cook according to directions on the package.

Let stand in the refrigerator for 3 days.

Strain off the juice into a saucepan, add ½ cup sugar, bring to a boil and cook for 10 minutes.

Add 1 cup port wine to the syrup and pour all back over the prunes.

Let stand in the refrigerator for another day.

Serve with whipped cream as a dessert.

BAKED RHUBARB

(Serves 6)

Rhubarb will stay in pieces if baked instead of boiled.

Preheat oven to 350° F.

Clean 2 pounds of young pink rhubarb, peel if necessary and cut into 1-inch pieces, discarding the root and green tops.

Add to 1 cup sugar a dash of salt and a dash of cinnamon.

Mix the sugar with the rhubarb.

Place in a large flat pyrex baking dish without adding any water.

Bake in a 350° F. oven until tender, about ½ hour.

There will be plenty of juice.

Serve warm or cold with heavy cream.

SLICED BANANAS

Slice ripe bananas and sprinkle with lemon juice and brown sugar.

BAKED BANANAS

Preheat oven to 450° F.

Peel bananas and place in a buttered baking pan.

Dot with butter and brown sugar.

Bake in a hot oven (450° F.) for about 15 minutes until soft and lightly browned.

Serve warm, sprinkled with moist coconut.

PART TWO

COUNTRY LIFE

AS I grew up, I tried more and more kinds of cooking. It became a hobby of mine, but never did I dream that it would lead to a business career in the food world.

At school I majored in mathematics and finance courses, and, fortunately for me, my business training started in a bank. Years later, when the Pepperidge Farm business began to expand, that banking experience was of tremendous value. I enjoyed six years of the banking and brokerage business before I married in 1923.

Then I really became serious about cooking.

My husband always has had a great sense of adventure and curiosity about everything. The result was that any whim or idea of his or mine usually became a real project, and we vied with each other for results.

One of our whimsical ideas was to live a real country life. In 1926 we bought 125 acres of land in Connecticut, part of which had once been a farm. One of the attractions of the place was a group of beautiful trees with unusually gorgeous coloring in the autumn, and when we discovered that they were a variety of the sourgum species and were known as pepperidge trees, we called the place Pepperidge Farm. We built a house and farm buildings and started our country life like babes-in-the-wood, for neither of us knew anything about country ways.

Pepperidge Farm really was a farm for us, and our first commercial venture was to put in an orchard of five hundred apple trees, which have been bearing beautiful apples for the past thirty years. I surely can tell you how to cook apples! We raised all our own vegetables, small fruits—pears, peaches and plums—and poultry—turkeys, chickens and capons. And we also raised three sons.

During the war we bravely tackled raising our own Porterhouse steaks and hams and bacon, which, by a miracle, turned out very well. We didn't know the first thing about it, but I wrote to the Department of Agriculture in Washington for the list of government pamphlets and ordered #1186, all about killing, curing and corning pork, and another one all about beef.

When the booklets came, we studied the instructions and were ready to try. We started off with a few baby pigs and one young steer, and when the pampered pigs and the fatted calf were in prime condition, the butcher came to slaughter them.

We equipped one farm building with refrigerating machinery so we could chill the meat properly at controlled temperatures. In addition, we put in a freezer room about six feet by ten feet, to be kept at ten degrees below zero so that after the meat had been properly prepared we could freeze it.

It really was very little trouble, and the quality of the meat was excellent.

The first lot of hams and bacon we did by the dry cure. We bought Dry Sugar Cure, read the instruction booklet and followed every word. But it was mighty hard, cold work in that chilly refrigerated building, and rubbing the salt into the pork made our hands purple and numb.

The next lot we did in brine, again following instructions, and that was much easier on us and made excellent products.

Pig's head is full of good meat, and our German gardener's wife always made delicious head cheese, or "souse," as she called it.

We made our own lard from the loin fat, sausage meat from all the small parts, and the liver was made into a pâté.

Our beef was really marvelous because we had good grass pastures and raised field corn for fattening up the cattle.

Like all husbands, mine became an expert at broiling steaks over charcoal—he likes to rub mustard over the surface and then sprinkle lightly with sugar, which burns off in the cooking but makes a nice crisp surface.

I always loved seeing a good supply of homemade foods in my store cupboards—jellies and jams from our own fruits, pickles and preserves, big crocks of our own sauerkraut, eggs kept in waterglass, and jars of my special mincemeat.

I'll never forget the first strawberry jam I made. I thought I might as well make a good big batch while I was at it, so I cleaned and hulled and crushed strawberries and sugar together for hours and filled up a huge pot. I stirred and stirred and thought it would never come to a boil. Well, it did—just when I had my back turned. Whoosh! Over the top it went, frothing and boiling all over the stove into sticky crimson puddles on the kitchen floor. That's how I discovered that small batches of jam cooked in a big pot come out better in more ways than one!

I must say I was very prideful about my homemade mincemeat, which always turned out well. The recipe was given to me when I was a bride by a very fussy friend of the family. She told me it was perfect just as it was, and I never made the slightest change in it, for she was right. For years and years on November 1st I made a big batch of it and put the filled jars away to ripen for Thanksgiving and Christmas.

In the early days at Pepperidge Farm we made our own sauerkraut. We had an old-fashioned hand cutter for the cabbage, which we placed over large earthenware crocks and shredded the cabbage right into them. Each layer of cabbage was sprinkled with salt, and when the crock was full, clean grape leaves were laid on the top and a plate with a big stone went on next to keep the cabbage under the brine which formed from the salt. A clean cheesecloth next, and then the crock was left to ferment.

When the sauerkraut was ready, we cooked it in various ways, sometimes with chopped onion and apple, sometimes with caraway seeds and tomatoes, and sometimes with stuffed cabbage rolls. A roast loin of pork with sauerkraut and applesauce is a grand dinner for a cold winter's evening.

During the war we made our own butter. As usual, I knew nothing about the subject, so again I wrote to Uncle Sam for a free booklet and found it very easy to follow instructions.

We bought a secondhand cream separator and a wooden barrel churn and made five pounds of butter at a time. We learned that a certain exact degree of temperature of the cream made the butter come very easily. Otherwise you might churn till your arm was stiff before you succeeded.

We were very popular during ration time because we could always give a present of some precious butter or a bit of bacon to our friends.

During the sugar rationing I used to make icing for cakes by whipping egg whites with jam or jelly or orange marmalade. Delicious! But you had to eat it right away before the egg whites deflated.

Now our children are married and off in their own homes and there's no need for that big storeroom, but I sadly miss the pleasures of those busy years.

I am adding to this chapter some of the recipes which were most popular during those early days of our country life.

CREAMY CHEESE DIP

Cocktail dips have become so popular that we try to include at least one when we have hors d'oeuvres. This is one of the easiest and most delicious we have served.

Combine 1 cup cottage cheese with half as much sour cream.

Add a little mashed Roquefort cheese to suit your taste and mix well.

Add 2 tablespoons Mayonnaise, finely chopped green onions, a dash of salt and freshly ground black pepper.

Serve well chilled with Melba toast.

FILLED ENDIVE

At a cocktail party in Belgium, the land of the lovely, delicate endive, we were introduced to these unusual hors d'oeuvres.

Spread stalks of endive with Mayonnaise and fill with a strip or two of anchovy fillets.

Or stuff the stalks with a savory mixture of softened cream cheese and crisp, crumbled bacon.

CHEESE CANAPES

(Makes 2 dozen small canapés)

One of our favorite cocktail accompaniments is plain Melba toast. Occasionally, however, we succumb and spread Melba toast with this zippy cheese mixture.

1 cup grated sharp Cheddar cheese
⅓ cup Mayonnaise
½ teaspoon dry mustard
⅓ cup chopped ripe olives
freshly ground black pepper

Combine all the ingredients.
Spread on Melba toast and heat in a hot oven (450° F.) for about 5 minutes.

CRABMEAT CANAPES

(Makes 1 dozen canapés)

Whenever I serve these canapés, I think of San Francisco, where I first tasted them. Perhaps San Franciscans use luscious King crab, but we have reproduced these canapés here in Connecticut with plain crabmeat, fresh, canned or frozen, and with great success.

½ pound crabmeat
⅓ cup lemon juice
1 package (3 ounces) cream cheese
¼ cup Mayonnaise
3 tablespoons finely chopped green onions
⅛ teaspoon garlic salt

Marinate the crabmeat in the lemon juice for an hour or so.
Meanwhile blend the remaining ingredients.
Drain the crabmeat and add to the cream-cheese mixture.
Serve well chilled, heaped high on crisp crackers or Melba toast.

SARDINE SPREAD

(Makes 2 dozen canapés)

½ pound cream cheese
3 tablespoons lime juice
2 tins filleted sardines
3 tablespoons finely cut chives
½ cup chopped parsley
salt to taste

Blend the cream cheese well with the lime juice.

Add the sardines mashed with their oil, chives (or onions) and chopped parsley.

Add salt to taste and spread on salty rye slices or bread cut in fancy shapes.

SHRIMP DIP

(Makes about 1½ cups)

1 can frozen condensed cream of shrimp soup
1 package (3 ounces) cream cheese, softened
1 teaspoon lemon juice
½ small clove garlic, pressed

Place the can of soup in a pan of hot water for about 30 minutes to thaw.

Then combine the soup with the other ingredients; beat until smooth with an electric mixer or rotary beater.

Chill.

Serve as a dip for crackers, potato chips, etc.

Note: This may also be used as a salad dressing by thinning with a little milk; or heat it and serve as a sauce over cauliflower, fish, etc.

CUCUMBER IN SOUR CREAM

(Serves 6)

Pare and thinly slice 3 firm, medium-size cucumbers.

Add 1 thinly sliced sweet onion.

Marinate for a few hours in lemon juice and salt and pepper.

Lay the marinated cucumbers in a shallow dish and pour over them a sauce made of Mayonnaise mixed equally with sour cream.

Sprinkle with finely chopped parsley or any other green herb and serve with lightly buttered slices of rye bread.

SEVICHE
(Serves 6)

6 fillets of raw flounder (white side only)
strained juice of 9 limes (1½ cups)
6 small bay leaves
4 hot dried red pepper pods
1 teaspoon salt
1 large Bermuda onion
¾ cup white vinegar
1 clove garlic
1 bunch watercress
1 extra lime

Crush the pepper pods and place in a small jar.

Cover with the white vinegar, adjust the cover on the jar and refrigerate overnight.

Wash the flounder fillets and pat dry on a paper towel.

Cut in very thin slices on the bias, and once again in half, and place in a rectangular glass dish.

Cover with the strained lime juice.

Bury in this the bay leaves.

Cover with waxed paper and refrigerate overnight.

At 4 o'clock on the afternoon of the party, add to the fish 1 clove garlic run through the garlic press.

Sprinkle with about 1 teaspoon salt and cover with the Bermuda onion, peeled, quartered and sliced paper thin.

Pour over this the white vinegar, having first strained out the hot peppers.

Cover with 1 lime cut paper thin. Cover with waxed paper and chill again until ready to serve. Garnish with crisp watercress and serve as a first course with whipped butter and crisp heated French bread.

BROTH FROM LEFTOVERS

Homemade soup is a good way to use up leftovers.

Meat bones, scraps of meat, leftover vegetables and water in which vegetables have been cooked are of little use except for soup. By slow simmering of these leftovers you can make a good broth which can then be used instead of water with many of the canned soups or canned vegetables, such as canned peas, making cream of pea soup.

Barely cover leftover roast beef bones, or turkey or chicken bones and scraps, with cold water or water in which vegetables have been cooked.

Add an onion, a few sprigs of parsley, a piece of celery with the celery leaves, any leftover cooked vegetables you have and pepper and salt to taste.

Bring just to the boil and simmer, covered, for about 2 hours. Strain and keep to use with canned soups.

CREAM OF PEA SOUP

(Serves 6)

*3 cups broth, made from leftover bones,
    meats and vegetables*
1 no. 2 can green peas, including juice
1 onion, sliced

1 bay leaf
1 teaspoon sugar
salt and pepper
2 tablespoons butter
2 tablespoons flour
1 cup light cream or milk

Add the peas with the canned juice to the broth.
Add the onion and seasonings and bring just to the boil.
Simmer slowly for ½ hour.
Rub through a strainer.
In a saucepan melt the butter, add the flour and cook, stirring constantly, for 3 minutes.
Remove the pan from the heat and add the pea soup.
Return to the heat and cook for 5 minutes, stirring constantly.
Add the cream or milk and reheat, but do not boil.

CORN CHOWDER

(Serves 6)

4 cups corn cut from cob, or 4 cups canned
  corn (not cream-style)
2 medium-size potatoes
1 small Bermuda onion (1 cup when cut)
1 cup water
2 cups clear chicken broth
5 tablespoons butter
2 cups hot milk
1 cup heavy cream
salt and pepper to taste
pinch cayenne

Prepare 4 cups corn cut from the cob, being careful not to cut too deep, or use canned corn.
Peel the potatoes and cut in ½-inch cubes.
Peel and cut fine the Bermuda onion.
Place the corn in a large (4-quart) pan.
Pour over it 1 cup water and the chicken broth.
Place on low heat and simmer for 15 minutes, counting from the time it comes to a boil.
Watch carefully to prevent scorching.

In the meantime boil the cubed potatoes in 1½ cups water until tender, or for about 15 minutes.

Cook the chopped Bermuda onion in 4 tablespoons butter, slowly, without browning, until soft, or for about 10 minutes.

Add to the corn the onion, well-drained potatoes and hot milk.

Put all this mixture through the electric blender, a cup or two at a time, running it at low speed for 1 minute and another minute at high speed.

Place in the top of a very large double boiler.

Season to taste with salt and coarsely ground pepper and a dash of cayenne.

Place over boiling water and heat thoroughly.

When scalding hot, stir in the heavy cream.

Place 1 tablespoon butter in a soup tureen, pour over it the corn chowder and serve at once.

BLACK BEAN SOUP

(Serves 6)

2 cups black beans
1 ham bone
1 stalk celery
parsley
4 tablespoons butter
1 onion, sliced thin
2 quarts water
¼ cup sherry

Soak the beans overnight.
Drain the beans and cover with 2 quarts fresh water.
Add the ham bone.
Add the sliced onion, parsley and celery to taste.
Simmer 3½ to 4 hours in a covered pot, until soft.
Rub the beans and liquid through a sieve.
Reheat, add butter, pepper, salt and sherry.

GUMBO CREOLE SOUP
(Serves 6–8)

2 quarts homemade clear beef consommé or
   canned consommé
1 pound fresh okra, washed and cut in fine slices
2 onions, chopped fine
1 bay leaf
salt and pepper to taste
1 no. 2 can tomatoes, chopped fine
½ cup rice

Simmer everything except the rice for 2 hours, covered.
Add the rice and cook 20 minutes until the rice is soft.

CHICKEN BROTH
(Serves 6)

4- to 5-pound boiling fowl
6 cups cold water
1 large onion, sliced
1 large stalk celery, sliced
¼ teaspoon peppercorns
¼ teaspoon powdered thyme
4 or 5 sprigs parsley
1 teaspoon salt

Wash and wipe dry the chicken, whole or cut in pieces.

In a large saucepan, cover the chicken with cold water and
add the vegetables and seasoning.

Bring just to the boiling point and let simmer for 2 hours, or
until the chicken is very tender.

Let the chicken cool in the broth, then lift out and take off
the skin.

Remove all the meat from the bones and set aside to use for
creamed chicken, chicken salad or chicken mousse.

Strain the broth and keep in the refrigerator until needed.

CREAM OF CHICKEN SOUP

(Serves 4–6)

4 cups chicken broth, homemade or canned
4 tablespoons butter or chicken fat
4 tablespoons flour
salt and pepper to taste
1 cup cream

Over direct heat, melt the butter in the top of a double boiler.
Add the flour and cook for 2 minutes, stirring constantly.
Remove the pan from the heat and add slowly, stirring constantly, the chicken broth.
Return to the heat and bring just to a boil, stirring constantly.
Place over boiling water and add the cream.
Taste for seasoning and add salt and pepper if needed.

CURRIED CREAM OF CHICKEN SOUP

(Serves 4–6)

4 cups chicken broth, homemade or canned
4 tablespoons butter or chicken fat
4 tablespoons flour
1 level teaspoon curry powder
salt and pepper to taste
1 cup cream

Over direct heat, melt the butter in the top of a double boiler.
Mix the curry powder with the flour, add to the hot butter and cook for 2 minutes, stirring constantly.
Remove the pan from the heat and add the chicken broth slowly, stirring constantly.
Return to the heat and bring just to a boil, stirring constantly.
Place over boiling water and add the cream.
Taste for seasoning and add salt and pepper if needed.

[76]

CREAM OF CAULIFLOWER SOUP

(Serves 6)

4 cups chicken broth, homemade or canned
1 small head cauliflower, cooked (about 3 cups)
4 tablespoons butter (2 ounces)
½ small onion, chopped
½ bay leaf
¼ cup flour
1 cup light cream
1 cup milk
salt and pepper to taste

Melt the butter and add to it the onion and bay leaf.
Cook until the onion is tender and yellow.
Remove the bay leaf.
Add the flour and cook for 3 minutes, stirring constantly.
Remove from the heat and add the chicken broth slowly, stirring constantly.
Add salt and pepper to taste.
Return to the heat and bring just to the boil, stirring constantly.
Rub the cooked cauliflower through a strainer to make a purée.
Add the strained cauliflower to the hot soup.
Add the cream and heat thoroughly.
If too thick, thin out with milk.

ONION SOUP

(Serves 4–6)

1 cup finely sliced onions
4 tablespoons butter
6 cups beef consommé, homemade or canned
grated Parmesan cheese
toast

Cook the onions in butter until very soft and yellow but not browned.
Add the consommé.

Simmer for 20 minutes.

Put a thick slice of crisp toast into each soup plate and pour soup over it.

Sprinkle with grated cheese.

CLEAR MUSHROOM SOUP

(Serves 4)

Here is a good way to use mushroom stems.

> mushroom stems
> 4 cups consommé, homemade or canned
> sherry
> whipped cream

Chop the stems left over from 1 pound mushrooms (1 cup).

Put into the consommé and simmer for 30 minutes, tightly covered.

Strain and reheat.

Add 1 teaspoon sherry to each serving and top with a spoonful of whipped cream.

SPINACH SOUP

(Serves 6)

> 1 package frozen spinach
> 2 cups clear chicken broth or 1 can (13¾ ounces)
> 1 small onion
> 3 tablespoons butter
> 3 tablespoons flour
> 2 cups milk
> ⅓ cup heavy cream
> salt and pepper to taste
> ¼ teaspoon grated nutmeg or mace
> 1 cup sour cream

Cook the spinach, following directions on the package, and chop fine.

Peel and chop fine the onion.

Melt the butter, add the onion and cook gently without browning, stirring with a wooden spoon until soft.

Add the flour, cook for a minute or two, then stir in the hot clear chicken broth.

When it comes to a lively boil, add the cooked spinach and any juice it may have.

Add the milk and continue cooking until it comes to a boil.

Remove from the fire, season to taste with salt, pepper and nutmeg or mace.

Stir in the heavy cream.

Serve at once, garnished with sour cream.

GREEK RICE SOUP
(Serves 6–8)

8 cups clear chicken broth
½ cup long-grain rice
4 egg yolks
8 thin strips lemon peel
1 cup heavy cream
3 tablespoons strained lemon juice
2 tablespoons butter
salt
coarsely ground black pepper

Heat the clear chicken broth until boiling in the top of a large (3-quart) double boiler over direct heat.

Wash the rice and add it gradually to the boiling broth.

Cook until the rice is very tender, about 20 minutes.

Place over boiling water.

Add the lemon peel.

Beat together in a bowl the egg yolks and heavy cream.

When ready to serve the soup, add a little of the chicken soup to the egg-and-cream mixture, then add this gradually to the soup, stirring constantly until thickened, about 5 minutes.

Stir in gradually the lemon juice and season to taste with salt and pepper.

Place the butter in a soup tureen, add the soup, stir until the butter has melted and serve.

POTAGE CRECY

(Serves 4–6)

6 large carrots
2 small white onions
2 large potatoes
2 cans beef bouillon
5 tablespoons butter
4–5 cups boiling water
salt and pepper to taste
2 teaspoons sugar

Wash, peel and slice fine the carrots.

Peel and chop fine the onions.

Wash, peel and cut in cubes the potatoes.

Cook the onions without browning for a minute or two in 4 tablespoons butter, add the carrots and potatoes and moisten with the hot beef bouillon diluted with 2 cups hot water.

Cook until the carrots are tender, about ½ hour.

Cool partially, thin with 1½ cups water and place in an electric mixer. Run at low speed for a minute or two, then at high speed until smooth.

Place in a pan and dilute to the desired consistency with about 1½ cups or more of boiling water.

Season to taste with about 1 teaspoon salt, 2 teaspoons sugar and a dash of pepper.

Bring to a lively boil, remove from the fire, stir in 1 tablespoon butter and serve in hot soup plates.

GAZPACHO
(Serves 4)

1 can condensed tomato soup
1 soup can water
1 cup thinly sliced cucumber (1 small cucumber)
½ cup finely chopped green pepper
¼ cup minced onion
½ cup olive oil
2 tablespoons wine vinegar
1 small clove garlic, pressed
dash Tabasco
dash salt
dash black pepper

Combine all the ingredients in a large bowl.

Cover and place in the refrigerator for at least 4 hours (longer if possible).

Stir gently.

Serve in well-chilled bowls, or in bowls set in containers of crushed ice.

Garnish with a lemon or lime slice.

VICHYSSOISE
(Serves 3)

1 can frozen condensed cream of potato soup
½ soup can chicken broth
½ soup can light cream

In a saucepan, heat the soup, broth and cream over low heat until the soup is completely thawed.

Beat until smooth with an electric blender or rotary beater.

Place in the refrigerator for at least 4 hours.

Serve in chilled bowls.

If you like extra seasoning, stir in a dash of nutmeg, thyme or Tabasco.

For a special garnish, use chopped chives, shredded vegetables, sliced olives, parsley or shredded cheese.

CLAM (QUAHAUG) CHOWDER

(Serves 4–6)

1 2-inch square of salt pork
1 large onion
2 or 3 stalks celery
⅛ pound butter
1 pint quahaugs (opened at the market)
1 cup potatoes, cut in cubes or sliced fine
1 quart milk or half milk, half cream
1 tablespoon chopped parsley
½ teaspoon paprika
1 tablespoon flour

Cut the salt pork into tiny cubes and fry in a frying pan on a very low flame.

Drain off the fat and place the crisp bits temporarily on paper toweling.

Do not wash the pan.

Peel, quarter and slice very fine the onion.

Prepare 1 cup potatoes peeled and cut in small cubes or sliced very fine.

Remove the strings from several stalks of crisp celery and dice fine.

Line a sieve with several thicknesses of cheesecloth and place it over a pan.

Drain off all the precious juice from the quahaugs and save it.

Wash each clam separately, in ½ cup cold water, going over them with your fingers in search of bits of shell, and when you are through, strain the ½ cup water through the cloth-lined sieve.

Likewise into a separate bowl strain the clam juice itself.

All this fuss is to avoid the sand sometimes encountered in carelessly prepared chowder.

When this is accomplished, chop the clams in a wooden bowl or put them through the meat grinder, using the medium cutter.

Prepare 1 tablespoon finely chopped parsley.

To the pan in which you fried the pork, add the butter.

Place on low heat, add the onion and celery and cook gently until soft, without browning.

Sprinkle with the flour and cook for a minute or two, stirring with a wooden spoon.

Set aside.

In the meantime cover the cubed potatoes with the strained clam juice and the strained water in which the clams were washed, and simmer until almost done, skimming them carefully.

Add the celery-and-onion mixture and the chopped clams, and simmer gently for 3 minutes.

Do not boil.

Scald the milk in a double boiler (or if a richer chowder is desired, make this half milk and half cream).

Add the clam-potato-celery mixture.

Place the chowder in a hot soup tureen, sprinkle with the paprika and parsley, and send to the table accompanied by the hot pork bits, to be scattered over each plate of chowder as it is being served.

POTATO-SPINACH SOUP

(Serves 3)

1 cup finely chopped fresh cooked spinach or half
  of a 10-ounce package frozen spinach
1 can frozen condensed cream of potato soup
1 soup can water or milk

Combine the soup and water or milk and the spinach.
Cover and heat slowly until thawed.

(If using fresh spinach, add to the soup after it thaws.)
Cover the soup and simmer for about 2 minutes.
Serve as is or pour into the blender and blend until smooth.
Serve immediately or chill before serving.

CHICKEN-POTATO POTAGE

(Serves 6–8)

1 cup chopped celery
2 tablespoons butter or margarine
2 cans frozen condensed cream of potato soup
2 soup cans water or milk
1 can (5 ounces) boned chicken or turkey, minced
2 tablespoons minced parsley

In a covered saucepan, cook the celery in butter over very low heat until tender but not browned.
Add the soup and water or milk.
Heat until the soup is thawed; stir occasionally.
Add the chicken and parsley.
Simmer a few minutes to blend the flavors.

PEASE PORRIDGE HOT

(Serves 4–6)

1 can condensed green pea soup
1 can condensed pepper pot soup
2 soup cans water

Blend the soups and water in a saucepan.
Heat, stirring occasionally.

MARYLAND BISQUE

(Serves 4–6)

2 cups diced raw potatoes
2 cups water
1 can frozen condensed oyster stew
1 can frozen condensed cream of shrimp soup
2 tablespoons chopped parsley

In a covered saucepan, cook the potatoes in the water until done.

Add the soups and parsley.

Heat, stirring occasionally.

BEAN AND BACON SOUP

(Serves 2–3)

1 or 2 small sausages
1 can condensed bean and bacon soup
1 soup can water
1 apple, peeled and cored, chopped in small cubes

Slice the sausage and brown in a saucepan.

Pour off all fat.

Blend in the soup and water.

Heat thoroughly.

In each dish, put a few tiny cubes of apple on top of the soup.

PEANUT-BUTTER BISQUE

(Serves 3)

2 tablespoons minced onion
1 tablespoon butter or margarine
¼ cup peanut butter (chunky or smooth)
1 can condensed cream of chicken soup
1 soup can water
¼ cup milk
minced parsley, celery or grated carrot

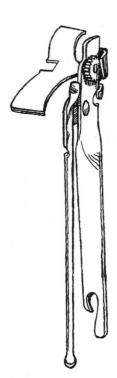

In a saucepan, cook the onion in the butter until tender but not browned.

Blend in the peanut butter.

Add the soup, water and milk.

Heat, stirring occasionally.

Garnish with one of the minced vegetables.

SEAFOOD BISQUE

(Serves 6–8)

¼ cup chopped onion
2 tablespoons butter or margarine
2 cans condensed cream of celery soup
1 soup can milk
1 soup can water
1 cup flaked salmon (7¾-ounce can, drained)
2 tablespoons chopped parsley
2 cups beef stock or canned bouillon
paprika, if desired

In a saucepan, cook the onion in butter until tender.

Blend in the soup, milk, water, salmon, parsley and pepper.

Heat thoroughly.

Garnish each serving with paprika.

For variation: Use condensed cream of mushroom soup instead of celery; and canned crab, lobster, shrimp or tuna instead of salmon.

COLD AVOCADO SOUP

(Serves 4)

3 cups chicken broth
1 large ripe avocado, peeled and cut in small pieces
1 teaspoon salt
pepper
½ cup cream
sherry

Put everything except the sherry and cream in a blender.

Cover and turn the blender on for 1 minute.

Put in a container and keep in the refrigerator to chill thoroughly.

In each cup of soup put 1 teaspoon sherry and stir well.

Put 1 tablespoon fresh cream on top.

PINK SOUP

(Serves 6–8)

This is a wonderful uncooked summer soup, served icy cold. It has a long Russian name, but we call it Pink Soup.

> *2 cups tomato juice*
> *2 cups beet soup (homemade or canned)*
> *2 tablespoons lemon juice*
> *dash black pepper*
> *1½ cups buttermilk*
> *½ cup cream*
> *2 scallions, sliced fine (include the tender part of the green tops)*
> *2 tablespoons chopped chives (about)*
> *chopped celery*
> *chopped cucumber*

Mix together all the ingredients except the celery and cucumber, and let stand in the refrigerator at least 24 hours. The longer it stands, the better.

When ready to use, add finely chopped celery and finely chopped cucumber in whatever quantity you want.

To this base you can then add, in whatever quantity you wish:

> *chopped cooked shrimp and hard-boiled egg slices, or*
> *chopped cooked chicken, or*
> *flaked fish and egg slices, or*
> *crabmeat and egg slices*

PATTY SHELLS

Making puff pastry is a tricky and time-consuming job, but patty shells, freshly baked from expertly prepared pastry, are the answer to every homemaker's dream. They make everyday dishes exciting and glamorous, and dress up favorite recipes into "party fare."

With an extra package or two of frozen patty shells in your freezer, you are always ready for the unexpected guest who comes to stay for lunch or dinner.

Pepperidge Farm Patty Shells are based on an ancient French recipe called "the pastry of one thousand leaves," made of one thousand tissue-thin layers of uncooked pastry that expand to seven times their height on contact with the oven's heat, turning golden and unbelievably fragile in the baking.

In less than thirty minutes from freezer to table you can produce these small delectable containers in which to serve anything from scrambled eggs to sweet creamy puddings or fresh fruit and ice cream.

Anything goes in a patty shell. Use them for

creamed poultry, fish or meat

cheese custard and rarebits

chicken, seafood, cheese and fruit salads

fresh fruit and ice cream or whipped cream

quick pudding mixes

individual pies, hot or cold

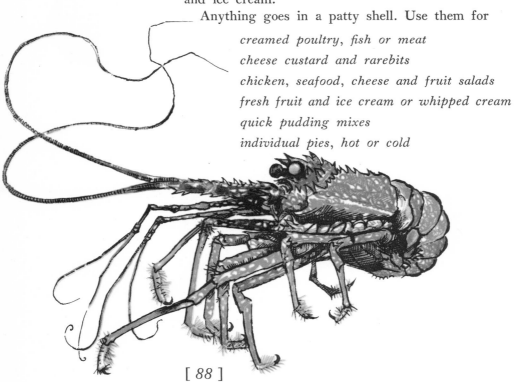

[88]

To help organize your meal planning, you can bake Pepper-idge Farm Patty Shells ahead of time so that you can use your oven for other dishes. Simply reheat baked patty shells in a moderate oven (350° F.) for 5 to 6 minutes. They can even be baked several days in advance, if stored in a tightly closed, moisture-proof container such as a cookie tin.

Do not fill patty shells until just before serving, except when specified in a recipe.

Do not refrigerate baked patty shells. The moisture from the refrigerator will spoil their flakiness.

The following are some of my favorite patty-shell recipes.

LOBSTER NEWBURG
(Serves 6)

Preheat oven to 350° F.

> *6 baked patty shells*
> *Newburg Sauce (p. 149)*
> *1 teaspoon brandy (optional)*
> *2 cups diced cooked lobster*

Make Newburg Sauce.

Stir in the brandy and lobster meat and cook over simmering water until the lobster is heated through.

Spoon the mixture into baked patty shells, replace caps and bake in a 350° F. oven for 15 minutes.

MUSHROOMS AU GRATIN
(Serves 6)

Preheat oven to 350° F.

6 baked patty shells
1 pound mushrooms
4 tablespoons butter
3 tablespoons flour
¾ cup chicken broth
¼ teaspoon dry marjoram
1 tablespoon chopped parsley
salt and pepper to taste
¼ cup heavy cream
1 tablespoon sherry (optional)
2 tablespoons grated cheese

Wash the mushrooms, remove and chop stems finely.

Slice the caps and cook stems and caps in butter over low heat for 15 minutes, stirring occasionally.

Stir in the flour and gradually stir in the chicken broth.

Add the marjoram, parsley, salt and pepper, and cook, stirring, for 5 minutes.

Stir in the cream and sherry, and cook, stirring, for 3 minutes longer.

Fill the baked shells with the mushroom mixture.

Crumble the baked patty-shell caps, mix with the cheese and sprinkle over the filling.

Bake in a 350° F. oven for 15 minutes.

CHICKEN A LA KING
(Serves 6)

6 baked patty shells
Sherry Cream Sauce (p. 149)
1 tablespoon minced onion
1 cup sliced mushrooms cooked in 1 tablespoon butter
1½ cups diced cooked chicken

Make Sherry Cream Sauce, but sauté the onion in the butter before adding the flour.

When the sauce is cooked, stir in the remaining ingredients. Heat over simmering water and serve hot in baked shells.

VEGETABLES MORNAY
(Serves 6)

Preheat oven to 350° F.

6 baked patty shells
1 package (10 ounces) frozen artichoke hearts
1 package (10 ounces) frozen French-cut string beans
1 tablespoon minced parsley
¼ teaspoon dry tarragon
Mornay Cream Sauce (p. 148)

Cook the vegetables according to directions on the packages and drain.

Combine with the parsley, tarragon and sauce and keep hot over simmering water.

Reheat the baked shells and caps in a 350° F. oven for 6 minutes.

Remove, fill with the sauced vegetables, replace the caps and serve immediately.

Note: 2 cups of any hot cooked vegetables may be used instead of the artichoke hearts and beans.

CRABMEAT LOUIS
(Serves 6)

Preheat oven to 350° F.

6 baked patty shells
2 green onions, sliced
¼ cup minced green pepper
½ teaspoon dry mustard
3 dashes Tabasco
½ cup shredded Cheddar cheese
1 tablespoon chopped parsley
1 can (6½ ounces) crabmeat
6 1-inch rounds sliced Cheddar cheese

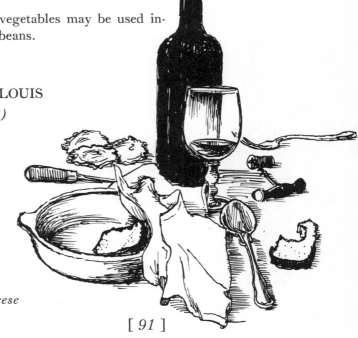

Make Cream Sauce (p. 34), but sauté the onion and green pepper in the butter before adding the flour.

When the sauce is finished, stir in the mustard, Tabasco, shredded cheese, parsley and crabmeat.

Fill the baked shells and replace the caps.

Cover each cap with a round of cheese and bake in a 350° F. oven for 8 minutes.

Serve hot.

Note: 2 cups cooked diced lobster or shrimp may be used in place of the crab.

CHEESE CUSTARD TARTS
(Serves 6)

Preheat oven to 350° F.

> *6 baked patty shells*
> *¼ cup chopped onions*
> *2 tablespoons butter*
> *½ cup diced cooked ham, lobster or crabmeat*
> *4 eggs*
> *1 cup hot heavy cream*
> *½ cup grated Swiss cheese*
> *1 tablespoon chopped parsley*
> *dash cayenne*
> *¼ teaspoon salt*

Sauté the onion in butter until transparent, then combine with the ham or fish.

Put a layer of the mixture in the bottom of each baked shell.

In the top of a double boiler, mix the eggs and cream.

Cook over simmering water, stirring, until as thick as a medium cream sauce.

Stir in the cheese, parsley, cayenne and salt, and cook, stirring briskly, until the cheese is melted.

Fill the shells with the cheese custard and bake in a 350° F. oven for 15 minutes.

Serve hot.

EGGS FLORENTINE
(Serves 6)

Preheat oven to 350° F.

>6 baked patty shells
>¾ cup cooked, chopped spinach
>1 tablespoon butter
>1 teaspoon lemon juice
>¼ teaspoon salt
>⅛ teaspoon pepper
>Mornay Sauce (p. 148)
>6 Poached Eggs (p. 104)
>1 tablespoon grated Parmesan cheese

Heat the spinach and butter and stir in lemon juice, salt and pepper.

Make a layer of spinach in the bottom of each baked shell.

Spoon 1 tablespoon sauce over the spinach and place a poached egg on top.

Fill the shells with the remaining sauce, sprinkle with cheese and bake in a 350° F. oven for 15 minutes.

SCALLOPS POULETTE
(Serves 6)

>6 baked patty shells
>3 tablespoons butter
>1 pound scallops, quartered
>½ bay leaf
>4 tablespoons flour
>⅛ teaspoon pepper
>2 egg yolks
>1 teaspoon minced onion
>½ cup white wine
>¼ pound mushrooms, chopped
>½ teaspoon salt
>½ cup heavy cream
>1 teaspoon lemon juice
>1 tablespoon chopped parsley

In a saucepan melt 1 tablespoon butter and in it cook the onion for 3 minutes.

Add the scallops, white wine and bay leaf, and bring the liquid to a simmer.

Cover tightly and poach the scallops for 2 minutes.

In a frying pan melt the remaining butter and in it cook the mushrooms for 6 minutes.

Stir in the flour.

Drain the liquid from the scallops into the frying pan and cook, stirring, until the sauce is thick.

Add salt and pepper and cook over low heat for 10 minutes, stirring occasionally.

Stir in the cream, lightly beaten with egg yolks.

Add the lemon juice, parsley and scallops and stir over low heat for 3 minutes longer.

Serve in baked patty shells.

Note: Cooked diced sweetbreads, flaked white fish or oysters may be used in place of scallops.

CHIPPED BEEF ROYALE

(Serves 6)

Shred 8 ounces chipped beef into a saucepan and cover with boiling water.

Drain and mix with Cream Sauce (p. 34) or Sherry Cream Sauce (p. 149).

Heat over simmering water and serve hot in baked patty shells.

VEGETABLES AU GRATIN

(Serves 6)

Preheat oven to 350° F.

Combine 1¾ cups chopped cooked spinach, broccoli, carrots or cauliflower with Cream Sauce (p. 34) or Mornay. Sauce (p. 148).

Fill the baked shells.

Crumble the caps and mix with 2 tablespoons shredded cheese, sprinkle over the filling and bake in a 350° F. oven for 15 minutes.

Serve hot.

EGGS BENEDICT
(Serves 6)

Preheat oven to 350° F.

> *6 baked patty shells*
> *1 cup shredded cooked ham*
> *6 fresh eggs*
> *Hollandaise Sauce (p. 406)*
> *parsley clusters*

Fill the baked shells loosely with the ham and heat in a 350° F. oven for 10 minutes.

Poach the eggs in a frying pan in enough salted water to cover (see p. 104).

When done, cut out the eggs with a 2-inch cookie cutter.

Place an egg on top of the ham inside each shell and cover with sauce.

Replace the cap and garnish with parsley.

CHICKEN LIVERS CHASSEUR
(Serves 6)

> *6 baked patty shells*
> *¼ cup chopped onion*
> *½ pound sliced mushrooms*
> *4 tablespoons butter*
> *¾ pound chicken livers, cut*
> *3 tablespoons flour*
> *1¼ cups hot water*
> *½ teaspoon salt*
> *⅛ teaspoon pepper*

Sauté the onion and mushrooms in the butter until the onion is transparent.

Dredge the livers in flour and add to the onion and mushrooms and continue to cook, stirring, until the livers are lightly browned.

Add the water, salt and pepper (⅛ teaspoon soy sauce may be added for extra flavor).

Bring to a boil and simmer for 5 minutes.
Serve hot in baked shells.

ASPARAGUS HOLLANDAISE
(Serves 6)

6 baked patty shells
cooked asparagus spears

For the sauce:
½ cup (1 stick) butter
2 egg yolks
2 tablespoons lemon juice
¼ teaspoon salt
pinch cayenne

Have the butter and eggs at room temperature.

In the top of a double boiler, beat the butter and egg yolks until smooth.

Beat in the lemon juice, salt and cayenne.

Place over simmering water and stir briskly for exactly 3 minutes (the water in the bottom of the boiler should not reach the upper pan).

Turn off the heat and continue to stir for 1 minute longer, or until the sauce is thick and smooth.

Arrange the asparagus in the baked shells and cover with the sauce.

WHITE FISH PROVENCALE
(Serves 6)

Preheat oven to 350° F.

6 baked patty shells
2 tablespoons butter
1 small onion, finely chopped
1 clove garlic, minced
1 can (4 ounces) mushrooms, drained
¼ teaspoon thyme
salt and pepper to taste

1 cup chopped canned tomatoes
½ cup dry white wine
1 pound cooked sole or haddock
2 tablespoons chopped parsley
2 tablespoons flour

Cook the onion and garlic in 1 tablespoon butter for 5 minutes.

Add the mushrooms, thyme, salt, pepper, tomatoes and wine. Sprinkle with the parsley, cover and simmer for 20 minutes. Break the fish into pieces with a fork and add to the sauce.

Mix the remaining butter and the flour to a smooth paste and stir into the liquid in the pan, bit by bit.

Cook, stirring, for 3 minutes.

Spoon into the baked patty shells, replace the caps and bake in a 350° F. oven for 15 minutes.

HOT APPLE TARTS

(Makes 6 tarts)

Preheat oven to 350° F.

6 baked patty shells
2 cups sliced tart apples
1 teaspoon lemon juice
1 cup apple juice or water
2 tablespoons water
¼ teaspoon cinnamon
⅔ cup sugar
pinch salt
3 tablespoons cornstarch
⅛ teaspoon nutmeg
¼ teaspoon lemon rind

Combine the apples, sugar, lemon juice, salt and apple juice or water.

Bring to a boil and simmer until the apples are tender.

Soften the cornstarch in 2 tablespoons water and stir into the juice.

Cook, stirring, until the juice is clear and thickened.

Stir in the spices and lemon rind.

Fill the baked shells; replace the caps.

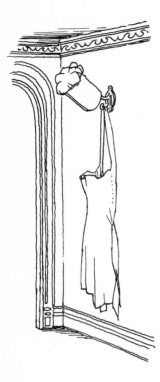

Place on a baking sheet and sprinkle with sugar.
Bake in a 350° F. oven for 15 minutes.
Serve hot or warm with whipped cream.

LEMON MERINGUE PUFF TARTS
(Makes 6 tarts)

Preheat oven to 350° F.

> *6 baked and cooled patty shells*
> *¾ cup sugar*
> *pinch salt*
> *1¼ cups water*
> *¼ cup lemon juice*
> *5 tablespoons flour*
> *2 egg yolks*
> *2 tablespoons butter*
> *grated rind of 2 lemons*
> *a two-egg meringue (see below)*

Combine the sugar, flour, salt and egg yolks.
Gradually stir in the water and cook, stirring, until the mixture thickens.
Cook over simmering water for 10 minutes, stirring occasionally.
Remove from the heat and stir in the butter, lemon juice and rind.
Cool.
Fill the baked shells with the lemon custard.
Cover with meringue and bake in a 350° F. oven for 10 minutes.

TWO-EGG MERINGUE

Beat the whites of 2 eggs until frothy.
Gradually beat in 4 tablespoons granulated sugar. Continue beating until stiff.
Flavor with ¼ teaspoon vanilla.

APRICOT CREAM TARTS
(Makes 6 tarts)

6 baked patty shells
½ pound dried apricots
pinch salt
2 teaspoons cornstarch
1 cup water
½ cup sugar
¼ cup shredded toasted almonds
1 cup sour cream
¼ cup light brown sugar

Simmer the apricots, water, salt and sugar for 20 minutes.

Stir into the juice the cornstarch dissolved in a little cold water and cook, stirring, until the juice is clear and thickened. Cool.

Sprinkle half the almonds into the baked shells.

Fill with the apricots and cover with the sour cream.

Sprinkle with the remaining almonds and brown sugar.

MINCEMEAT PUFF TARTS
(Serves 6)

Preheat oven to 350° F.

Fill six baked patty shells with mincemeat, replace the caps and sprinkle with sugar.

Bake in a 350° F. oven for 20 minutes.

Remove from the oven, raise the caps with a fork and sprinkle the filling with 1 teaspoon brandy.

Serve with hard sauce.

HARD SAUCE

8 tablespoons (1 stick) sweet butter
1½ cups sifted confectioner's sugar
¼ cup brandy

Cream the butter with an electric mixer and gradually add the sugar.

[*99*]

Add the brandy and continue beating until light and fluffy.

BAKED ALASKA
(in Patty Shells)

Preheat oven to 450° F.

Place baked and cooled patty shells on a bread board or cookie sheet.

Fill each patty shell with ice cream.

Cover each patty shell completely with Meringue (page 98).

Place on a bread board and bake in a 450° F. oven for 5 minutes until delicately browned.

Decorate with candied violets and serve immediately.

VANILLA CREAM FILLING
(for Patty Shells)

Cook 1 package vanilla pudding mix with 1½ cups milk and 1 tablespoon sugar.

Cool and add ½ teaspoon vanilla.

Beat until smooth.

Fold in 1 cup heavy cream, whipped, and chopped nuts, if desired, and fill baked and cooled patty shells.

EGGS

Only strictly fresh eggs should be used for poaching, boiling, omelettes, meringue, etc.

Eggs should always be kept in the refrigerator.

Eggs should be taken out long enough before using to remove the chill.

When eggs are low in price in the spring, you can put a supply into waterglass to preserve them.

Buy a 1-pound can of prepared waterglass.*

Boil 11 quarts of water and cool it.

Pour the water into a large stoneware crock.

Pour the waterglass into the water and stir well.

Do not wash the eggs.

Place the eggs carefully in the liquid in layers, preferably on end to keep the yolks in place.

Keep the jar in a very cool place and keep at least 2 inches of the liquid over the top layer of eggs.

The eggs will keep for 3 to 6 months, but should be used only for cooking (puddings, cakes, sauce), not for boiling or poaching.

TO BOIL EGGS

Bring to a full boil enough water to cover the number of eggs you are going to boil.

Place the eggs in the boiling water. Reduce heat and simmer:

> *3 minutes for very soft*
> *4 minutes for medium soft*
> *15 minutes for hard*

Put hard-cooked eggs in cold water immediately to prevent discoloration of the yolks.

---

* Waterglass, according to Webster's Collegiate Dictionary, is "a substance consisting usually of sodium silicate, but sometimes of potassium silicate, or of both ('double' waterglass), found in commerce as a glassy mass, a stony powder, or dissolved in water as a viscous sirupy liquid. It is used as a cement, as a protective coating and fireproofing agent, and in preserving eggs, etc."

CODDLED EGGS

Place eggs in boiling water, cover the pan tightly, remove from heat.

Let stand 5 to 10 minutes according to preference.

Place each egg in the small end of an egg cup and serve, to be coped with at the table.

Or, if you want to be popular, open the eggs in the kitchen by giving each egg a skillful whack through the center and scoop out with a teaspoon into a hot egg cup or plain cup, and serve at once.

SCRAMBLED EGGS

These should be cooked only in a double boiler if you want them soft and creamy.

For 1 portion

Beat 2 eggs, add 4 tablespoons milk and salt and pepper to taste.

In the top of a double boiler, melt 1 tablespoon butter.

Add the egg mixture and cook over boiling water, stirring constantly with a small wire whisk or a fork until thick and creamy.

Pile onto a slice of hot buttered toast.

MY SPECIAL OMELETTE

I don't like wet, leaky omelettes, so I make mine this way.

For 1 portion

Beat 2 eggs, add 2 tablespoons milk, salt and pepper.

Drop 1 tablespoon butter in an 8-inch omelette pan and, when sizzling hot, pour in the egg mixture.

Cover the pan and cook on medium heat for 1 minute.

Take off the cover and lift the edges which have cooked a bit, tip the pan slightly and let the liquid egg run under the edge.

Cover again and cook until set but still soft, and browned on the bottom, about 2 minutes more.

Fold over and slide out of the pan onto a very hot plate.

Make several small omelettes rather than a big one.
A 4-egg omelette for 2 people should be the maximum.
Use a 10-inch omelette pan for 4 eggs.
An omelette pan should not be used for anything else.
The new pans which require no greasing are excellent for
this purpose.

OMELETTE VARIATIONS

Use a filling when you fold the omelette over.

Prepare in advance:
A few stalks of hot cooked asparagus, cut in small pieces and blended with a little hot cream.

A few tablespoons of cooked peas, reheated in butter with a tablespoon of cream.

A couple of tablespoons of creamed mushrooms.

A couple of chicken livers, cooked in butter and chopped into small bits.

A little crisp cooked bacon, broken into small bits.

Any leftover meat—chicken, lamb or beef—chopped fine and heated in gravy or cream.

Any leftover fish, flaked into small pieces and heated in cream.

Sprinkle two tablespoons of grated Parmesan or Cheddar cheese over a hot omelette just before folding over.

A few tablespoons of cooked tomatoes, canned or fresh, with plenty of chopped onion.

Cut stale bread into small cubes, fry in the butter in the pan until crisp and brown, add another tablespoon of butter to the pan and pour the omelette mixture over the bread and cook until set.

Cut cooked potatoes into small cubes, fry in the butter in the pan until crisp and brown, add another tablespoon butter to the pan, and pour the omelette mixture over the potatoes and cook until set.

Cut cooked ham into small cubes, cook in the butter in the pan just until heated through so as not to dry it out, then pour the omelette mixture over the ham and cook until set.

EGGS IN CREAM

Butter a frying pan and for each egg to be cooked put in 1 tablespoon cream.

Break eggs one at a time and drop into the cream.

Cover the pan and cook for 3 minutes.

The cream and butter will be absorbed by the eggs.

Serve on buttered toast.

PLAIN POACHED EGGS ON TOAST

Heat 1 quart water or more in a frying pan, and salt it slightly.

Break an egg into a saucer and slip it gently into the water. Repeat until the desired number of eggs are in.

Remove the pan from the fire, or turn the heat down very low, and, with a spoon, gently ladle the water over the yolks until a white film covers the yolks and the whites are set; this takes about 3 minutes.

Remove gently, one by one, from the water, using a perforated spoon, and slip onto thin pieces of hot buttered toast.

Serve at once.

POACHED EGGS WITH SAUCE

(Serves 4)

1 *sliced onion*
2 *tablespoons butter*
½ *cup thinly sliced mushrooms*
2 *chicken livers, sliced thin*
2 *cups consommé*
2 *cups canned tomatoes*
½ *teaspoon salt*
1 *teaspoon sugar*
¼ *teaspoon oregano*
4 *eggs*

In a saucepan, cook the onion in the butter until clear but not browned, stirring constantly.

Add the mushrooms and chicken livers and cook for 5 minutes.

[*104*]

Add the consommé, tomatoes, salt, sugar and oregano.

Cover and simmer for 20 minutes.

Drop in the eggs, one at a time.

Cover tightly again and poach for 4 minutes.

Carefully lift each egg out of the liquid with a slotted spoon and place each egg on a slice of hot buttered toast.

Serve immediately with the sauce from the pan.

EGGS WITH PEPPERS
(Serves 4)

3 green peppers
3 tablespoons olive oil
1 onion, chopped
3 tomatoes
1 clove garlic, crushed
salt
black pepper
4 eggs

Slice the peppers thinly and sauté slowly in the olive oil and chopped onion.

When half cooked, add the tomatoes (peeled), garlic, and salt and black pepper to taste.

Simmer until it is a soft, mushy purée, crushing it with a fork.

Add the eggs, stir quickly and constantly until eggs are cooked and serve at once on toast triangles.

CHEESE SOUFFLE
(Serves 6)

Preheat oven to 325° F.

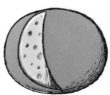

3 tablespoons butter
3 tablespoons flour
1½ cups milk
½ teaspoon salt
dash ground pepper
¾ cup grated sharp American cheese
6 eggs, separated

In the top of a double boiler over direct heat, melt the butter; add the flour and cook, stirring constantly, for 2 minutes.

Remove from the heat and add the milk gradually, stirring constantly.

Place over boiling water and cook till thick and smooth.

Add the cheese and stir till melted.

Add salt and pepper.

Remove from the fire and cool.

Beat the yolks of the eggs until thick and light in color.

Add to the cheese mixture, stirring in well.

Beat the egg whites until stiff.

Fold the whites into the yolk-and-cheese mixture.

Pour into a buttered 2-quart round dish.

One inch from edge of the dish, run a knife around the soufflé mix, making a cut about an inch deep. This keeps the soufflé from spilling over the edge and makes it rise in the center.

Bake at 325° F. for 30 to 40 minutes until high and golden brown.

CHEESE SOUFFLE SURPRISE

(Serves 6)

This is a specialty of the Ritz in Paris.

Preheat oven to 325° F.

First poach 6 eggs for not more than 3 minutes (see p. 104).

Remove carefully from the water and lay on a clean towel to cool and drain.

Make a regular cheese-soufflé mix (p. 105).

In a rectangular baking dish (size 12 by 6 inches) put a layer of half the soufflé mix.

Gently lay the poached eggs on the soufflé mix in 2 evenly spaced rows parallel to the long sides of the dish.

Carefully cover the eggs with the rest of the mix.

Bake at 325° F. for 30 minutes until golden brown.

To serve, carefully cut around the places where you hid the poached eggs and lift each portion out with a large serving spoon without breaking the poached eggs.

You can do it if you space the eggs in the mix evenly.

MACARONI AND CHEESE FAMILY STYLE

(Serves 4)

Preheat oven to 350° F.

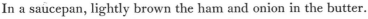

½ cup ground or finely chopped cooked ham
¼ cup chopped onion
2 tablespoons butter or margarine
1 can condensed cream of mushroom soup
½ cup milk
1 cup shredded sharp Cheddar cheese
2 cups cooked macaroni
2 tablespoons buttered bread crumbs

In a saucepan, lightly brown the ham and onion in the butter.
Stir in the soup, milk and ¾ cup cheese.
Heat until the cheese melts.
Blend the sauce with the macaroni.
Pour into a buttered 1½-quart casserole.
Sprinkle the remaining cheese and crumbs on top.
Bake in a moderate oven (350° F.) about 30 minutes, or until nicely browned and bubbling.

QUICK CHEESE SOUFFLE

(Serves 4–6)

Preheat oven to 300° F.

1 can condensed cream of celery soup
1 cup shredded sharp process cheese
6 eggs, separated

In a saucepan, combine the soup and cheese; heat slowly until the cheese melts.

Beat the egg yolks until thick and lemon-colored; stir into the soup mixture.

In a large bowl, using a clean egg beater, beat the egg whites until stiff; fold the soup mixture into the egg whites.

Pour into an ungreased 2-quart casserole.

Bake in a slow oven (300° F.) 1 to 1¼ hours, or until the soufflé is golden brown.

Serve immediately.

Note: Or bake in a hot oven (400° F.) for 30 minutes.

My special cheese pies are very quick to make and are fine for a lunch or supper dish with a salad on the side. Here are three of them.

CHEDDAR CHEESE PIE

(Serves 4)

Preheat oven to 350° F.

> *slices of white bread*
> *butter*
> *½ pound sharp Cheddar cheese*
> *2 eggs*
> *1 cup milk*

Butter a 9- or 10-inch pyrex pie pan generously.

Butter enough slices of white bread, crusts removed, to line the pan's bottom and sides, buttered side down, cutting the bread to fit and overlapping here and there if necessary.

Slice the cheese into small pieces and lay evenly over the bread in the pie pan.

Beat the eggs in a small bowl.

Add the milk and pour over the cheese.

Bake at 350° F. about ½ hour until bubbly and golden brown.

Serve hot.

TOMATO CHEESE PIE

(Serves 4)

Preheat oven to 350° F.

> *bread slices, buttered, crusts trimmed off*
> *4 tablespoons dry bread crumbs*
> *canned tomatoes*
> *1 tablespoon grated onion*
> *salt and pepper*

1 teaspoon sugar
4 ounces grated Cheddar cheese
2 eggs
1 cup milk
1 extra egg white, slightly beaten

Butter generously a 9-inch pyrex pie pan.

Line the pan with the bread, buttered side down, cutting strips to fit around the sides.

Brush the bread surfaces with beaten egg white and sprinkle with the dry crumbs.

Drain the tomatoes from their juice and lay the tomatoes on the crumbs. Reserve the juice for other use.

Sprinkle with the salt, pepper, sugar and grated onion.

Add the grated cheese all over evenly.

Beat the eggs and milk together and pour over the cheese.

Bake for ½ hour at 350° F.

CARROT CHEESE PIE

(Serves 4)

Preheat oven to 350° F.

bread slices, buttered, crusts trimmed off
4 ounces grated carrots
4 ounces grated Cheddar cheese
2 eggs
1 cup milk

Butter generously a 9- or 10-inch pyrex pie pan.

Line the pan with the slices of bread, buttered side down, cutting to fit the bottom and sides.

Put the grated cheese and carrots on top of the bread.

Beat the eggs with the milk.

Pour over the cheese mixture.

Bake in a moderate (350° F.) oven for 30 minutes.

STUFFED SHAD WITHOUT BONES
(Serves 4)

Preheat oven to 225° F.

1 large sheet aluminum foil
1 shad weighing 3½ pounds before dressing
1 large yellow onion
3 carrots
3 shallots
1 clove garlic
bouquet of parsley, ½ teaspoon thyme, 1 bay leaf
2 thin slices boiled ham
⅔ cup olive oil
½ teaspoon salt
¼ teaspoon pepper
3 lemons
2–3 tablespoons cognac

Buy 1 fine fresh buck shad, weighing about 3½ pounds.

Have it prepared for baking, with head, tail and center bone removed.

Five and a half hours before you will be serving the fish, prepare the following ingredients:

Peel and chop fine the onion, shallots and carrots.

Make a bouquet of parsley, ½ teaspoon thyme, 1 bay leaf.

Peel the clove of garlic and cut the boiled ham into tiny pieces.

Squeeze and strain the juice of 1½ lemons.

Heat ⅓ cup olive oil in a small frying pan on low heat. Add the chopped onion and cook for a minute or 2. Add the chopped carrots and cook 3 or 4 minutes, stirring with a wooden spoon. Add the ham and continue cooking 10 minutes, stirring frequently. Last of all, add the shallots and season to taste with pepper and salt.

Spread a large sheet of aluminum foil over a shallow jelly-roll baking pan.

Wash the fish inside and out with cold water and pat dry on paper toweling.

Oil the center of the foil generously with 2–3 tablespoons olive oil.

Lay the fish, skin side down, on the foil.

Trickle the strained lemon juice over the whole, and spread the cooked vegetable stuffing over one half of the fish.

Cover with the other half, enclosing the vegetables.

Dribble another 2 tablespoons olive oil over the fish, and tuck the garlic and the parsley bouquet by its side.

Now very carefully enclose the fish securely, folding the foil, making double seams, over the top and at both ends.

Place in a very slow (225° F.) oven and bake for 5½ hours, leaving it strictly alone.

Ten minutes before it will be done, split the foil down the center to expose the fish, and pour over it 2 or 3 tablespoons good cognac.

Continue cooking 10 minutes, then pour off all the oil and, with the aid of a pancake turner, transfer the fish to a hot fish platter, discarding the foil.

Don't worry if the bottom skin sticks to the foil, for this is all to the good.

The fish may lose its shape, but this doesn't matter.

Just reshape it a bit and garnish prettily with parsley and quartered lemons.

Serve at once with boiled new potatoes and hot Clarified Butter (p. 152).

The long, slow cooking completely dissolves the tiny bones, one of the disadvantages of shad.

Serve a well-chilled white wine with this.

FILLET OF FLOUNDER ON A BED
OF MUSHROOMS

(Serves 6)

Preheat oven to 350°–375° F.

> *1½ pounds fillet of flounder*
> *1 pound fresh mushrooms*
> *2 shallots*
> *½ cup dry white wine*
> *½ cup cold water*
> *10 tablespoons (1¼ sticks) butter*
> *2 tablespoons flour*
> *8 black peppercorns*
> *1 bay leaf*

strained juice of 1 lemon
1 tablespoon chopped parsley
salt and pepper to taste
¼ teaspoon nutmeg
pinch cayenne
½ cup heavy cream

Wash, dry and remove the tough part of the stems from the mushrooms—chop fine.

Melt 4 tablespoons butter in a frying pan, add the shallots, peeled and cut fine, and cook without browning for about 3 minutes.

Add the chopped mushrooms and cook gently for about 5 minutes.

Set aside.

Butter 2 rectangular dishes, 10 by 6 by 1½ inches, using 1 tablespoon butter for each.

Season the mushrooms to taste with about ¼ teaspoon salt, a pinch of nutmeg and a dash of pepper.

Spread over the bottom of one of the dishes.

Wash the flounder and pat dry on paper toweling.

Place in the second dish and pour over it the cold water and the white wine.

Add the peppercorns, bay leaf and, last of all, the lemon juice.

Dot with 2 tablespoons butter.

Place the dish in a moderate (350°–375° F.) oven and bake until the fish is opaque throughout, or for about 25 minutes.

Remove from the oven and drain off the juice into a small pan.

With the help of a pancake turner, spread the fillets over the bed of mushrooms.

Keep warm while you make the sauce.

Melt 2 tablespoons butter in a small pan, and stir in 2 tablespoons flour, using a wooden spoon.

Cook for a minute or two, then add gradually the fish juice, making a smooth sauce.

Remove from the fire when thickened and add gradually, stirring constantly, the heavy cream.

Season to taste with salt and pepper and about ¼ teaspoon nutmeg and a pinch of cayenne.

Pour over the fish.

Increase the heat of the oven to 450° F. and place under the grill until slightly browned.

Watch carefully.

Sprinkle with the parsley and serve at once, accompanied by buttered fresh or frozen peas.

FILLET OF SMOKED COD OR HADDOCK
(Finnan Haddie)
(Serves 6)

1½ pounds fillet of smoked cod or haddock
6 tablespoons butter (¾ bar)
1½ quarts milk
6 poached eggs (optional)
freshly ground black pepper

Wash the fillets in cold water, place in a shallow pan large enough to hold them comfortably.

Cover with the milk.

Bring slowly to the boiling point but do not allow to boil.

Simmer for 10 minutes, turn the fillets over with a pancake turner and simmer for 10 to 15 minutes longer.

Remove the pan from the fire.

Place the fillets temporarily on a plate and pull apart into large bite-size flakes.

Place the milk in the top of a double boiler over boiling water to keep hot.

Add the fish and a little freshly ground black pepper.

When ready to serve, cut ¾ bar butter into 6 pieces, place in a hot soup tureen, pour the fish and milk over the butter, and send to the table to be served in soup plates, accompanied by heated and buttered French bread.

Poached eggs may be served with this if desired, in which case the soup is served in the kitchen, placing it over a freshly poached egg in each soup plate.

KEDGEREE

(Serves 4–6)

If by chance you have any smoked cod or haddock left over, it may be made into kedgeree, an excellent breakfast or luncheon dish.

> *1–1½ cups flaked cooked smoked cod or haddock*
> *½–¾ cup rice*
> *2–3 hard-boiled eggs*
> *pinch cayenne*
> *¼ teaspoon freshly ground pepper*
> *¼ teaspoon curry powder*
> *¼ teaspoon nutmeg*
> *⅛ pound butter (½ bar)*
> *1 tablespoon chopped parsley*

Cook the rice, following the directions on the box.

Hard-boil the eggs, peel and chop coarsely.

Place the well-drained fish in the top of a double boiler with the butter and heat over boiling water.

Season with the pepper, curry powder, nutmeg and cayenne.

Add the well-drained rice and the chopped egg.

Stir lightly with a fork and, when piping hot throughout, garnish with chopped parsley and serve.

CODFISH BALLS

(Serves 4)

> *½ pound salt codfish*
> *3 large potatoes*
> *1 egg*
> *¼ cup milk*
> *1 tablespoon chopped parsley*
> *salt and pepper to taste*

Wash the codfish well and soak in cold water for at least 4 hours.

Drain and pull it apart in search of any bones that may remain.

Peel the potatoes, wash and quarter them.

Add to the fish and cover with cold water.

Bring to a boil, skim carefully and continue cooking gently until the potatoes are well done.

Drain well and mash the fish and potatoes together at once with a wire masher or, better still, an electric rotary beater.

Beat the egg with the milk and add to the fish, mixing well.

Season to taste with pepper and salt if necessary and stir in the parsley.

Heat sufficient vegetable shortening in a deep heavy saucepan with straight sides.

The temperature of the fat should be about 390° F. and the depth of the fat when melted should be 4 inches.

With a spoon and a fork, form small balls of the mixture and drop into the fat, not more than 6 at a time, and cook until a golden brown all over, or for about 5 minutes.

Turn the cakes once with the aid of a slotted spoon.

Remove from the fat with the same slotted spoon and place on paper toweling.

Keep warm while you fry the rest.

Serve with Coleslaw (p. 146).

FISH CAKES WITH EGG SAUCE

(Serves 6)

> 1 cup salt codfish
> 2 cups sliced raw potatoes
> 2 eggs, beaten well
> 1 tablespoon butter

Wash the fish well in running cold water for 10 minutes; soak for 1 hour if very salt.

Drain and shred into fine pieces.

Slice the potatoes thin.

Cover the fish and potatoes with boiling water and cook until the potatoes are soft.

Drain and shake the pan over heat to dry.

Mash the fish and potatoes together, adding the butter.

Add well-beaten eggs and beat till smooth.

Drop by spoonfuls into hot fat and cook about 1 minute until golden.

Drain well on absorbent paper.
Serve with Egg Sauce (p. 152).

CREAMED SALT CODFISH

(Serves 4)

½ pound salt codfish
4 tablespoons butter
4 tablespoons flour
2 cups hot milk
2 eggs
salt and pepper to taste
¼–½ cup heavy cream
1 teaspoon chopped parsley

Wash and soak the fish in cold water for at least 6 hours, or overnight, changing the water occasionally.

When ready to cook it, drain and with your fingers pull it apart in search of bones, which must be discarded.

Cover again with fresh cold water and bring gently to the boiling point.

Reduce the heat and simmer ½ hour.

Drain and cool.

Hard-boil the eggs, cooking them gently for 10 to 15 minutes.

Plunge into cold water for 5 minutes or so.

In the meantime melt the butter in the top of a double boiler over direct low heat.

Stir in the flour and cook for a minute or two, stirring constantly with a wooden spoon, then add gradually the hot milk, making a smooth cream sauce.

Season lightly to taste with about ½ teaspoon salt and ¼ teaspoon pepper.

Remove the shells from the eggs and slice the eggs into the sauce.

Also add the codfish, going over it once more in search of bones.

Stir lightly with a fork, then place over boiling water until ready to serve, at which time add heavy cream to thin to desired consistency.

Sprinkle with chopped parsley and serve.

SHRIMPS PIRAEUS

(Serves 6)

4 pounds fresh cooked shrimps, shelled and deveined
1 can (2 pounds 3 ounces) Italian tomatoes with basil
1 can (7 ounces) tomato paste
2 cans (8 ounces) whole pimientos
1 teaspoon dried basil
¼ teaspoon powdered marjoram
1 tablespoon chopped parsley
¼ teaspoon pepper
juice of 1 lemon
¾ cup olive oil
2 cloves garlic
¾ pound imported Feta cheese *
salt
Tabasco sauce
2 large Bermuda onions

Peel and chop fine the onions.

Heat the olive oil in a large (12-inch) iron frying pan.

Add the onions and cook very gently, stirring with a wooden spoon, until soft—not brown, just golden.

Press into this the garlic, using a garlic press.

Blend in 1 can of tomato paste, then add the pimientos, chopping them and including their juice.

Then add the peeled Italian tomatoes with basil, chopping the tomatoes likewise.

Add the pepper, basil, marjoram, a generous dash of Tabasco and salt to taste.

Simmer gently for ½ hour, stirring occasionally to prevent sticking.

Transfer to the top of an extra-large double boiler and stir in the strained lemon juice.

---

* Feta cheese may be bought in certain shops specializing in imported cheese. It should be kept in milk until ready to use.

Keep hot over boiling water.

When ready to serve, drain the prepared cooked shrimps, add to the sauce and allow to heat through (about 10 minutes).

In the meantime cut the Feta cheese into 1-inch cubes.

Drop them gently into the sauce, turn off the heat, cover and allow to stand 5 minutes, or just long enough to have the pieces begin to melt.

Do not stir.

Place the whole in a large hot soup tureen, sprinkle with chopped parsley and serve at once at the table in large soup plates.

Crisp, warm French bread should accompany this, also a well-chilled white wine.

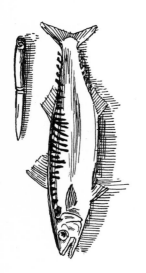

FRESH MACKEREL IN WHITE WINE
(Serves 4)

A delicious cold dish!

Preheat oven to 450° F.

> *4 mackerel, medium-size, cleaned, boned, split*
> *3 carrots*
> *8 small white onions*
> *thyme*
> *1 bay leaf*
> *pepper and salt*
> *parsley*
> *1 cup white wine*
> *¼ cup olive oil*

Cut the carrots into thin slices.

Chop the onions and sprinkle them with the white wine.

Add freshly ground pepper, salt, a pinch of thyme, a bay leaf.

Cook for 5 minutes over low heat.

Put the mackerel on a flat ovenproof dish.

Pour the carrot-and-onion mixture over.

Sprinkle the olive oil over the fish.

Bring to a boil over direct heat and finish cooking in a hot oven for 10 minutes.

Cool and sprinkle with chopped parsley.

Leave in the refrigerator overnight.

CHOPPED BEEF RING
(Serves 6)

Preheat oven to 450° F.

> *2 pounds ground beef*
> *¾ cup butter*
> *½ cup grated onion*
> *4 slices white bread*
> *1½ teaspoons salt*
> *2 teaspoons paprika*
> *1½ teaspoons prepared mustard*
> *few grains cayenne*
> *1 tablespoon finely chopped parsley*
> *1 tablespoon finely chopped chives*
> *⅔ cup tomato juice or soup*
> *⅓ cup tomato ketchup*
> *creamed mushrooms*

Mix together the beef, butter, grated onion, bread (broken into small pieces), salt, paprika, prepared mustard, cayenne, parsley and chives.

Mix thoroughly and moisten with ⅔ cup tomato juice or soup.

Pack the mixture into a generously buttered ring mold.

Spread tomato ketchup over the top of the mixture and bake the ring in a hot oven (450° F.) for 45 minutes, or until the top is delicately brown and the meat shrinks from the sides of the mold.

Unmold on a heated platter fill the center of the ring with creamed mushrooms and serve with boiled potatoes and broiled tomato slices.

STUFFED GREEN PEPPERS
(Serves 6–8)

Preheat oven to 425°–450° F.

> *4 large green peppers*
> *4 cups leftover roast lamb, ham, chicken, veal,*
>   *pork or beef*
> *1 tablespoon chopped parsley*

2 large shallots, chopped fine
¼ teaspoon pepper
¼ teaspoon dried marjoram
salt to taste
8 tablespoons butter (¼ pound)
3 tablespoons tomato ketchup
1 teaspoon Worcestershire sauce
½ cup beef, chicken or veal broth

Split the peppers in half lengthwise.

Remove stems and seeds.

Wash and parboil for 10 minutes in salted boiling water.

Drain, run cold water over them, and place on a towel while you prepare the stuffing.

Put sufficient cold roasted meat through a meat grinder, using the medium cutter, to make 4 cups.

Stretch it if necessary with cold boiled rice or soft bread crumbs.

Season with the shallots, marjoram, pepper, tomato ketchup, Worcestershire sauce, chopped parsley and salt to taste (about ½ teaspoon) and moisten with 5 tablespoons melted butter.

Stuff the peppers with this mixture, and place side by side in an ovenproof rectangular glass baking dish 12 by 7½ by 1½ inches, well buttered with 1 tablespoon butter.

Dot with 2 tablespoons butter and pour into the dish the beef, chicken or veal broth.

Bake in a 425°–450° F. oven for about 20 minutes, or until sizzling hot and well browned, basting once or twice with the juice in the bottom of the dish.

HOT SAUSAGE CREAM TART

(Serves 4–6)

Preheat oven to 450° F.

Plain Pastry
1 tablespoon butter
1 teaspoon curry powder
1 cup milk
2 tablespoons chopped onion
½ pound tiny fresh pork link sausages

[*120*]

1 tablespoon flour
4 whole eggs
2 cups heavy cream

Make Plain Pastry (p. 153) and line a deep 9-inch pie pan.

Place the pastry shell in the refrigerator to chill while preparing the filling.

In a saucepan melt the butter and stir in the curry powder.

Add the milk and finely chopped onion.

Simmer for 20 minutes.

Cool.

While this is cooking, fry the tiny fresh pork sausages (or regular-size sausages cut into quarters) until they are browned.

Cool the cooked sausages.

Place the cooled sausages in the pastry shell.

Blend the flour gradually into the beaten eggs.

Add the curried milk.

Add the heavy cream.

Pour this mixture carefully over the sausages in the pastry shell.

Bake for 10 minutes in a 450° F. oven; reduce the heat to 350° and bake for about 40 minutes more, or until the custard is set.

CALF'S LIVER SWISS STYLE

(Serves 3–4)

1 pound sliced calf's liver
flour
pepper and salt
2 ounces butter

Cut the liver into small strips about 1½ inches long by ½ inch wide.

Toss in flour to coat all sides.

Melt the butter, drop in the liver strips and stir and toss over low heat for 2 minutes, adding salt and pepper to taste.

Remove the liver to a hot plate and add a little boiling water to the pan, stirring constantly.

Pour the gravy over the liver.

CALF'S LIVER WITH BACON
(Serves 3–4)

Prepare the liver as for Calf's Liver Swiss Style (above).

Fry 6 or 8 slices of bacon; when done, remove from the pan.

Drop the liver strips into the hot bacon fat and cook for 2 minutes, stirring and tossing to cook all sides.

Serve with the crisp bacon.

VEAL KIDNEYS IN MUSTARD
(Serves 4)

5 veal kidneys
6 tablespoons butter
⅓ cup brandy
salt and pepper to taste
2 heaping teaspoons chopped parsley
3 teaspoons dry mustard

Remove the fat and the veil-like skin from the veal kidneys.

Slice into small pieces, being careful not to include any of the hard white substance in the center.

Melt 2 tablespoons butter in a frying pan.

When sizzling hot, add the kidneys and cook quickly just for a minute or 2, shaking the pan so that they cook on all sides.

Remove from the pan, using a slotted spoon; place temporarily on a hot plate, cover and keep warm.

Add 2 tablespoons butter to the remaining juice in the pan and when it has melted, stir in the dry mustard, ¼ to ½ teaspoon salt and a dash of pepper.

Stir in the brandy, and when it begins to boil, avert your face and ignite the sauce with a lighted match. Let burn until the flame turns yellowish green.

Cover the pan to extinguish the flame.

Add the kidneys and 1 teaspoon chopped parsley.

Simmer for a minute or 2, stir in another 2 tablespoons butter, turn into a hot serving dish, sprinkle with another teaspoon of parsley and serve at once, accompanied by tiny plain boiled potatoes or French bread.

STEAK ROLL-UPS
(Serves 4)

2 pounds thinly sliced round steak or flank steak
2 cups Bread Stuffing (p. 29)
2 tablespoons shortening
1 can condensed cream of mushroom soup
½ cup water
½ cup sour cream, if desired

Pound the steak with a meat hammer or the edge of a heavy saucer.

Cut the steak into 8 pieces long enough to roll.

Place about ¼ cup stuffing near the center of each piece of steak; roll, pinwheel fashion, and fasten with a toothpick or skewer.

In a large skillet, brown the roll-ups in shortening.

Add the soup and water.

Cover and cook over low heat about 1½ hours, or until tender.

Spoon the sauce over the meat occasionally during the cooking.

Remove the roll-ups from the pan.

Stir sour cream into the sauce; heat and serve.

TOP-STOVE SHORT RIBS
(Serves 4–6)

3 pounds short ribs of beef
¼ cup flour
2 tablespoons shortening
1 can condensed beef broth
1 cup dried apricots

> 2 tablespoons brown sugar
> 2 tablespoons vinegar
> ¼ teaspoon ground cinnamon
> ¼ teaspoon ground cloves
> ¼ teaspoon ground allspice

Dust the ribs with flour; brown in shortening in a large, heavy pan.

Pour off the excess drippings.

Combine the remaining ingredients; pour over the ribs.

Cover.

Cook over low heat about 2½ hours, or until the ribs are tender; turn the ribs and baste with the sauce occasionally.

BOEUF STROGANOFF WITHOUT PANIC
(Serves 6–8)

To be made the day before serving.

> 1 tablespoon chopped parsley
> 1 pound onions (3 large), sliced very fine
> 2 pounds top round, cut in narrow strips about
>   the size of a little finger
> 6 ounces butter
> 1 tablespoon dry mustard
> 1 teaspoon salt
> ¼ teaspoon pepper
> 1 tablespoon flour
> 1 cup sour cream
> 2 bay leaves

Sauté the sliced onions slowly in 8 tablespoons butter until a light golden color, or for about 20 minutes.

Remove into a casserole.

Sauté the beef strips in 4 tablespoons butter, just long enough for them to turn gray and give out their juice.

Strain this juice over the onions and stir in the dry mustard, salt and pepper, and 1 tablespoon sour cream.

Bury in this the bay leaves and add the meat.

Mix well, place on low heat, cover and simmer very gently for 45 minutes, stirring lightly occasionally.

Remove from the heat, cool and refrigerate overnight.

Fifteen minutes or so before serving, simmer again on a low flame until done (time depending on the quality of the meat).

Sprinkle with flour, stir well, then add 1 scant cup sour cream, and continue cooking on a very low flame, stirring constantly until well incorporated, but be careful not to allow it to actually boil.

Garnish with chopped parsley and serve with cooked broad or fine noodles.

GROUND BEEF A LA LINDSTROM

(Serves 6)

> *2 pounds ground beef*
> *2 large cold boiled potatoes*
> *2 egg yolks*
> *2 pickled beets, finely chopped*
> *1½ tablespoons grated onion*
> *2 tablespoons chopped capers*
> *salt and pepper to taste*
> *6 tablespoons butter*
> *12 slices pickled beets*
> *12 sprigs fresh dill (optional)*

Crush the potatoes and work them into the ground meat (preferably top sirloin).

Season lightly to taste with salt and pepper.

Work in gradually the egg yolks.

Add the chopped beets, grated onion and chopped capers.

Form into 12 rather thick patties and fry immediately in 4 tablespoons butter, cooking them about 10 minutes in all, adding 2 additional tablespoons butter toward the end.

Place on a hot serving dish, pour a drop or two of water into the frying pan to make a bit of pan gravy and pour over the patties.

Top each with an additional slice of pickled beet, and garnish, if you like, with a sprig of fresh dill on each patty.

[*125*]

LAMB STEW WITH DILL
(Serves 6)

3 pounds shoulder of lamb cut up for stew
1 large bunch dill (5 ounces)
1 quart water
4 white peppercorns
1 bay leaf
2 tablespoons butter
2 tablespoons flour
1 tablespoon vinegar
2–3 teaspoons salt
coarsely ground black pepper
1 teaspoon sugar
1 egg yolk
2 tablespoons finely cut fresh dill

Wash the dill (keep out sufficient of the green feathery part to make 2 heaping tablespoons when cut fine).

Make a bouquet of the rest, enclosing the peppercorns and bay leaf.

Tie securely.

Place the bouquet in a large pan.

Add the salt and water.

.Bring to a boil, cover and simmer for 15 minutes.

In the meantime cut away the excess fat from the lamb, but do not remove the bones.

Add the meat to the dill-flavored water, stand by until it comes to the boiling point, reduce the heat and skim carefully.

Cover and simmer until the meat is tender, or for about 2 hours.

Discard the bouquet of dill, drain off almost all the broth and keep the meat hot on a very low flame while you make the sauce.

Melt the butter in the top of a double boiler over low direct heat, stir in the flour, cook for a few seconds, then add gradually 2 cups of the dill-flavored broth.

Cook until thickened.

Add the vinegar, sugar and a dash of pepper.

Beat the egg yolk with a wire whisk in a small bowl, then add the hot broth gradually, stirring constantly.

Place over boiling water and stir in the finely cut dill.

Place the meat, well drained of any remaining broth, in a hot serving dish, pour the dill sauce over all, and serve piping hot, accompanied by plain boiled potatoes, and buttered fresh asparagus cut in 1-inch pieces.

BLANQUETTE DE VEAU
(Serves 6–8)

3 pounds leg of veal, cut in 1-inch squares
salt and pepper to taste
1 small peeled onion
1 whole clove
1 large carrot, scraped
bouquet: parsley, celery leaves, 1 bay leaf,
*   ¼ teaspoon thyme*
1 quart water (or more)
½ pound small white mushrooms
1 lemon
6 ounces butter
12 small white onions
½ cup flour
1 tablespoon chopped parsley
2 egg yolks
¼ cup heavy cream
pinch nutmeg

Soak the veal squares in enough cold water to cover for 2 hours.

Drain and place the meat in a deep pan—the top of a 3-quart double boiler is ideal.

Pour over it 1 quart fresh cold water, or sufficient to cover the meat.

Add 1 teaspoon salt, place on low heat, and bring very slowly to the boiling point. This is a slow process and will take about ½ hour. Stand by and skim carefully.

Add the peeled onion studded with the clove; the peeled carrot cut in chunks; and a bouquet, securely tied, of a few celery leaves, parsley, ¼ teaspoon thyme and 1 bay leaf. Cover partially and simmer gently for 1½ hours.

In the meantime remove the stems from ½ pound small, fresh, white mushrooms. Wash them carefully.

Have ready a saucepan containing ¼ cup cold water, the juice of ½ lemon and 1 tablespoon butter.

Peel the mushrooms, quarter them and place immediately in the saucepan containing the water, lemon and butter.

When all is prepared, place the pan on the fire, cover and bring to a brisk boil. Cook 4 to 5 minutes, shaking the pan occasionally. Watch carefully so that they don't boil dry. Remove from the fire and keep warm.

Now place 12 little white onions of uniform size in a pan and cover with boiling water.

Let them stand 1 minute, drain, allow cold water to run over them and with a sharp knife remove a small bit from both ends, then pull off with the fingers the first layer of onion.

Place in a little pan just large enough to hold them comfortably, then add 1 tablespoon butter and ¼ cup broth from the veal.

Cover and place on low heat and cook gently until just tender through, about 35 minutes.

Watch carefully and add additional hot water if necessary to keep them from boiling completely dry.

When the veal is done, remove the bouquet, carrots and onion and strain off most of the broth into another little pan. Dot the meat with 2 tablespoons butter, place over boiling water, cover and keep warm while you make the sauce.

Melt ¼ pound butter, add the flour, cook together a minute or 2, stirring constantly to make a white roux, then add gradually the hot broth, of which there should be 3 cups (if there is not enough, add boiling water to make up the difference).

Now add the mushrooms and their juice and the onions and their juice to the meat.

Break the egg yolks into a little bowl, add the heavy cream and beat together; add gradually a little of the hot sauce, and in turn add this mixture gradually back to the sauce.

Do not allow to boil.

Season to taste with salt, coarsely ground pepper, a pinch of nutmeg and the juice of ½ lemon.

Also drain into it all the remaining juice on the meat.

Pour the sauce over the meat.

Place in a hot deep serving dish.

Garnish with chopped parsley and serve at once accompanied by a big bowl of flaky, boiled white long-grain rice.

MARINATED VEAL SCALLOPS AMANDINE
(Serves 6)

12 veal scallops
1 cup blanched almonds
4 eggs
2 tablespoons cream
2 teaspoons flour
½ cup olive oil (or more)
2 lemons
¼ teaspoon salt

For the marinade
2 tablespoons sherry
juice of 1 lemon
⅛ teaspoon mace
⅛ teaspoon pepper
½ teaspoon salt
½ teaspoon oregano
¼ cup olive oil
2 teaspoons sugar

Ask your butcher to make small equal-sized veal scallops (12) cut from rib chops ⅜ inch thick, pounded between waxed paper not too vigorously.

Place the veal in a bowl and pour over it the marinade. Cover and marinate overnight in the refrigerator.

Before cooking, drain and dry the scallops thoroughly on paper toweling.

Run the blanched almonds through the meat grinder, making a fine powder of them.

Make a light batter by beating together the eggs, cream, flour and salt.

Heat ½ cup olive oil, or more, in a very large heavy iron frying pan over low heat.

Now dip the meat into the batter, piece by piece, and then into the grated nuts, pressing down firmly on both sides to pick up an even coating of nuts.

Place in the frying pan, working as quickly as possible, and cook gently until well browned, turning them over with a pancake turner.

They should cook at least 10 to 15 minutes on each side.

Place on a hot serving platter, garnish with quartered lemons and serve at once, with buttered peas.

A well-chilled white wine would be good with this.

LAMB CURRY

(Serves 6–8)

¼ cup flour
2 teaspoons curry powder
2 pounds cubed lean lamb
2 tablespoons shortening
1 can condensed onion soup
½ can water
1 cup sliced celery
1 unpeeled tart red apple, cubed
¼ cup seedless raisins
hot cooked rice
chutney
shredded coconut
chopped peanuts

Combine the flour and curry powder; roll the lamb in the flour mixture.

In a skillet, brown the lamb in the shortening.

Blend in any remaining flour.

Add the soup, water, celery, apple and raisins.

Cook covered over low heat for about 1 hour, or until the lamb is tender.

Stir often during cooking.

Serve over hot rice (about 4 cups cooked).

Garnish with chutney, coconut and peanuts.

ROAST BEEF

Preheat oven to 300° F.

Buy a two or three rib roast of beef, preferably the first cut.

Place the roast, fat side up, in an uncovered roasting pan.

Sprinkle with salt and pepper.

Roast in a slow oven (300° F.).

Do not baste or turn it.

There will be less shrinkage than in a hot oven, and the meat will be deliciously browned but juicy and never dry.

Rare: roast 18 to 20 minutes per pound.
Medium: roast 22 to 25 minutes per pound.
Well done: roast 30 minutes per pound.

It is well to use a meat thermometer.

ROAST LEG OF LAMB

Preheat oven to 300° F.

1 leg of lamb—6 to 7 pounds
garlic or garlic salt
salt and pepper

Place the leg of lamb, fat side up, in an uncovered roasting pan and rub all over with garlic or sprinkle with garlic salt.

Sprinkle with pepper.

Roast in a slow oven (300° F.).

Do not baste or turn it.

There will be less shrinkage, and the meat will be pink and juicy if you like it rare.

Rare: roast 20 minutes per pound.
Well done: roast 30 minutes per pound.

CHICKEN A LA KING SUPREME

(Serves 4–6)

2 tablespoons chopped celery
⅓ cup chopped green pepper
3 tablespoons butter

1 tablespoon flour
1 can condensed cream of chicken soup
1½ cups sliced mushrooms (2 3-ounce cans)
¾ cup diced chicken (1 5½-ounce can)
¼ cup chopped pimiento
seasoning to taste

Sauté the celery and peppers in the butter till tender.
Stir in the flour, soup and mushrooms.
Cook till thick, stirring fairly constantly.
Add the pimiento, chicken, salt and pepper.
Heat.
Serve on golden toasted triangles of bread.

MINUTE CHICKEN

(Serves 4)

1 3-pound chicken cut into quarters
1 tablespoon butter
1 tablespoon oil
½ shallot, chopped
1 large ripe tomato, peeled and diced
¼ pound mushrooms, sliced
salt
pepper
thyme
1 bay leaf
chopped parsley

In a skillet brown the pieces of chicken lightly on both sides in the butter and oil.
Add the chopped shallot.
Add the diced tomato, the sliced mushrooms, salt, pepper, a pinch of thyme and the bay leaf.
Cover tightly and cook over moderate heat for about 30 minutes.
Taste for seasoning.
Place the pieces of chicken on a platter, pour the sauce over them and sprinkle with chopped parsley.

CHICKEN WINGS

(Serves 4–6)

4 tablespoons butter
1 large white onion
pepper and salt
12 chicken wings

In a saucepan put a layer of sliced onions, a layer of chicken wings; dot over with half the butter, salt and pepper.

Another layer of onions, another layer of chicken wings, salt and pepper and the rest of the butter.

Add ½ cup water and cover the saucepan tightly.

Cook over moderate heat for 30 minutes.

Serve with buttered rice with the sauce formed by the butter and the chicken broth.

CHICKEN WITH ORANGE SAUCE

(Serves 6)

6 breasts of chicken, boned
4 tablespoons butter
4 tablespoons flour
1 cup chicken broth
1 teaspoon salt
pepper
1 cup orange juice
2 tablespoons lemon juice
grated orange rind

Poach the breasts of chicken by covering them with boiling water, salt and pepper to taste.

Simmer gently until tender, or for about 45 minutes.

Remove from the water and keep hot while you make the sauce.

Melt the butter, add the flour and cook 2 minutes, stirring constantly.

Add the chicken broth, orange juice, lemon juice, salt and pepper.

Cook till thick, stirring constantly.

Add a little grated orange rind.

Drop the chicken pieces into the hot sauce, heat thoroughly and serve hot.

BOILED MARINATED DUCKS
(Serves 6)

2 6-pound Long Island fresh-killed ducks

For rubbing

1 lemon
1 cup salt
¾ cup sugar
½ teaspoon saltpeter (obtainable at drugstores)

For marinade

6 quarts water
3 cups salt
3 cups granulated sugar

For boiling

6 quarts water
12 white peppercorns
3 bay leaves
6 peeled carrots
1 Bermuda onion, sliced

For stuffing

4 apples
24 pitted tenderized prunes
4 leeks and 2 carrots—parboiled, cut in 1-inch slices

Time required for preparation: 32–40 hours.

This recipe sounds complicated, but is actually very easy to accomplish and worth the slight bother.

Not all drugstores carry saltpeter, so start by locating this. A very small amount is needed, but it is necessary.

If you intend to serve the ducks hot, start 32 hours ahead for preparation; for cold, about 40 hours.

Wash the ducks carefully, inside and out, and pat dry with paper toweling.

Rub the inside of each with ½ lemon.

Rub inside and out with a combination of 1 cup salt, ¾ cup sugar and ½ teaspoon saltpeter.

Place on a large platter, cover with waxed paper and leave in a cool place.

(I put mine in the refrigerator, right or wrong.)

Twelve hours later drain the birds and place in a large roasting pan, 5 inches deep, with a cover to fit.

In a large separate pan, heat 6 quarts water to the boiling point.

Add 3 cups salt and the same amount of sugar.

Pour over the ducks, and keep in a cool place for 18 hours this time.

(Again I use the refrigerator.)

However, before refrigerating, place a weight or a heavy plate on top of each bird, the idea being to keep them submerged in the marinade—and, of course, wait until the marinade has cooled completely before putting them in the refrigerator.

About 2½ hours before you will be serving the birds hot (or 10 hours if they are to be served cold), prepare the following:

Scrape 8 carrots, cut two in 1-inch slices and put the others aside.

Peel and slice 1 Bermuda onion.

Cut the green part away from 4 leeks, wash, remove the root ends, cut in 1-inch pieces and add to the sliced carrots.

Parboil both together for 10 minutes, and drain.

Pit 24 tenderized uncooked dried prunes, and add to them the carrot and leeks.

Peel, quarter and core 4 large apples and add them to the prunes, etc.

Drain the ducks thoroughly and discard the liquid.

Stuff the ducks with the prunes, apples and parboiled vegetables.

Sew up securely, using trussing needle and fine twine.

Place the birds side by side in the roasting pan again, breast side up.

Heat 6 quarts water to the boiling point and pour sufficient over the birds to cover.

Bring to a brisk boil again and skim carefully.

Add the 6 peeled whole carrots, the sliced Bermuda onion, 3 bay leaves and 12 white peppercorns.

Reduce the heat, cover and simmer ½ hour.

In the meantime preheat the oven to 425°–450° F.

Uncover the birds, place in the oven and continue simmering for another 1¼ hours, basting once or twice.

If the ducks are to be served hot, place on a hot platter, remove all strings and garnish prettily with parsley and lemon.

Cut in thin slices as you would any duck—and serve with this either Cumberland Sauce (p. 151) or Unfrozen Sauce of Whipped Sweet Cream and White Horseradish (p. 151).

Boiled Red Cabbage is usually served with this (p. 137).

If you prefer to serve the birds cold, allow them to cool completely in their juice—breast side down, however.

Then place the pan, tightly covered, in the refrigerator for 6 to 8 hours.

When about ready to prepare the birds for serving, remove the pan from the refrigerator and with a spoon carefully remove the solidified fat which will have risen to the surface.

The juice under the birds will be lightly jellied.

Lift the birds out of the jelly and place breast side up on a serving platter.

Remove all the strings.

Wipe off any remaining fat, using paper toweling.

Spoon some of the jelly over the birds, garnish with the carrots and thin slices of lemon and parsley, and serve.

Carve at the table in paper-thin slices.

Serve with this the following Frozen White Horseradish Sauce Made with Sweet Cream.

FROZEN WHITE HORSERADISH SAUCE MADE WITH SWEET CREAM

1 cup heavy cream
2 tablespoons white grated pickled horseradish
½ teaspoon pepper
½ teaspoon salt
2 teaspoons French mustard

Whip the cream until stiff.

Mix together the grated pickled horseradish, French mustard, salt and pepper.

[*136*]

Mix this thoroughly into the whipped cream.

Place in a serving bowl, cover tightly with waxed paper and place in the freezing compartment until firm, or for about 2 hours.

Slice and serve with cold Boiled Marinated Duck (above).

RED CABBAGE
(Serves 6)

6 cups finely cut red cabbage (about 2 pounds)
3 tablespoons finely cut shallots or onion
6 tablespoons butter
6 tablespoons light brown sugar
6 tablespoons tarragon vinegar
1 tablespoon caraway seeds
salt and pepper to taste

Soak the finely cut red cabbage in cold water while you prepare the finely cut shallots or onion.

Cook these gently for a minute or 2 in 4 tablespoons butter.

Add the light brown sugar, tarragon vinegar and caraway seeds.

Drain the cabbage and add it to the cooked shallots.

Cook gently, stirring frequently, for 25 minutes.

Season to taste with about 1½ teaspoons salt and ¾ teaspoon coarsely ground pepper.

Place over boiling water until ready to serve, at which time add 2 additional tablespoons butter.

Stir until butter is melted, place cabbage in a hot vegetable dish and serve at once.

CREAMED ONIONS
(Serves 4–6)

2 pounds small white onions
4 tablespoons butter
4 tablespoons flour
2 cups hot milk
½ cup heavy cream
salt to taste
paprika

Pour boiling water over the onions to cover, and allow to stand a minute or 2.

Drain and cover with cold water.

With a sharp knife cut away the top and bottom of each, removing as little as possible. Then slip off the outside skin and first onion layer, using your fingers.

Pierce the root ends twice, forming a cross. This is to prevent the onions from bursting.

Place them in a large saucepan, add ½ teaspoon salt and cover generously with boiling water.

Cook uncovered until tender through, or for about 30 minutes.

In the meantime make a smooth cream sauce of the butter, flour and hot milk.

Season to taste with salt and keep hot over boiling water.

When the onions are done, drain them thoroughly.

Stir the heavy cream into the hot sauce and pour over the onions.

Place in a serving dish, sprinkle with paprika and serve at once.

CARROTS IN ORANGE JUICE

(Serves 4)

1 bunch carrots (5 or 6)
½ cup orange juice
1¾ cups cold water
½ teaspoon salt
2 tablespoons granulated sugar
3 tablespoons butter
1 tablespoon flour
½ cup additional boiling water

Wash, peel and slice fine the carrots.

Place in a saucepan and add the orange juice, salt, sugar and cold water.

Bring to a boil, skim carefully, reduce heat, cover and simmer until tender, about 1¼ hours.

Watch carefully and shake the pan occasionally to prevent sticking.

When tender, add ½ cup additional boiling water.

Stir in 3 tablespoons butter creamed with 1 tablespoon flour.

Cook for a minute or 2 and serve.

ASPARAGUS WITH BROWNED BUTTER

(Serves 4)

2 pounds fresh asparagus
½ teaspoon salt
1¼ cups boiling water
4 tablespoons butter

Break off the tough part of the asparagus.

Wash the tender part and scrape or peel carefully.

Wash again and cut in ½-inch pieces.

Place in a saucepan, add ½ teaspoon salt and barely cover with about 1¼ cups boiling water.

Cook until tender, or for about 10 minutes.

In the meantime prepare 4 tablespoons Browned Butter (see below).

Drain the cooked asparagus thoroughly, place in a hot serving dish and pour the browned butter over all.

Serve at once.

BROWNED BUTTER

Place the required amount of butter in a saucepan and cook slowly over moderate heat, skimming off the white foam as it forms.

Continue cooking until brown specks begin to form on the bottom of the pan.

Watch carefully and remove from the heat when well browned—but don't let it burn, for then it will be bitter.

Use a deep pan if you are browning much butter, for it foams way up and might overflow and catch fire.

BAKED YAMS AND APPLES

(Serves 4)

Preheat oven to 475° F.

3 small yams or sweet potatoes (1 pound)
3 large apples (1 pound)
6 tablespoons butter

½ cup light brown sugar
¼ cup water

Wash the yams or sweet potatoes and boil them with their skins on until just barely tender, or for about 20 minutes.

Drain and cool.

Wash, peel, core and cut the apples into eighths.

Butter a 10-inch ovenproof glass pie plate with 2 tablespoons butter.

Peel the sweet potatoes and cut into pieces the approximate size of the apples.

Arrange the apples and sweet potatoes attractively in the dish, dot with 4 tablespoons butter, and sprinkle with the light brown sugar and cold water.

Bake in a 475° F. oven until the apples are tender and beginning to brown, or for about 40 minutes.

Baste once or twice as they cook.

Serve hot, with ham or pork.

BROILED EGGPLANT

(Serves 4–6)

Preheat broiling unit.

2 small firm eggplants
6 tablespoons creamed butter
1 teaspoon chopped parsley
salt and pepper to taste

Remove the stem ends of the eggplants.

Peel and slice in pieces ½ inch thick.

Butter both sides of each piece with the creamed butter.

Place on a flat shallow jelly-roll pan, sprinkle lightly with salt and pepper and place under preheated moderate broiler.

Broil until lightly browned on one side, or for about 15 minutes; turn over with a pancake turner and continue cooking until soft through and brown.

Transfer to a hot serving platter, sprinkle with the chopped parsley and serve.

STRING BEANS A LA POULETTE
(Serves 4)

1 pound tender fresh stringless string beans
2 tablespoons butter
2 tablespoons flour
salt and pepper to taste
2 teaspoons strained lemon juice
1⅛ cups chicken broth or consommé
1 egg yolk
1 tablespoon chopped parsley
¼–½ cup heavy cream

Stem the beans, wash thoroughly, place in a large pan and cover with boiling water.

Bring to a boil, skim carefully and cook until just tender through, or for about 20 to 25 minutes.

Drain thoroughly while you make the sauce.

Melt the butter, add the flour and cook for a minute or 2 without browning.

Add gradually the hot clear chicken broth, or consommé, making a smooth sauce.

Season to taste with salt, pepper and about 2 teaspoons strained lemon juice.

Beat the egg yolk in a bowl, using a wire whisk, and add gradually the hot sauce.

Place the well-drained beans in the top of a double boiler, over boiling water, to heat through.

Stir about ¼ cup heavy cream into the sauce and pour over the beans.

Heat thoroughly.

Place in a hot serving dish, sprinkle with parsley and serve piping hot.

Good with roast chicken.

CREAMED BRUSSELS SPROUTS WITH CELERY
(Serves 4)

1 package frozen Brussels sprouts
1 bunch of pascal celery

1 teaspoon caraway seeds
½ cup boiling water
½ teaspoon salt
5 tablespoons butter
1 tablespoon flour
¾ cup heavy cream

Separate the stalks from the celery, wash and cut away the leaves and stringy part.

Cut in ¼-inch cubes.

Soak in cold water while you cook the frozen Brussels sprouts in ½ cup boiling salted water, following directions on the box, but adding the caraway seeds and cooking 10 minutes instead of 6.

Set them aside while you melt 4 tablespoons butter in a small frying pan.

Drain the celery and cook it gently in the butter without browning for about 10 minutes.

Drain the water from the sprouts onto the celery and continue cooking 5 minutes longer.

At the same time add ½ cup heavy cream to the sprouts and simmer gently for a minute or 2, then add 1 tablespoon butter creamed with 1 tablespoon flour.

Cook for a minute or two, then add the celery, shake the pan over low heat and stir in an extra ¼ cup cream, but do not allow it to boil.

Serve at once with roast pork or pork chops.

STUFFED ARTICHOKE HEARTS

(Serves 6)

Preheat oven to 400° F.

6 large artichoke hearts, canned
1 package frozen baby artichokes
1 can cream of mushroom soup
grated Parmesan cheese
¼ cup milk

Cook the frozen artichokes, following instructions on the package.

[*142*]

Chop the cooked artichokes into small pieces.

Place the artichoke hearts on a flat pan.

Cover each artichoke heart generously with the chopped cooked artichokes.

Make a smooth sauce of the cream of mushroom soup and the milk.

Put a few spoonfuls of the mushroom sauce over each artichoke.

Sprinkle with Parmesan cheese.

Cook in a 400° F. oven for about 10 to 15 minutes until the cheese melts.

Serve very hot.

SLICED BEETS

(Serves 6)

2 pounds small young beets
4 tablespoons butter
4 tablespoons sugar
salt and pepper
4 tablespoons lemon juice

Wash the beets, but do not try to peel them.

Cook in boiling water until tender, 30 to 40 minutes.

Drain and run cold water over them.

Slip off the skins.

Cut into slices.

Melt the butter, add the sugar, salt, pepper and lemon juice.

Heat the sliced beets in the sauce.

CREAMED SCALLIONS

(Serves 6)

18 scallions
pepper and salt
cream

Clean the scallions by cutting off the roots and the top of the green part.

Wash carefully.

Leave whole and cover with boiling water.
Cook until tender.
Drain and add just enough cream to moisten.
Serve on toast.

CREAMED MUSHROOMS

(Serves 4)

*1 pound mushrooms (preferably field-
   grown for marvelous flavor)*
4 tablespoons butter
salt and pepper
2 tablespoons flour
1 cup cream

Wash and stem the mushrooms; keep the stems aside for soup.
Cut the mushrooms into thin slices.
Melt the butter and cook the mushrooms in the butter for 3 minutes.
Sprinkle with flour and stir well.
Add salt and pepper.
Add the cream and cook a few minutes more, stirring constantly.

COUNTRY SALAD

*On a hot day I love a salad which can be a whole meal, either
a hearty luncheon or supper salad. Lima beans with bacon or
ham make this main-dish salad.*

Combine freshly cooked lima beans with either crisp lean
bacon or slivers of cooked ham. Add minced sweet onion, a dash
of sugar, salt and freshly ground pepper. Stir in enough sour
cream to moisten thoroughly and serve in lettuce cups with deviled eggs.

SERVE-YOURSELF SALAD

On a table that guests can reach from any angle, set large
bowls of crisp greens such as chicory, escarole, romaine, Boston

or iceberg lettuce. In smaller bowls, place any or all of the following: green and red pepper rings, julienne strips of carrots
and celery, button mushrooms, artichoke hearts, pitted ripe
olives, anchovy fillets, cottage cheese. Offer a variety of dress-
ings such as plain and wine French dressing, sour cream and
lemon wedges. Use luncheon-size plates, and be sure that they
and all the ingredients for the salad are thoroughly chilled.

Brown-and-serve French rolls cut into thick slices, spread
with garlic butter, broiled until brown and bubbly, and served
piping hot, make an excellent accompaniment for this salad.

LOBSTER SALAD

(Serves 4)

*Lobster salad is greatly improved by the addition of pieces
of ripe melon or some white grapes. The combination of flavors
is interesting.*

> 1 pound cooked lobster, cut in pieces
> 1 cup diced ripe melon (cantaloupe or honeydew)
>   or 1 cup white seedless grapes
> 1 cup Mayonnaise
> 1 cup sour cream

Mix together the mayonnaise and sour cream.

Toss together the lobster and fruit and mix with the mayonnaise and cream.

Chill well before serving.

CHILLED VEGETABLE SALAD

(Serves 6)

*Fresh vegetables usually eaten cooked and hot are delightfully
different, I think, when served raw and chilled as in this crisp
salad.*

> ½ pound green beans
> 2 zucchini or summer squash
> 2 scallions
> 3 stalks celery
> 3 tomatoes

salt and pepper
oil
wine vinegar
Mayonnaise, if desired

Wash the vegetables thoroughly.

Remove the ends and strings from the beans and slice thinly lengthwise.

Blanch for a few minutes in boiling water, if desired.

Set aside to cool.

Do not peel the squash, but slice wafer-thin.

Slice the scallions and celery, stalks and leaves.

Peel the tomatoes and cut in wedges.

Combine all the vegetables; season with salt and pepper and pour on a small amount of oil and vinegar or favorite French dressing.

Chill in the refrigerator for several hours.

Just before serving, stir in a small amount of mayonnaise, if desired, and serve in lettuce cups.

COLESLAW

(Serves 6)

1 small cabbage
¾ cup heavy cream
6 tablespoons sour cream
1 tablespoon French-style prepared mustard
2 tablespoons granulated sugar
¼ cup strained lemon juice
salt and pepper to taste
1 teaspoon caraway seeds (optional)

Remove the outer leaves from a small head of cabbage.

Quarter and core it and slice very, very fine.

Mix together in a bowl the heavy cream, sour cream, mustard, lemon juice and granulated sugar.

Beat with a rotary beater until almost stiff.

Season to taste with about ¼ teaspoon coarsely ground pepper and ¼ teaspoon salt.

Add this to the cabbage and stir lightly with 2 forks.

Chill until ready to serve.

Note: If you like caraway seeds, soak 1 teaspoon of them in 1 tablespoon lemon juice for half an hour or so and add them to the coleslaw before serving.

LOW-CALORIE DRESSING

(Makes about 2 cups)

Two tablespoons of this dressing contain 25 calories and 2⅔ grams protein.

> 1 cup cottage cheese
> 1 can condensed tomato soup
> 1 tablespoon India or sweet pickle relish
> 1 tablespoon lemon juice
> grated lemon rind, if desired

Blend all the ingredients; chill.
Stir well and serve over crisp salad greens.

BOILED SALAD DRESSING

(Makes 2 cups)

> 1 teaspoon salt
> 2 tablespoons granulated sugar
> 1 tablespoon flour
> dash pepper
> ½ cup cider vinegar
> ¼ cup water
> ⅛ pound butter
> 4 egg yolks
> ½ to ¾ cup heavy cream or
>   1 cup sour cream

Put in a small bowl the salt, granulated sugar, flour and pepper.

Add to it, stirring until smooth, the cider vinegar and water.

Beat the egg yolks well and add them to the mixture, then strain the whole into the top of a small double boiler.

Add the butter, place over boiling water and cook, stirring furiously, until well thickened, but be careful to remove immediately from the fire the second it is done, so it won't curdle.

It should be quite thick, as it is to be thinned when cold with about ½ cup to ¾ cup heavy cream or 1 cup sour cream.

Especially good for boiled potato salad.

BASIC SAUCE
(Makes 1 cup)

3 tablespoons butter
½ teaspoon salt
3 tablespoons flour
⅛ teaspoon pepper
1 cup hot milk, beef stock or chicken stock

In the top of a double boiler melt the butter over low heat. Remove from the heat and stir in the flour, salt and pepper. Add the hot liquid, return to the heat and cook, stirring, until the sauce is thick.

Cook over simmering water, covered, for 10 minutes.

RICH CREAM SAUCE
(Makes 1 cup)

Make Basic Sauce (above) with milk.
When cooked, stir in ½ cup heavy cream.

ANOTHER RICH CREAM SAUCE
(Makes 1 cup)

Mix 1 beaten egg yolk with 3 tablespoons of hot Rich Cream Sauce (above), and then stir into balance of Rich Cream Sauce.

MORNAY CREAM SAUCE
(Makes 1 cup)

Add to Cream Sauce (above) 2 tablespoons grated Swiss cheese and 2 tablespoons Parmesan cheese.

Cook, stirring, until the cheese is melted.

SHERRY CREAM SAUCE
(Makes 1 cup)

Make Basic Sauce (p. 148) with chicken stock.

When cooked, stir in ½ cup heavy cream and 1 to 2 tablespoons cooking sherry to taste.

NEWBURG SAUCE
(Makes 1 cup)

Make Basic Sauce (p. 148) with milk.

When cooked, stir in ½ teaspoon paprika, dash cayenne, 2 egg yolks lightly beaten with ¼ cup cream and 2 tablespoons sherry.

WARM MUSTARD SAUCE
(Makes 1½ cups)

juice of 1 lemon
4 tablespoons cider vinegar
pinch each of white pepper and salt
2 tablespoons cold water
4 egg yolks, slightly beaten
½ pound butter
2 tablespoons dry mustard
coarsely ground black pepper

Squeeze and strain the juice of 1 lemon.

Put the cider vinegar in the top of a double boiler with a pinch of salt and white pepper, and reduce to 2 teaspoons by simmering on a low flame.

Add the cold water and the egg yolks.

Add 4 tablespoons of the butter, cut into small pieces.

Place over a very low flame and beat constantly with a wire whisk until the mixture thickens slightly.

Remove from the fire immediately.

Place over a pan of hot (not boiling) water and add, little by little, the remaining butter, stirring vigorously all the while.

Stir together in a cup the dry mustard and the strained lemon juice.

[*149*]

Add gradually to the sauce and season to taste with additional salt and coarsely ground black pepper.

Remove the top of the double boiler from the bottom until ready to serve, at which time place the top again over hot water on a low flame and stir constantly until warm (not hot) and serve with broiled or fried fish.

COLD MUSTARD SAUCE

(Makes 1 cup)

3 tablespoons French-style prepared mustard
1 cup sour cream
1 tablespoon finely cut fresh tender chives

Fold the mustard into the sour cream.
Add the chives.
Stir lightly with a fork and serve with hot boiled tongue, corned beef, boiled or baked ham or broiled frankfurters.

HOT MUSTARD SAUCE

(Makes 1 cup)

1 small onion, chopped fine
1 tablespoon butter
½ jar French-style mustard (8-ounce size)
¼ cup cream
1 teaspoon Worcestershire sauce

Cook the chopped onion in the butter until soft but not brown.
Add the mustard and the cream.
Stir well until heated through.
Add the Worcestershire sauce.

FROZEN WHITE HORSERADISH SAUCE MADE WITH SOUR CREAM

(Serves 6)

1 cup sour cream
2 tablespoons white pickled horseradish

Drain the horseradish well and fold into the sour cream.

Place in a cup-size mold and place in the freezing compartment of the refrigerator until hard.

Fifteen minutes before you will be ready to serve it, allow to stand at room temperature.

Run a knife around the edge to loosen, and turn out into a serving dish.

Send to the table to be cut into slices with a sharp knife.

Delicious on any cold fish, including fillets of smoked trout.

UNFROZEN SAUCE OF WHIPPED SWEET CREAM AND WHITE HORSERADISH

(Makes 1 cup)

1 cup heavy cream
2 tablespoons white grated pickled horseradish
½ teaspoon pepper
½ teaspoon salt
2 teaspoons French-style mustard

Whip the cream until stiff.

Mix together the horseradish, mustard, salt and pepper.

Mix this thoroughly into the whipped cream.

Place in a serving dish and serve with hot Boiled Marinated Duck (p. 134).

CUMBERLAND SAUCE FOR HAM

(Makes 2 cups)

peel from ½ orange and ½ lemon
4 tablespoons currant jelly
1 cup port wine
juice of 1 orange
juice of ½ lemon
1 teaspoon dry mustard
1 tablespoon light brown sugar
¼ teaspoon powdered ginger
dash cayenne
½ cup white sultana raisins
½ cup blanched, slivered almonds

With a sharp knife remove the thin peel from ½ orange and ½ lemon, being careful not to include any of the white part.

Cut in tiny slivers, put into cold water and bring to a boil; drain and repeat the process 3 times.

Melt the currant jelly in the top of a double boiler, add ½ cup port wine, the orange and lemon peel, the strained orange and lemon juice, the dry mustard mixed with the light brown sugar, the powdered ginger and a dash of cayenne.

Bring to a boil on low direct heat.

Place over boiling water to keep warm.

In the meantime boil the sultana raisins in ½ cup port wine until plump.

Add to the sauce, and, last of all, add the blanched, slivered almonds.

Serve with hot ham, boiled or roasted, or with hot Boiled Marinated Duck (p. 134).

CLARIFIED BUTTER

To clarify butter, place the desired amount of butter (not less than ¼ pound) in a small pan over a low flame and let it melt slowly.

When melted, skim off the foam that rises to the surface.

Remove from the fire, let it settle a few minutes and then ladle or pour off the clear butter, being careful not to include any of the milky sediment in the bottom of the pan.

HARD-BOILED EGG SAUCE

(Serves 6)

2 Hard-boiled Eggs (p. 101)
4 tablespoons all-purpose flour
4 tablespoons butter
2 cups hot milk
salt and pepper to taste

Hard-boil the eggs.

Melt the butter in the top of a double boiler over direct low heat.

Stir in the flour and cook for a minute or 2, stirring constantly with a wooden spoon.

Add gradually the hot milk, making a smooth cream sauce.

Season lightly with about ½ teaspoon salt and ¼ teaspoon pepper.

Keep hot over hot water.

Remove the shells from the eggs and slice them into the sauce.

Good with boiled salmon—or any boiled fish.

PLAIN PASTRY
(For a 2-crust pie)

I make a plain pastry for my crust, using good lard and the all-purpose flour with which I also make bread. I use a 9-inch pie pan.

Preheat oven to 450° F.

> *2½ cups sifted flour*
> *1 teaspoon salt*
> *6 ounces lard*
> *6 tablespoons ice water*

First sift the flour onto a piece of paper.

Then measure 2½ level cups of the sifted flour into a bowl.

Add the salt to the flour and stir well.

Cut the lard into small pieces, and as you cut, let them drop into the bowl.

Mix the lard into the flour with 2 knives or a pastry mixer until evenly distributed in very small bits.

Add the water bit by bit, stirring each moistened part with a fork.

This will seem very dry, but after all the water has been stirred in, press the dough together with your hands into a ball.

Wrap in waxed paper and chill while preparing your filling.

Roll out the pastry on a sheet of waxed paper lightly dusted with flour.

There are several gadgets available to help shape the pastry. I use a round wire circle, and I place half my dough in the cen-

ter of it and roll out quickly in each direction to fill out the circle.

The bottom crust should be slightly larger than the top crust and should fit in the pan loosely. Trim off the edges, leaving about ½ inch to come up over the edge of the top crust.

Brush the inside of the bottom crust with egg white.

Fill carefully.

Roll out the top crust and fit it over the filling.

Fold up the edge of the lower crust and seal all around by pressing with your fingers.

Prick the top crust in several places.

Brush with beaten egg yolk or milk and bake in a very hot oven (450° F.) for 15 minutes, then reduce heat to 350° to finish baking, the time depending upon the filling.

PLAIN PASTRY WITH BUTTER

(For a 2-crust pie)

2½ cups sifted all-purpose flour
1 teaspoon salt
6 tablespoons vegetable shortening
6 tablespoons (¾ bar) sweet butter
6 tablespoons ice water

Sift together the flour and the salt.

Add the vegetable shortening and butter.

Work the shortening into the flour lightly, using your fingertips.

When mealy in consistency, moisten with 6 tablespoons ice water.

Form into 2 flat balls, wrap in waxed paper and chill until ready to use.

GRAHAM CRACKER CRUST

Preheat oven to 375° F.

1½ cups rolled graham crackers
¼ cup confectioner's sugar
6 tablespoons melted butter
¼ teaspoon powdered cinnamon

Put sufficient graham crackers through the meat grinder, using the medium blade, to give 1½ cups.

Add to these crumbs the confectioner's sugar sifted with the cinnamon.

Stir in the melted butter.

Pat the mixture firmly on the bottom and around the sides of a buttered 9-inch pie pan.

Bake in a 375° F. oven for about 15 minutes.

Cool before filling.

APPLE PIE

Preheat oven to 450° F.

Mix 1 recipe of Plain Pastry (p. 153).

> *6 to 8 tart apples, preferably Greening,*
> *Baldwin or Northern Spy*
> *1 tablespoon flour*
> *¾ cup sugar*
> *¼ teaspoon nutmeg*
> *¼ teaspoon salt*
> *1 tablespoon butter*
> *grated rind of ½ lemon*

Roll out the pastry for the bottom crust and line a 9-inch pie pan.

Brush with egg white.

Peel and slice the apples into a bowl.

Mix together the sugar, flour, nutmeg and salt, pour over the apples and toss well together.

Place the sugared apples in the pastry, dot with butter and lemon rind.

Wet the edge of the pastry.

Roll out the top crust and place over the apples.

Press the edges together.

Prick in several places and brush with beaten egg or milk so it will brown nicely.

Bake in a 450° F. oven for 15 minutes, then reduce heat to 350° and bake for 45 minutes more.

RHUBARB PIE

Preheat oven to 450° F.

Mix 1 recipe of Plain Pastry (p. 153).

> *2 cups rhubarb*
> *¾ cup sugar*
> *3 tablespoons flour*
> *dash nutmeg*

Line a 9-inch pie pan with pastry.
Peel and cut the rhubarb into small pieces.
Mix the sugar, flour and nutmeg together.
Mix the rhubarb with the sugar mix and place in the pie pan.
Cover with a pastry top.
Prick the top with a fork and brush with beaten egg or milk.
Bake in a hot oven (450° F.) for 15 minutes.
Reduce heat to 350° and bake 45 minutes more.
Serve warm with thick cream to pour over it.

BLUEBERRY PIE

Preheat oven to 450° F.

Mix 1 recipe of Plain Pastry (p. 153).

> *4 cups blueberries*
> *4 tablespoons flour*
> *¾ cup sugar*
> *¼ teaspoon salt*
> *⅛ teaspoon mace*

Line a 9-inch pie plate with pastry.
Mix together the flour, sugar, salt and mace.
Sprinkle this mixture over the berries.
Cover with a pastry top.
Prick the top with a fork and brush with beaten egg or milk.
Bake in a 450° F. oven for 15 minutes.
Reduce heat to 350° and bake for 45 minutes more.

CUSTARD PIE

Preheat oven to 450° F.

Mix ½ recipe of Plain Pastry (p. 153).

4 eggs
¼ cup sugar
¼ teaspoon salt
2 cups milk
1 cup cream
nutmeg

Line a 9-inch pie pan with pastry.

Brush the inside with white of egg.

Chill.

Beat the eggs slightly with a fork, add the sugar and salt and stir till blended.

Add the milk and cream and blend well.

Place the pie pan on the oven shelf and gently pour in the custard.

Sprinkle a slight amount of nutmeg on the top.

Bake at 450° F. for 10 minutes, then reduce heat to 300° and bake for 50 minutes more, or until firm when tested with a knife.

COCONUT CUSTARD PIE

Use the recipe for Custard Pie (above).

Add ½ cup moist grated coconut to the egg mixture.

Sprinkle the top with more coconut.

DEEP-DISH BLUEBERRY PIE

This is a great favorite and we have it often during the blueberry season because all we have to do is go out and pick our own berries.

Preheat oven to 400° F.

Mix ½ recipe for Plain Pastry (p. 153).

1 quart fresh blueberries
½ cup sugar
2 tablespoons flour
¼ teaspoon salt
½ teaspoon nutmeg
2 tablespoons lemon juice
1 tablespoon butter

Wash the blueberries in cool water and pick over if necessary. Drain.

Mix together the sugar, flour, salt, nutmeg and lemon juice, and add to the blueberries, mixing very gently until the fruit is coated.

Turn into a deep 6-cup baking dish; dot with butter.

Cover with pie crust and bake in a hot oven (400° F.) for about 30 minutes until the crust is golden brown.

This is delicious either warm or chilled.

PRUNE OR APRICOT PIE

Preheat oven to 450° F.

Mix ½ recipe of Plain Pastry with Butter (p. 154).

> *¾ cup cooked sweetened prunes or apricot purée*
> *½ teaspoon grated lemon rind*
> *1 tablespoon strained lemon juice*
> *½ cup granulated sugar*
> *3 egg whites*
> *⅛ teaspoon salt*
> *1 cup slightly whipped cream*

Line a 9-inch pie plate with pastry.

Crimp the rolled-under edges prettily.

Prick with a fork and bake for about 15 minutes, or until lightly browned.

Cool and fill with the following mixture:

Rub cooked sweetened dried apricots or prunes through a sieve.

To ¾ cup of the purée, add ½ teaspoon grated lemon rind and 1 tablespoon strained lemon juice.

Add ⅛ teaspoon salt to 3 egg whites and beat until stiff, then beat in gradually ½ cup granulated sugar.

Fold this into the fruit purée and fill the cooked tart shell.

Reduce the heat of the oven to 325° F. and bake for about 20 minutes.

Serve soon after baking, while still warm, accompanied by a bowl of slightly beaten heavy cream.

RICH APPLE AND ALMOND PIE

(Serves 6–8)

Preheat oven to 400° F.

> *5 large apples*
> *1 cup butter (2 bars)*
> *1 cup sifted flour*
> *1 cup blanched almonds, finely grated*
> *1¾ cups granulated sugar*
> *I cup heavy cream, whipped*

For the pastry, cream the butter with 1 cup granulated sugar and beat until very light, then add gradually the sifted flour and almonds.

When well blended, shape into 2 balls, one slightly larger than the other.

Wrap in waxed paper, flatten a bit and chill until firm.

In the meantime, peel, quarter and core the apples.

Slice fine into a bowl, sprinkling with ¾ cup granulated sugar as you go along.

Now, working quickly, roll out on a floured pastry cloth the larger ball of pastry, making it about 12 inches in diameter.

Roll it up onto your rolling pin and unroll over a 10-inch pie plate.

Place immediately in the refrigerator for 5 minutes to prevent softening, then fill with the prepared apples.

Refrigerate again while you quickly roll out the smaller ball of pastry, making it just large enough to cover the apple-filled crust.

Roll up on the pin, working quickly, and unroll over the apples.

Press the edges together and crimp prettily.

Prick with a fork, place immediately in a 400° F. oven and bake for 15 minutes.

Reduce heat to 350° F. and continue cooking until the juices flow, or for about 1 hour in all.

Serve hot with plenty of whipped cream.

MY MINCEMEAT FOR PIES AND TARTS
(Makes 16–18 quarts)

4-pound piece of the round of beef
1 fresh beef tongue
4 pounds beef suet
5 pounds raisins
2 pounds currants
1 pound citron
5 pounds brown sugar
3 quarts sweet cider
1 quart molasses
1 quart wine
1 quart brandy
¼ pound candied lemon peel
¼ pound candied orange peel
12 soda crackers, rolled to crumbs
24 tart green apples, chopped
2 tablespoons salt
2 tablespoons ground cloves
1 tablespoon cinnamon
1 tablespoon mace
4 lemons, grated rind and juice
1 8-ounce glass currant jelly
1 8-ounce glass quince jelly
1 8-ounce glass plum jelly
1 8-ounce glass crabapple jelly

Cover the beef with boiling water and simmer until tender.

Cool it and put through the meat chopper, using the fine blade.

Cover the tongue with boiling water and simmer for 2 hours.

Remove from the water, take off the skin and cut off the root end.

Put the tongue meat through the meat chopper, using the fine blade.

Put the beef suet through the meat chopper.

In a large pot mix the molasses, cider, chopped apples and spices together and bring to a boil.

Add the chopped meat and suet and everything else except the wine and brandy.

Bring to a full rolling boil, remove from the heat and add the wine and brandy.

Fill immediately into hot sterilized jars and seal at once.

STRAWBERRIES

Clean the strawberries, sprinkle with several spoonfuls of kirsch and powdered sugar, and let them stand for several hours.

Mix them with whipped cream perfumed with kirsch and sprinkle shredded toasted almonds on top.

Chill in the refrigerator several hours before serving.

The same may be done with sliced pears or peaches in season.

STRAWBERRIES WITH WHITE CUSTARD CREAM
(Serves 6)

2 quarts strawberries
1 12-ounce jar strawberry jam
¼ cup kirsch liqueur

Wash and stem the strawberries.

Drain well and place in a pretty dessert bowl.

Chill.

Have ready 1 12-ounce glass strawberry jam softened with ¼ cup kirsch.

When ready to serve, be sure there is no water in the bottom of the dish.

Pour the softened jam over the strawberries.

This makes them look so pretty and shiny and gives them a heavenly taste.

Serve accompanied by White Custard Cream (below).

WHITE CUSTARD CREAM

2 cups heavy cream
2 tablespoons granulated sugar
4 egg whites
1 teaspoon vanilla

Scald 1 cup heavy cream in the top of a double boiler.

Sweeten with the granulated sugar.

Beat together the egg whites and the remaining cup of cream (100 turns of a hand rotary beater will be sufficient).

Add a little of the hot cream to the egg-white-and-cream mixture, stir well, then add this gradually to the hot cream.

Cook over boiling water, stirring constantly, until thickened, or for about 4 minutes.

Remove from the fire and cool, stirring occasionally.

Flavor with the vanilla, pour into a covered glass jar and chill thoroughly.

This will be a very thick and heavenly concoction to glorify the already delectable strawberries (above).

WHITE GRAPE DESSERT

seedless white grapes
sour cream
brown sugar

Mix the grapes and sour cream together and chill for a few hours in the refrigerator.

Just before serving, sprinkle brown sugar over the surface, shaking the sugar through a sieve to make an even surface.

APPLE TRIFLE

This is a good way to use up a little leftover cake and applesauce too. A favorite with our family.

Spread leftover plain cake with tart red currant jelly.

Place on the bottom (and sides, if possible) of a dessert serving dish.

Sprinkle with a small amount of sherry, brandy or cordial and let stand until the liquor is absorbed by the cake.

Spoon tart applesauce over the cake.

Cover with another layer of cake, sprinkle the cake with the liquor and cover with a layer of applesauce; then cover completely with chilled Custard Sauce (p. 164).

Top with whipped cream and garnish with toasted slivered almonds.

BAKED APPLES

(Serves 6)

Preheat oven to 350° F.

> *6 tart apples*
> *2 cups sugar*
> *2 cups water*
> *½ cup currant jelly*
> *2 tablespoons brandy or Cointreau*
> *finely chopped almonds*

Peel and core the apples thoroughly.

Make a syrup of the sugar, water and jelly and boil for 5 minutes.

Drop the apples into the syrup and cook gently for 15 minutes.

Transfer to a deep baking dish, pour the syrup over them, cover with foil and bake slowly ½ hour, or until tender.

Remove from the oven and let cool in the syrup.

When cool, pour the brandy or liqueur over the apples and sprinkle with finely chopped almonds.

QUINCE CREAM

(Serves 4–6)

> *3 large ripe quinces (2½ pounds)*
> *1 cup sifted powdered sugar*
> *4 egg whites*
> *6 cups water*
> *1 8-ounce jar quince preserves*
> *(optional)*

Wash, quarter, peel and core the quinces.

Slice fine, and cook gently in 6 cups water for about ¾ hour, or until almost no juice is left.

Rub through a fine sieve, using a wooden spoon.

This should give you about 3 cups purée.

Cool and refrigerate for at least 1 hour.

Beat the egg whites with a rotary beater until stiff enough to hold a peak, then add gradually the sifted powdered sugar.

Continue beating until very stiff, or for about 5 minutes, then fold in the quince purée.

Continue beating with the rotary beater for another 5 minutes.

Pile into a pretty serving dish, and chill until ready to serve.

Garnish with quince preserves if desired, and serve with either plain heavy cream or the following Heavy-Cream Custard Sauce.

HEAVY-CREAM CUSTARD SAUCE

2 cups heavy cream
4 egg yolks
3 tablespoons granulated sugar
2 teaspoons vanilla

Scald together in the top of a double boiler the heavy cream and sugar.

Beat the egg yolks with a rotary beater about 100 times, then add a little of the hot cream to the eggs, stirring constantly.

Add this to the remaining hot cream, stirring constantly over boiling water.

Cook until well thickened, or until it coats the spoon—about 3 to 4 minutes.

Remove from the fire and cool, stirring occasionally.

When cold, flavor with the vanilla.

Chill until ready to serve.

LOW-CALORIE "WHIPPED CREAM"

You can have excellent "whipped cream" on your desserts with only one-third the calories. This is made from dried skim milk and is an excellent product for fat-free low-calorie diets.

½ cup dried-milk powder
½ cup ice water
2 tablespoons lemon juice

Mix the dried milk and water in a bowl.

Whip 3 to 4 minutes, until soft peaks form.

Add the lemon juice and continue to beat 3 to 4 minutes more.

Serve immediately.

CHOCOLATE SOUFFLE
(Serves 4)

This is the favorite dessert of one daughter-in-law, and we always have it for dinner when she comes.

Preheat oven to 350° F.

> 2 *squares unsweetened chocolate*
> 3 *tablespoons butter*
> 2 *tablespoons flour*
> ¼ *teaspoon salt*
> 1 *cup milk*
> ½ *cup sugar*
> 1 *teaspoon vanilla*
> 2 *tablespoons rum*
> 4 *egg yolks*
> 4 *egg whites, stiffly beaten*
> ½ *pint heavy cream, whipped stiff*

Butter a 2-quart soufflé dish and sprinkle the bottom and sides with granulated sugar.

Melt together the chocolate and butter.

Blend in the flour and salt to make a smooth paste.

Gradually add the milk, sugar and vanilla, and cook, stirring constantly, until thick and smooth.

Remove from the heat and cool slightly.

Stir in the rum.

Add the egg yolks and beat well.

Fold in the beaten egg whites and pour into the soufflé dish.

Set in a pan of hot water and bake in a moderate oven (350° F.) for about 45 minutes.

Serve warm, with the whipped cream passed separately.

CAKE

There's only one way to make good homemade cake, and that is to measure everything exactly.

Use cake flour and double-acting baking powder. I prefer to sift my flour once before measuring it.

Use level measurements for everything, leveling off spoons or cups with a spatula.

Get your pans ready before you start mixing. Butter the pan, then sprinkle with flour and tip the pan back and forth until the flour coats the pan evenly. Then shake off the surplus flour.

Do not butter angel-food or sponge-cake pans except on the bottom.

Be sure your oven is the correct temperature. Check it with an oven thermometer.

Cooling cakes perfectly is very important. When you turn out a layer of cake onto a rack, it will be upside down. Don't leave it that way. Turn it and let it cool resting on the bottom flat side.

Sponge cakes and angel cakes can be cooled in the pan by turning the pan upside down on a cake rack for 1 hour. Then loosen the sides gently by running a knife or spatula around the side of the cake and around the center tube. It should slide out easily.

TWO-LAYER CAKE

Preheat oven to 375° F.
Butter and flour 2 9-inch layer-cake pans.

> *2 cups sifted cake flour*
> *2 teaspoons double-acting baking powder*
> *½ teaspoon salt*
> *½ cup butter (¼ pound)*
> *1 cup sugar*
> *3 eggs*

½ cup milk
1 teaspoon vanilla

Sift the flour once and measure.

Add the baking powder and salt and sift together.

Cream the butter and sugar in your electric mixer until soft and fluffy.

Separate the eggs and add the yolks to the butter and sugar, one at a time, beating well.

Remove the bowl from the mixer and add the flour and milk alternately by hand. This is best because overbeating after the flour is added makes a less tender cake.

Add the vanilla and mix well.

Beat the egg whites till stiff and place them on top of the batter.

Then carefully fold them into the batter, lifting it from the bottom up over and over. Do not beat or stir, just fold over and under.

Spoon evenly into the pans.

Bake at 375° F. for 25 minutes, or until brown and shrunken a little from the sides of the pan.

Turn out onto cake racks and immediately turn right side up by putting another cake rack on top and reversing them.

Let cool thoroughly.

COCONUT LAYER CAKE

Make a Two-Layer Cake (p. 166).

Seven-Minute Coconut Frosting
2 egg whites, unbeaten
1½ cups fine granulated sugar
5 tablespoons water
1 teaspoon vanilla
1 can moist coconut

Put all the ingredients except the coconut and vanilla in the top of a double boiler and mix well.

Place over boiling water and beat with a rotary egg beater or electric hand beater for 7 minutes, no more, no less.

The frosting should be shiny and thick.

Remove from the heat.

Add the vanilla and beat a few turns more.

Spread one layer of cake with frosting and sprinkle with some of the coconut.

Cover the top layer and sides with frosting and sprinkle the rest of the coconut all over.

CHOCOLATE LAYER CAKE

Make a Two-Layer Cake (p. 166).

When the cake layers are cool, frost with Old-fashioned Chocolate Frosting (below).

OLD-FASHIONED CHOCOLATE FROSTING

1 cup sugar
4 level tablespoons cake flour
4 ounces unsweetened chocolate, cut into small bits
1½ cups milk
2 tablespoons butter

Put all the dry ingredients in a saucepan.

Mix well and add the milk.

Cook until it boils, stirring constantly, until thick and smooth.

Remove from the heat and add the butter, stirring well.

Cool and use to cover layers.

DEVIL'S-FOOD CAKE

Preheat oven to 350° F.

Butter and flour 2 9-inch layer-cake pans.

¼ pound butter, very soft
2 cups sifted cake flour
¾ teaspoon salt
1 teaspoon baking soda
1¼ cups sugar
3 squares unsweetened chocolate, melted
1 teaspoon vanilla
¾ cup milk
2 eggs

Put the soft butter into a mixing bowl.

Put the sifted flour, salt, soda and sugar into a sifter and sift them right over the butter.

Add the milk and beat for 2 minutes.

Add the vanilla, melted chocolate and whole eggs.

Beat 1 minute.

Pour evenly into the pans.

Bake in a 350° F. oven for 25 minutes, or until slightly shrunken from the sides of the pan.

Turn out onto cake racks and immediately turn right side up.

Let cool thoroughly.

Ice with Seven-Minute Vanilla Frosting (p. 170).

CHOCOLATE ICEBOX CAKE

(Serves 8)

2 3½-ounce packages ladyfingers (24 double ones)
2 4-ounce packages sweet chocolate
12 tablespoons sweet butter (1½ bars) plus 1 extra
*   tablespoon*
3 eggs
¾ cup powdered sugar
3 tablespoons warm water
¼ cup granulated sugar
¼ cup water
¼ cup light rum

Butter a 2-quart straight-sided soufflé dish with 1 tablespoon butter.

Moisten the granulated sugar with ¼ cup water and boil for 5 minutes.

Remove from the fire and add the rum.

Cool partially.

Dip the ladyfingers quickly in and out of the syrup and stand them around the inside of the soufflé dish.

Lay 2 or 3 over the bottom.

Now melt the chocolate in 3 tablespoons warm water over hot (not boiling) water, stirring until smooth.

Stir in gradually the powdered sugar.

Separate the egg yolks from the whites.

Add the yolks, one at a time, beating well with a spoon.

Last of all, add .1½ bars sweet butter, a tablespoon at a time, being careful not to allow the water in the bottom of the double boiler to actually boil.

When all has been well blended, remove the top of the double boiler from the bottom.

Beat the egg whites until stiff but not dry, and fold them into the chocolate mixture.

When all the whites have disappeared, pour the whole into the ladyfinger-lined dish.

Cover and refrigerate overnight.

When ready to serve, turn out carefully onto a serving platter and send to the table.

SEVEN-MINUTE VANILLA FROSTING

1 egg white, unbeaten
⅔ cup fine granulated sugar
¼ teaspoon cream of tartar
2 tablespoons cold water
½ teaspoon vanilla

Put all the ingredients except the vanilla in the top of a double boiler.

Stir well until the sugar is dissolved.

Place over boiling water, but do not let the bottom of the top pot touch the water.

Beat with a rotary egg beater for about 7 minutes, beating continuously until the frosting is thick.

Remove from the heat and add the vanilla.

BROWN-SUGAR FROSTING

Use the recipe for Seven-Minute Vanilla Frosting (above), but substitute sifted light brown sugar for the white sugar.

CREAM CHEESE FROSTING

(Makes enough to top 2 8-inch layers)

Blend a 3-ounce package cream cheese with 1 tablespoon milk.

Gradually add 2½ cups sifted confectioner's sugar; blend well.

Mix in ½ teaspoon vanilla extract, if desired.

GATO-ALMOND CAKE (SPANISH)
(Serves 8)

Preheat oven to 325° F.

2 4½-ounce cans blanched almonds
6 eggs (separated)
grated rind of 1 lemon
½ teaspoon powdered cinnamon
1 cup granulated sugar
½ box vanilla cookies
5 tablespoons butter
confectioner's sugar in which you have kept a vanilla bean

Butter a round 9-inch cake tin with straight sides, using 1 tablespoon butter.

Grind or roll out a generous half-box of plain vanilla cookies and add to them 4 tablespoons melted butter.

Mix with a fork and line the sides and bottom of the pan, spreading the crumbs evenly. This takes a bit of patience.

Grind through a meat grinder, using the smallest cutter, the blanched almonds.

Separate the egg yolks from the whites.

Grate the rind of 1 lemon and add to the yolks.

Also add the cinnamon and granulated sugar.

Stir well with a wooden spoon until thoroughly mixed.

Add the ground almonds and stir well.

Beat the egg whites until stiff but not dry.

Stir these into the yolk-and-almond mixture.

Place evenly in the crumb-lined cake pan and bake in a 300°–325° F. oven for about ½ hour.

The mixture should be set but still soft, not dry.

Cool a bit, run a knife around the edge, and turn out carefully onto a large round serving platter.

Sift copiously with confectioner's sugar.

Serve cold, with hot black coffee.

[*171*]

CHEESE CAKE

Preheat oven to 450° F.

Make 1 recipe Plain Pastry (p. 153) or Graham-Cracker Crust (p. 154).

1½ pounds dry cottage cheese
1 cup sour cream
½ cup sugar
2 tablespoons cornstarch
¼ teaspoon salt
2 eggs, separated
cinnamon sugar

Line a 9-inch pie pan with plain pastry or graham-cracker crust.

Mix the cornstarch, sugar and salt.

Put the cottage cheese and sour cream in a mixer bowl and beat till smooth.

Add the sugar mixture.

Beat the yolks and add.

Remove from the mixer.

Beat the egg whites stiff but not dry, and fold into the cheese mix.

Fill the pie pan and sprinkle lightly with cinnamon sugar.

Bake at 450° F. for 10 minutes, then at 350° for 45 minutes more.

EARLY AMERICAN SUGAR COOKIES

(Makes approximately 2 dozen cookies)

Preheat oven to 375° F.

½ cup butter
1 cup sugar
2 eggs, well beaten
½ teaspoon salt
2 teaspoons baking powder
1 teaspoon vanilla or lemon extract
1 tablespoon milk
1½ cups unbleached sifted white flour
(about)

Cream the butter, add the sugar, eggs, milk, and 1 cup flour mixed and sifted with the baking powder and salt.

Add enough more sifted flour to make of the right consistency to roll out.

Chill, roll, sprinkle with sugar, cut and bake in a moderately hot oven (375° F.) for about 8 minutes.

SAND COOKIES

(Makes 18 cookies)

Preheat oven to 375° F.

> *¼ pound butter*
> *1¼ cups unbleached sifted white flour*
> *1½ teaspoons double-acting baking powder*
> *⅓ cup granulated sugar*
> *1 teaspoon vanilla*

Melt the butter over low heat and continue cooking, stirring occasionally, until golden brown, or for about 7 to 8 minutes.

Remove from the fire and stir with a wooden spoon until cool.

Sift together the flour and baking powder.

Add to this the sugar and sift again.

When the butter is cool, add the flour and sugar to the butter, a heaping tablespoon at a time, and work into a smooth paste.

Flavor with the vanilla.

Form into 1-inch balls, using your fingers, pressing the mixture firmly together.

Place on a buttered cookie sheet, making 18 balls.

Bake in a 375° F. oven until lightly browned, or for about 18 minutes.

Remove from the oven and cool, before removing from the tin with a spatula.

CHOCOLATE COCONUT MACAROONS

(Makes 2½ dozen cookies)

Preheat oven to 325° F.

> *1 square unsweetened chocolate*
> *1 4-ounce package sweet cooking chocolate*

2 egg whites
½ cup granulated sugar
pinch salt
2 3½-ounce cans flaked coconut
1 teaspoon vanilla

Melt together in the top of a small double boiler, over hot water, the unsweetened chocolate and sweet cooking chocolate.

Stir until smooth, remove from the heat and cool.

Beat the egg whites with a rotary beater until stiff.

Then beat in gradually the sugar.

Add the vanilla and salt, and beat 4 to 5 minutes until very stiff.

Add the cooled chocolate and continue beating until well mixed.

Fold in the flaked coconut.

Drop by teaspoonfuls onto well-buttered cookie sheets, making 2½ dozen.

Bake in a 325° F. oven until stiff on the outside but still a little soft on the inside, or for about 16 minutes.

Remove from the oven and shortly after loosen with a spatula.

Remove from the pan when cold.

OATMEAL COOKIES

(Makes 4 dozen cookies)

Preheat oven to 325° F.

2 eggs
1 cup sugar
1 cup melted butter
2 tablespoons molasses
1 teaspoon baking soda
1 teaspoon cinnamon
2 cups rolled oats
1 cup raisins
3 cups unbleached white flour
¼ cup hot water

Beat the eggs, add the other ingredients and mix well.

Drop on a buttered cookie sheet.

Press flat.

Bake in a slow oven (325° F.) for about 15 minutes.

EXTRA-SPECIAL COOKIES
(Makes 16 cookies)

Preheat oven to 350° F.

⅓ cup pecans, chopped very fine
¼ cup granulated sugar
2 cups sifted flour
½ cup confectioner's sugar
¼ teaspoon baking soda
¼ pound sweet butter
1 whole egg
1 egg yolk
grated rind of 1 lemon
1 teaspoon vanilla
¼ cup thick jam, apricot or strawberry

Butter 2 large cookie tins lightly.

Mix together in a shallow saucer the chopped pecans and the granulated sugar.

Sift some all-purpose flour and measure out 2 cups.

Add to the flour the confectioner's sugar and baking soda, and sift into a large bowl.

Cut the butter into the flour mixture.

Work the butter into the flour and sugar, using a large silver fork.

Beat together in a cup the yolk of 1 egg with the vanilla and lemon rind.

Add this gradually to the first mixture.

It should be crumbly.

Gather the whole into a ball.

Work it with your hands, squeezing the dough until it sticks together and is smooth and well blended.

In a separate saucer break the whole egg and beat it well with a fork.

Place the dough in the center of a lightly floured pastry cloth or board and roll out to about ³⁄₁₆ inch thickness.

With a lightly floured 3-inch scallop-edged cookie cutter, stamp out 16 rounds.

It will be necessary to gather up the scraps and press them together and roll them out again in order to make the required number.

Place 8 of them on one of the buttered cookie sheets.

With a 1½-inch cutter, make holes in the centers of the other 8, and put the small rounds aside temporarily.

Now dip the 8 circles you have made, one side only, first into the beaten egg and then into the nuts and sugar.

Place them on the second buttered cookie sheet, nut side up.

Paint the plain ones, including the tiny rounds, with a thin coating of the remainder of the egg yolk.

Tuck the small ones between the big ones wherever you can, then place both pans in a 350° F. oven and bake until lightly browned and firm to the touch, or for 15 to 20 minutes.

The ones with sugar and nuts will cook slightly faster than the others, so watch carefully.

Remove the pans from the oven and almost immediately loosen the cookies, using a pancake turner.

Allow to cool.

When cool, spread the plain ones with a coating of thick jam, using about a heaping teaspoon for each cookie.

Top each with a nut-topped cookie circle.

These are very pretty, generous, life-sized cookies and extra-specially good.

CARAMEL CUSTARD

(Serves 6)

It is most important to cook custard in a very slow oven in order to have it smooth and tender. Never let the water in the pan boil.

Preheat oven to 300° F.

> ½ cup granulated sugar
> ¼ cup boiling water
> 3 eggs
> ½ cup sugar
> ¼ teaspoon salt

3 cups milk
nutmeg

Put ½ cup sugar in a small frying pan and melt over low heat, stirring constantly.

Add the boiling water very slowly and simmer for 10 minutes.

Put 1 tablespoon of this syrup in the bottom of each of 6 custard cups.

Beat the eggs, ½ cup sugar and salt together in a bowl.

Add the milk.

Pour into the cups to ½ inch from the top.

Put a dash of nutmeg on top.

Place the cups in a shallow baking pan with 2 inches of hot water in the pan and bake for 50 to 60 minutes.

Test with a silver knife. If the knife comes out clean, the custard is cooked.

SPECIAL BROWN BETTY

(Serves 6)

6 tart cooking apples
½ cup water
½ cup orange juice
¼ cup sugar
½ teaspoon nutmeg or mace
16 square graham crackers
½ cup sugar
1 teaspoon grated orange peel
¼ cup chopped almonds
butter

Peel, core and cut the apples into eighths.

Add the water and orange juice and cook until slightly tender.

Add the sugar and spice.

Put in a shallow baking dish.

Roll out the graham crackers to fine crumbs and mix with the sugar, orange peel and nuts.

Sprinkle on top of the apples and dot all over with butter.

Bake at 375° F. until the top is crusty.

Serve with heavy cream or Sabayon Sauce (p. 178).

SABAYON SAUCE

(Serves 4–6)

6 egg yolks
½ cup granulated sugar
⅓ cup kirsch liqueur

Beat the egg yolks in the top of a double boiler until very light, adding gradually the sugar.

When light and creamy in color, add the kirsch.

Place over boiling water and beat continuously with a rotary beater until the mixture foams up and is heated through, but be careful not to overcook it.

Pour into a bowl and serve at once.

APPLE AND ORANGE COBBLER

(Serves 6)

Preheat oven to 450° F.

6 large apples
juice and rind of 1 large orange
4 tablespoons butter
1 cup granulated sugar
1 cup heavy cream (or more)
5 tablespoons butter
2 cups sifted flour
2 tablespoons granulated sugar
½ cup milk
3 teaspoons baking powder

Grate the rind of 1 large orange and cover immediately with the strained juice of the orange.

Peel, quarter and core the apples and slice fine.

Place in a well-buttered round baking dish (1½-quart size).

Stir in 1 cup granulated sugar and dot with 4 tablespoons butter.

Pour orange juice and rind over all.

Cover with rich biscuit dough made as follows:

Sift together 2 cups flour, 2 tablespoons granulated sugar and 3 teaspoons baking powder.

Work into this with fingertips 5 tablespoons butter.

Moisten with about ½ cup milk.

Turn out on a lightly floured pastry cloth and pat out to the size of the baking dish.

Place over the apple-and-orange mixture and bake for 15 minutes in a hot (450° F.) oven; reduce heat to 350° and bake for 30 minutes longer.

Serve with heavy cream.

OZARK PUDDING

(Serves 4)

Preheat oven to 350° F.

> *1 egg*
> *¾ cup granulated sugar*
> *2 tablespoons flour*
> *1¼ teaspoons baking powder*
> *⅛ teaspoon salt*
> *½ cup chopped pecan meats*
> *1 apple, peeled, cored and chopped fine*
> *1 teaspoon vanilla*
> *1 cup heavy cream*

Butter copiously a 10-inch pie plate.

Prepare the chopped pecan meats.

Peel, core and chop fine the apple.

Beat the egg until light and beat in gradually the granulated sugar.

Combine the flour with the baking powder and salt.

Stir into the egg mixture, and beat well.

Add the nuts and apple, and flavor with the vanilla.

Spread evenly in the pie plate and bake in a moderate (350° F.) oven for 35 minutes.

Serve while still hot, accompanied by the heavy cream.

COLD BANANA MOUSSE

(Serves 6)

2½ tablespoons granulated sugar
2 egg yolks
1 cup light cream
1½ cups heavy cream
1 envelope plain gelatin
¼ cup milk
1 teaspoon vanilla
2 large ripe bananas

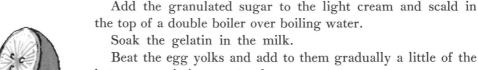

Add the granulated sugar to the light cream and scald in the top of a double boiler over boiling water.

Soak the gelatin in the milk.

Beat the egg yolks and add to them gradually a little of the hot cream, stirring constantly.

Then add the egg and cream to the rest of the scalded cream gradually, stirring constantly, and cook until thickened.

Remove from the fire, add the soaked gelatin and stir until completely melted.

Cool, stirring occasionally.

In the meantime peel the bananas, slice them into a large bowl and crush with a fork or wire potato masher.

Stir in the cooled custard and flavor with the vanilla.

Beat the heavy cream until very stiff, and fold it into the egg-and-gelatin mixture.

Place in a mold (1-quart size) and refrigerate until well set, or for about 6 hours.

Turn out into a pretty serving dish and serve on cold plates.

LIME MOUSSE

(Serves 6)

5 limes
1½ cups granulated sugar
2 cups milk
2 cups heavy cream

Grate the rind of 3 limes and strain over it immediately the juice of the 3 limes.

Add to this the sugar, stir and add gradually the milk.

Beat the heavy cream until almost stiff and fold into the milk-lime-sugar mixture.

Place in 2 shallow refrigerator trays in the freezing compartment, turn the control to coldest and freeze until partially frozen (about ¾ hour).

Remove from the freezing compartment, scrape down the sides, mix well with a spoon and allow to freeze until solid.

This takes about 2 hours in my refrigerator.

Reduce the temperature control to normal and allow to remain ½ hour or so until ready to serve, at which time place in a well-chilled dessert bowl and quickly grate over the surface the thin rind (green part only) of 2 additional limes.

Serve at once with angel cake.

WHITE WINE JELLY
(Serves 6)

¾ cup granulated sugar
grated rind and juice of 2 lemons
1½ cups warm water
2½ cups cold water
2 cups white wine
2 cups Madeira wine
2 egg whites
3 envelopes plain gelatin

Grate the rind of 2 lemons and add the strained juice of the lemons immediately.

Soak the gelatin in 1½ cups warm water.

Mix together the sugar, lemon rind and juice, 2½ cups cold water and the white wine.

Heat and, when warm, stir in the gelatin.

Beat the egg whites until stiff and add them to the warm mixture.

Bring to a boil, stirring constantly.

When it comes to the boil, remove from the fire and add the Madeira wine.

Strain through a cloth-lined sieve and pour into a 1½-quart mold.

Refrigerate when cold.
Serve with whipped cream.

DESSERT PANCAKES

(Makes 12 small pancakes)

1 cup sifted flour
¼ cup powdered sugar, sifted
½ teaspoon salt
¾ cup milk
3 eggs, beaten

Mix the flour, sugar and salt.
Add the milk.
Add the beaten eggs.
Cook in a slightly buttered small frying pan, one by one, tipping the pan to spread the batter over the surface.

Rolled Pancakes

Roll the cooked pancakes and serve with Orange Sauce (see below).

Filled Pancakes

On each pancake place 1 teaspoon black currant jam or strawberry jam, fold over and sprinkle with granulated sugar.
Serve with thick heavy cream.

Nuts-and-Cream Pancakes

On each pancake place 1 tablespoon whipped cream, sprinkle the cream with finely chopped almonds, fold over and sprinkle with brown sugar and more nuts.

ORANGE SAUCE FOR DESSERT PANCAKES

¼ pound butter
½ cup sugar
grated rind and juice of 1 large orange

grated rind and juice of 1 lemon
¼ cup brandy or Cointreau

Melt the butter.
Add the sugar and cook until blended.
Add the rind and juice of the orange and lemon.
Cook for a few minutes.
Remove from the fire and add the brandy or Cointreau.

BLACK CHERRY JAM

(Makes 3–4 pints)

10 cups pitted ripe black cherries
6⅔ cups granulated sugar
1⅓ cups water
1 cake paraffin for sealing the jars

Sterilize 3 or 4 1-pint jars.
Pit large black cherries until you have 10 cups of them.
Moisten the granulated sugar with the cold water and boil 5 minutes, skimming carefully.
Pour it over the cherries in a big preserving kettle, bring quickly to a boil again, skim carefully and frequently, and cook until thick and transparent, or about 40 to 50 minutes.
Pour into the sterilized jars, adjust rubbers and, when cold, cover with melted paraffin, cover and seal tight.

APRICOT JAM

(Makes 5 pints)

6 pounds fresh apricots
9 cups granulated sugar
2 cups cold water
1 cake paraffin for sealing the jars

Split the apricots and remove but save the pits.
Put the halves in cold water as you go along.
Next crack open the pits, take out the kernels, put them in a bowl, pour boiling water over them, cover and allow them to steep for 5 minutes, then pinch off the brown skins.
Now put the sugar in a large pan, moisten it with the cold

water, bring to a boil, skim well and boil for 5 minutes.

Then add the well-drained apricots and continue boiling, skimming carefully, stirring frequently to prevent sticking.

When the juice sheets from the side of the spoon and the jam is thick and transparent, add the blanched kernels and pour or ladle the jam into hot sterilized pint-size jars.

Adjust the scalded rubbers and, when cold, cover with a little hot paraffin, put on the top and seal tight.

It should take about 50 minutes for the jam to cook to the right consistency, but be careful not to overcook it, as jam thickens when it cools.

PEACH CHUTNEY

(Makes 3 pints)

8 large peaches, peeled, sliced
⅔ cup almonds, blanched and split
7 sweet red peppers, seeded and chopped
3 medium-size onions, peeled and chopped
peel and pulp of 1 orange, chopped
peel and pulp of 1 lemon, chopped
1 clove garlic, peeled and chopped
4 ounces candied ginger, chopped
1 cup seedless raisins
1 teaspoon salt
1 teaspoon powdered ginger
1⅔ cups granulated sugar
1¾ cups cider vinegar

Measure and prepare the above ingredients, leaving the peaches until last.

Moisten the sugar with 1¼ cups vinegar, bring to a boil and cook for 5 minutes.

Skim well, add the peaches and cook for 10 minutes, skimming again.

Then add the peppers, onions, garlic, ginger, salt, raisins and orange and lemon peel and pulp, and cook for 30 minutes, stirring frequently and skimming as necessary.

Add the almonds, powdered ginger and another ½ cup vinegar and continue cooking ½ hour, watching carefully and stirring frequently to prevent sticking.

[*184*]

In the meantime sterilize 3 pint-size jars.

When the chutney is done, pour immediately into the well-drained jars, adjust the rubbers and seal tight.

GRAPE CONSERVE

(Makes 4 pints)

4 pounds blue Concord grapes
1 cup walnut meats
4 cups granulated sugar
1 large navel orange
1 scant teaspoon salt
1 cup seedless raisins
1 cake paraffin

Wash and sterilize 4 pint-size jars.

Prepare the walnut meats, cutting them in two.

Wash, drain and pick off the grapes from 4 pounds Concord grapes.

Slip the skins from the grapes, keeping them separate from the pulp.

Cut the orange in 4, remove any seeds there may be, then put the orange, skin and all, through the meat grinder, using the coarse cutter. Be careful not to lose any of the juice.

Boil the grape pulp for about 10 minutes, stirring constantly.

Press through a sieve to remove the seeds.

To the resultant pulp, add the granulated sugar, seedless raisins, ground-up orange and salt.

Boil rapidly, stirring to prevent burning, for about 10 minutes, or until the mixture begins to thicken.

Add the grape skins and boil for 10 minutes longer, stirring constantly, skimming if necessary.

Add the walnut halves and pour immediately into hot sterilized jars, adjust the rubbers and, when cold, cover with melted paraffin and seal tight.

TOMATO CONSERVE

(Makes 6–7 half-pints)

4 pounds ripe red but firm tomatoes
2 small navel oranges

1 lemon
1 5-inch stick of cinnamon
12 whole cloves
sugar (equal to weight of tomatoes when ready to cook)
⅓ cup sliced candied ginger
1 cake paraffin, melted over very low heat

Sterilize 7 ½-pint jars.

Wash, blanch, skin and slice fine the tomatoes, and set aside.

Quarter and slice fine the oranges and lemon, discarding any seeds you find.

Drain off any juice that may have formed on the tomatoes and weigh them.

Place in a large kettle and add an equal weight of granulated sugar.

Put on the stove and stir until the sugar is dissolved.

Add the oranges, lemon, cinnamon (broken into several pieces) and cloves.

Bring quickly to a boil over high heat and skim carefully.

Reduce the heat slightly and cook until it sheets from the side of a silver spoon, or for about 1¼ hours; watch carefully, stirring frequently, as it scorches *very* easily.

Ten minutes before you think it will be done, add the sliced candied ginger.

Place in the sterilized jars and allow to cool before covering with a thin coating of melted paraffin.

Allow the paraffin to set before covering with screw-on lids.

DILL CUCUMBER PICKLES

25 medium-size cucumbers
2 stalks fresh dill
1½ bay leaves
½ tablespoon peppercorns
grape leaves
½ cup vinegar
½ cup salt
2½ quarts water

Soak the cucumbers overnight in cold water.

Make a brine of the water, salt, and peppercorns.

Bring to a good rolling boil and cool.

In a large crock put a layer of cucumbers, a few pieces of the dill and a bay leaf. Repeat until the cucumbers are all used.

Put dill on the top layer and pour the brine over all.

Cover with grape leaves, put a large plate on top and weight down to keep the cucumbers under the brine.

After a week add ½ cup vinegar.

Ready to use after 2 weeks more.

Keep the scum cleaned off the surface of the brine.

DILL TOMATOES

Choose small green tomatoes, but do not soak overnight.

Use same formula as for Dill Cucumber Pickles (above).

DILL BEANS

Choose green stringless beans or wax beans.

Cook in boiling salted water for 7 minutes and use the same formula as for Dill Cucumber Pickles (p. 186).

SPREADS FOR SANDWICHES

Salmon Spread

To 1 cup flaked cooked or canned salmon, add ¼ cup each finely chopped celery, green pepper and lettuce.

Moisten with French dressing and season to taste.

Tuna Spread

Mash ¾ cup tuna and mix with 2 tablespoons chopped chutney, 1 tablespoon sieved egg yolk and 1 teaspoon lemon juice.

Add Mayonnaise to bind, and season to taste.

Egg and Anchovy

Chop together 6 hard-cooked eggs, 3 celery stalks and 8 anchovy fillets.

Add Mayonnaise to bind, paprika and pepper to taste.

Pineapple-Cheese Spread

Blend 1 3-ounce package cream cheese with 3 tablespoons Mayonnaise, add ½ cup chopped pecans and ½ cup drained, crushed pineapple.

Avocado Spread

Mash to a paste ¼ cup Roquefort cheese, add 1 cup avocado purée and 1 tablespoon lemon juice, and mix thoroughly.

Mushroom Filling

Cream 6 ounces cream cheese with 1 tablespoon onion juice. When light and fluffy, add 1 cup finely chopped raw or canned mushrooms and season with salt and pepper to taste.

Bacon and Pickle

Combine ¼ cup Mayonnaise with 3 dill pickles, chopped, and 6 slices crumbled crisp bacon.

Chicken and Olive

Combine 2 cups ground dark chicken meat with ½ cup chopped ripe olives, add a little Mayonnaise to bind, and salt and pepper to taste.

Lobster Spread

Mix together 2 cups lobster meat, 1 hard-cooked egg and 1 large tomato, peeled and seeded.

Chop these together finely, season with salt and pepper, and bind with Mayonnaise.

Meat and Chili

Combine 1 cup chopped cooked meat or canned luncheon meat with ½ cup chili sauce.

Tongue and Gherkin

Combine 1 cup chopped cooked tongue, ½ cup chopped gherkins or drained chopped relish, ¼ cup Mayonnaise or salad dressing.

Lamb and Chutney

Combine 1 cup chopped cooked lamb, ¼ cup chopped Chutney (p. 184), 3 tablespoons Mayonnaise or whipped cream cheese.

Corned Beef and Horseradish

Combine 1 cup chopped cooked corned beef, 1 tablespoon prepared horseradish, 3 tablespoons Mayonnaise or whipped cream cheese.

Add a little dry mustard to taste.

Ham and Cream Cheese

Cream ½ teaspoon dry mustard with ½ cup cream cheese. Add 1 cup chopped cooked ham.

Chicken or Turkey with Celery

Combine 1 cup chopped cooked chicken or turkey, 1 cup chopped celery, ½ cup Mayonnaise or whipped cream cheese.

The addition of ½ cup chopped fennel, when available, will impart a distinctive tang to this recipe.

Tuna and Nut

Combine 1 cup flaked tuna, ½ cup chopped celery, ¼ cup chopped walnuts or pecans, ½ cup Mayonnaise.

Salmon and Cucumber

Combine 1 cup flaked salmon, ½ cup diced cucumber (no seeds), ¼ cup Mayonnaise.

Sardine and Lemon

Combine 1 can sardines, juice of ½ lemon, ⅛ pound softened butter or margarine.

Shrimp and Chutney

Combine 1 cup diced shrimp, ¼ cup chopped Chutney (p. 184), ¼ cup ketchup.

Crab and Avocado

Combine 1 cup flaked crabmeat, 1 cup mashed avocado, lemon juice and Tabasco to taste, Mayonnaise or creamed cheese.

Lobster and Celery

Combine 1 cup diced lobster, 1 cup diced celery, 2 tablespoons ketchup, ½ cup Mayonnaise.

Anchovy and Olive

Combine 1 small can anchovy fillets chopped with an equal amount of chopped stuffed olives or ripe olives, and 1 cup softened cream cheese.

Egg and Bacon

Combine chopped hard-cooked eggs with chopped crisp bacon and a little Mayonnaise or ketchup.

Egg and Liverwurst

Spread 2 slices bread with butter or margarine.
Spread liverwurst on one side.
Cover other slice with sliced egg.
Make sandwich, cut and serve.

Egg and Anchovy Paste

Sieve or chop 6 hard-cooked eggs.
Mix in a tablespoon of anchovy paste and add ⅓ cup Mayonnaise.

Egg and Sardine

Combine chopped hard-cooked eggs with mashed sardines and a little softened butter.
Season to taste.

WESTERN BURGER

(Serves 6)

½ cup coarsely chopped green pepper
¼ cup chopped onion
2 tablespoons butter or margarine
1 cup chopped cooked ham
1 can (10½ ounces) condensed cream
  of mushroom soup
6 eggs, slightly beaten
dash pepper
12 slices toast

Cook the green pepper and onion in butter or margarine until tender.

Add the ham; cook until lightly browned.

Blend the soup, eggs, and pepper; add to the ham and vegetables.

Cook over low heat, stirring occasionally, until the eggs are set.

Serve on toast.

CORNMEAL MUFFINS

(Makes 15 2½-inch muffins)

Preheat oven to 425° F.

1½ cups sifted white unbleached flour
4 teaspoons baking powder
½ teaspoon salt
2 tablespoons granulated sugar
¾ cup cornmeal
1 egg, beaten
1 cup milk
4 tablespoons melted shortening

Sift together the flour, baking powder, salt and sugar, and mix well with the cornmeal.

Combine the egg, milk and shortening.

Turn the milk mixture into the dry ingredients all at one

time, and stir quickly and vigorously until the dry and liquid ingredients are just mixed.

Fill greased muffin pans about ⅔ full of batter, and bake in a hot oven (425° F.) for 25 minutes.

WHOLE-WHEAT MUFFINS
(Makes 12–15 2½-inch muffins)

Preheat oven to 425° F.

> *1½ cups whole-wheat flour*
> *½ cup sifted unbleached white flour*
> *4 teaspoons baking powder*
> *½ teaspoon salt*
> *2 tablespoons brown sugar or molasses*
> *1 egg, beaten*
> *1½ cups milk*
> *4 tablespoons melted shortening*

Combine the dry ingredients and mix well.

Combine the brown sugar or molasses, egg, milk and shortening.

Then turn into the dry ingredients all at one time and stir quickly and vigorously until the dry and liquid ingredients are just mixed and the mixture has a lumpy appearance.

Fill greased muffin pans about ⅔ full of batter and bake in a hot oven (425° F.) for 25 minutes.

SPOON BREAD
(Serves 6)

Preheat oven to 425° F.

> *4 cups milk*
> *1 cup cornmeal*
> *2 tablespoons butter*
> *1¾ teaspoons salt*
> *4 eggs, well beaten*
> *2 tablespoons unbleached white flour*

Scald the milk in a double boiler.

Mix the flour with the cornmeal.

Gradually stir in the cornmeal and flour mixture and cook until it has the consistency of mush.

Add the butter and salt and pour over the well-beaten eggs gradually, while stirring.

Pour into a greased or oiled 1½-quart casserole.

Bake in a hot oven (425° F.) for 45 minutes.

Serve at once with plenty of butter.

BUCKWHEAT CAKES

(Makes 1 dozen cakes)

¾ cup buckwheat flour
¾ cup sifted unbleached white flour
2¼ teaspoons baking powder
3 tablespoons granulated sugar
¾ teaspoon salt
1 cup milk or ½ cup evaporated milk and ½ cup
   water
1 egg, beaten
3 tablespoons melted shortening

Combine all the dry ingredients.

Add the milk, egg and melted shortening and stir until smooth.

Drop on a hot griddle and bake until brown on both sides.

WHOLE-WHEAT GRIDDLE CAKES

(Makes 1 dozen 4-inch cakes)

1½ cups whole-wheat flour
3 teaspoons baking powder
¾ teaspoon salt
3 tablespoons brown sugar
1 egg, beaten
1¼ cups milk
3 tablespoons melted shortening

Thoroughly combine the dry ingredients.

Combine the egg, milk and shortening, and add the dry ingredients gradually, stirring until smooth.

Drop the mixture from the tip of a spoon onto a hot griddle which has been greased or not, according to manufacturer's directions.

Cook on one side, ahd when puffed and full of bubbles and cooked on the edges, turn and cook on the other side.

CORNMEAL WAFFLES

(Makes 1 dozen waffles)

1 cup cornmeal
1 cup unbleached sifted white flour
2 tablespoons granulated sugar
4 teaspoons baking powder
½ teaspoon salt
2 eggs
⅞ cup milk
6 tablespoons melted shortening

Combine the cornmeal and the remaining dry ingredients which have been sifted together in a bowl.

Beat the eggs until light, add the milk and shortening, and combine with dry ingredients, stirring until smooth and well blended.

Bake in a waffle iron, following the manufacturer's directions.

QUICK NUT BREAD

Preheat oven to 325° F.

2 cups whole-wheat flour
1 cup sifted unbleached white flour
¾ cup brown sugar
1 teaspoon salt
4 teaspoons baking powder
2 cups milk
4 tablespoons melted butter
1 cup nut meats, finely cut

To the whole-wheat flour add the flour, sugar, salt and baking powder.

When thoroughly mixed, add the remaining ingredients.

Turn into a buttered bread pan, cover and let stand for 20 minutes.

Bake in a moderately slow oven (325° F.) for 50 to 60 minutes.

PART THREE

PEPPERIDGE FARM

IN 1937 the most amazing period of my life started purely by chance.

I had become intensely interested in the study of proper nutrition, particularly for young children. Searching for medical advice about treating a special allergic condition, I was told by an allergy specialist that a basic diet of natural foods was most important, not only for children but for adults as well. In some allergy cases the only flour or starch in the diet should be made from fresh, stone-ground, whole wheat.

The stone-ground whole-wheat flour was new to me. It contains the wheat germ, rich in the miraculous Vitamin B_1.

My husband and I worked out a diet that used only fresh fruits and vegetables, fresh meat and fish, natural sugars (honey and molasses) and the fresh, stone-ground, whole-wheat flour which I bought from an old New England grist-mill—no white flour, no white sugar.

We used the flour first in delicious whole-wheat pancakes and muffins. Then, even though the flour seemed quite coarse in texture, I decided one day to try making some bread. I had never made a loaf of bread in my life, but I got out all the cookbooks I owned, read all the directions and started in. That first loaf should have been sent to the Smith-sonian Institution as a sample of bread from the Stone Age, for it was hard as a rock and about one inch high. The trou-

[*199*]

ble was that I had never before used yeast, which needs careful temperature control.

So I started over again. After a few more efforts by trial and error, and with a few competitive experiments by my husband, we achieved what seemed like good bread. I was generous in my use of butter and milk, honey and molasses, and invented a recipe which resulted in a delicious bread, pleasant for anyone to eat without being told "Eat it because it's good for you."

All the family liked it, and pretty soon we ate nothing but homemade whole-wheat bread. When I told the doctor I was making bread from the stone-ground flour, he wouldn't believe me because he said it was too coarse and I would have to add white flour to it. To convince him, I brought him some samples and told him exactly what I put in with the flour. Immediately he wanted to order it for himself and for his other patients.

I was quite taken aback by this idea, but I knew the bread was nutritious, unique, and delicious and was indeed an important part of the whole diet.

I decided to work only through doctors. Armed with a letter from my specialist, I approached three or four doctors. Before I realized what could happen, they began telling patients about my product, and very soon I had a sizable mail-order business.

I had to employ a young girl to help, and I taught her how to bake, for she had never made bread either. There we were on the farm in the hot August days of 1937, a pair of amateur bakers, mixing and kneading and baking like mad and then, when the loaves were cooled, making neat little packages to send by parcel post to our beloved customers. It was about the hottest summer I remember, and tears flowed when a batch of dough just didn't come out right and had to be discarded after all our toil and trouble.

That girl celebrated her twenty-fifth year with the Pepperidge Farm Company last summer. Soon I employed her sister, her brother, her sister-in-law, her cousins, and at one time ten members of her family were Pepperidge Farm employees. Some of the girls married, but there are six of the family with us now.

Now, all of this couldn't continue in my kitchen, so we moved ourselves into one of our farm buildings.

I believe that success is often the result of an accidental circumstance and an opportunity to take advantage of it. My accidental circumstance was my interest in proper food for children, and the opportunity to take advantage of it lay in the fact that we had space and facilities to work with, and a ready-made name for products from Pepperidge Farm.

In 1929, when we had built our house at Pepperidge Farm, my husband had also built a large garage and a large stable for his polo ponies. But in 1932, after a bad riding accident, polo and riding had had to be abandoned, and in 1937 we had lots of empty space to use.

First I walled off some space in the garage and made a nice room about twenty feet square, painted it pale green, hung up some curtains, put linoleum on the floor and installed a few pieces of equipment. Of course, this was all just a hobby, for I never dreamed of developing a business. I didn't spend a dollar if I could avoid it, and just used odds and ends I had in the house. I had a small gas stove in which we could make eight loaves at a time, an old table, a few mixing bowls, the old baby scale brought down from the attic to weigh the dough, a few bread pans and a few wire-mesh trays for cooling the bread. All these objects are now in the Pepperidge Farm Museum in one of our bakeries.

On we went with our mail-order business, and our operations soon took over all the space in the garage. Eventually we made the old stable building into a model bakery.

More and more friends and neighbors demanded our bread, so I decided to take a dozen loaves to our local grocer and ask if he would like to sell it. Regular commercial bread was then selling at ten cents a loaf, but I calmly announced that the price to him was twenty cents and that he could sell it at twenty-five. He told me later that he had thought I was just plain daft, but I was a good customer and he hadn't wanted to tell me he knew no one would pay that much for one loaf of bread.

I had thought that might be his reaction, however, so I had come prepared with some butter and a bread knife. I sliced a loaf and buttered the slices, and he and his clerks sampled my product. The look on their faces told the story. They all reached for more and said, "Well, that's bread!" I then gave my well-rehearsed sales talk about the ingredients I used and the high quality of the product and left my loaves. Before I got home my grocer friend had telephoned to say he was all sold out and wanted more.

Within a week people were talking about this new kind of bread, and every grocery store in our neighborhood called and wanted to sell our homemade product.

Up to November of 1937 we made only whole-wheat bread, but by then I thought there was also a market for old-fashioned white bread of fine quality for those people who preferred it to whole-wheat.

However, I would make it only of unbleached white flour, which very few commercial bakers were using because unbleached white flour must be slowly aged before it is ready for baking good bread. The chemical bleaching process had come into use because it not only made the flour super white but changed the baking quality of the flour in some way which eliminated the time needed for aging.

With the creamy-colored unbleached flour I used only honey as a sweetener, grade-A butter and fresh whole milk, salt and yeast—nothing to make it puff up and look big. The result was my loaf looked small, but it tasted good and people liked it.

By this time our New York City mail orders had grown to a size that was difficult to handle. I went into New York one day and walked into Charles and Company, the famous old food specialty shop.

My husband had always said, "When you want something go right to the top man." So I asked for the manager. The manager came out, looking rather skeptical, to see a woman with a package under her arm, another package in one hand (which was a quarter-pound of butter) and in the other hand a bread knife. I was petrified with fright, and he probably was also when he saw my knife—but I told him about my homemade bread and about the doctors' patients who were ready-made customers that I could send to him. He still looked skeptical.

But I said, "Can I give you a sample?" So we went into his office and I cut a slice, buttered it and gave it to him. As soon as he tasted it, he said, "My goodness, that's just the kind of bread my mother made when I was a boy." So, of course, I was in! He ordered twenty-four loaves a day, and I promised to tell the mail-order customers to come to the shop for their bread.

I went across the street to the Grand Central Station, and got on a train, just delighted with myself. But on the train I got to thinking, "My goodness, he said to get twenty-four loaves to him early tomorrow morning—how am I going to do that?" Then I thought, "It's all right, don't I have a commuting husband who goes on the train to Grand Central every morning? And what's a couple of packages between friends?"

When I reached home, the girls and I made the bread and packaged it, and I hid it behind the door. I didn't tell my husband anything that night, but just as he was about to leave in the morning, I said, "By the way, Henry, won't you just take this little package"—it weighed twenty-five pounds —"in to Grand Central and send it across the street to Charles and Company?" If he had stopped to argue, he would have missed the train, so off he went with the package.

For several weeks he and the package rode in the club car to Grand Central, where a porter met him and for twenty-five cents took the package across the street to Charles and Company. Orders increased, and soon Henry was taking two packages each day. Well, that was all right —he had two hands. But when we got to three packages a day, what were we going to do?

Then we discovered that the Railway Express people make a business of delivering packages, and we started do-

ing business with them.

And so we grew at first from store to store by word-of-mouth praise from customers because people talked about this unusual product. Gradually, other stores began asking for some of our bread to sell.

There was no planning, no theory, just: What is necessary to do next? Well, let's do it and see what happens. It was fun.

After a few months I decided that the little loose sheets of paper on which I kept my records were not very businesslike, and a neighbor offered to come around and set up some books for me.

I said, "Fine—how long will it take?"

"Oh," he said, "about half a day."

He finished the little bookkeeping set-up for me, and when he was about to leave he said, "I think a store I know would love to sell the bread," and I said, "Good. I will hire you as a salesman. Take some samples with you." Off he went, and he came back in the evening so excited he could hardly talk. He'd opened ten stores!

And he was rarin' to go the next day, too, so I said, "Well, all right, go ahead, go ahead." And he kept right on going! He came for half a day in 1937 and stayed for twenty-four years.

When we appeared on the market there was nothing like our product; today we have many imitators, but I suppose imitation is the greatest form of flattery and I believe competition is good for us. It prevents complacency and keeps us alert.

By 1940 we needed far more space than we had on the farm, and we rented some buildings in Norwalk just for a year while we bought land and drew up plans for a real bakery. But the war came along and we had to stay in those buildings until it was over. And that was torture, because they became much too small as we grew. Completely inefficient, and really a headache.

Now, how did we get enough stone-ground flour from old mills as we grew? Well, there was only one way—to find several old mills and either give them enough grinding business to warrant improvements and additions or operate them ourselves. We have had four old grist mills restored to full activity.

Three of them, owned by other people, did grinding for us; one of them we run ourselves; and, in addition, we bought old grinding stones and built a mill right into our newest bakery, the one outside Chicago.

And there we efficiently grind our own whole-wheat flour right in the bakery, which is my dream for all the other plants someday.

By either grinding the whole-wheat flour ourselves or having it done under our close supervision, we control the freshness and quality of the flour—it is very important that this flour be kept cool during grinding and not heated by too rapid revolutions of the stones.

THE STORY OF BREAD

IT IS believed that wheat was growing in the highlands of Abyssinia about five thousand years ago. It must have been growing in Egypt also, for grains of wheat were found in an Egyptian pyramid tomb dating back to 3000 B.C.

Bread was used as currency in Egypt, and at one time the salary of the chief priest was paid in "fine loaves" as well as "coarse loaves." The "fine loaves" must have been made of fine or white flour from which all the rough bran had been sifted by the hand labor of slaves.

When the Romans invaded Egypt in 47 B.C. the use of wheat was brought back to Rome and its conquered countries. But the Romans didn't conquer the Germans, so perhaps that is why nowadays rye bread is more popular than wheat bread in Germany.

The early records of Egyptian life—around 3000 B.C.— show that the baking of bread was considered important. The supervisor of the royal bakeries enjoyed a position of privilege. White bread at one's table was a mark of luxury, for slaves were needed for the long labor of sifting out by hand all the roughage from the ground whole wheat.

In ancient times bread was used as an offering to the gods. Pliny the Elder told of an urn in a temple in Rome which was always full of fresh bread, taken by the temple visitors as a gift to the gods.

The Greeks and Romans made baking more of an art and changed from the flat loaves of the Egyptians. The Romans had strict laws, and every baker who sold bread underweight was fined and put in prison.

Since prehistoric times some form of bread made from grains has been man's staple article of diet. All civilizations have had breads and cereals as principal foods, especially where meat was scarce or was forbidden for religious reasons. Of all the grains, wheat and corn (maize) appear in all civilizations as man's favorites. Barley, oats, rye, rice and millet are ground for flour but have much less gluten content, so the bread made from them is heavy.

The hard seeds of the grains were probably chewed by the cave men, until someone thought of grinding the seeds between stones. The upper and nether millstones spoken of in the Bible were considered an important part of a man's fortune if he was lucky enough to own a set.

In making stone-ground whole-wheat flour today for Pepperidge Farm Bread we use the upper and nether millstones. The lower stone is rigid and the upper stone revolves. The surfaces of both stones are intricately ground to create the passage of air, so that the flour, as it is ground, is forced off the edge of the stone into a bin underneath. Today's process for milling white flour is just a refinement of the basic operation. To separate the rough husks from the ground grain, the sifter was invented. Sifting out the bran and roughage makes smooth flour.

Many superstitions refer to bread.

To drop a slice of bread buttered side up means you will have a visitor.

If you dream about bread, you will make money.

If by chance you must take the last slice of bread on the plate, you will be an old maid or a bachelor. On the other hand, it is also said that if a girl deliberately waits for the last slice, she is waiting for a handsome husband.

When you are moving, the very last thing to put in the moving van is a loaf of bread, and it must be the first thing off at the new house so there will always be food in your house.

A crust of bread in a newborn baby's crib will keep evil spirits away.

When traveling in dangerous country, a crust in your pocket serves as a good-luck charm.

The Mohammedans never cut bread with a knife, but break it.

In Russia guests were welcomed with bread and salt.

"He knows which side his bread is buttered on" means he's a pretty keen fellow.

"It's my bread and butter" refers to the source of your income.

"It's not my bread and butter" means something is not important to you.

Ben Franklin said, "Never spare the parson's wine or the baker's bread."

"He butters his bread on both sides" means an extravagant chap.

The Spanish say, "With bread, troubles are less."

WHOLE-WHEAT BREAD

In my opinion, bread made from fresh, stone-ground, whole-wheat flour offers the best nutrition and the best flavor. This flour is not easy to find, but it can be purchased by mail direct from small mills that advertise in home-type magazines or special food magazines.

Bread made from fresh whole-wheat flour has more nutritional qualities than bread made from highly refined, unenriched flour. This is because whole-wheat flour is just what its name implies—all of the wheat, including the wheat germ, which is rich in Vitamin B_1. But wheat germ is perishable, so whole-wheat flour must be used soon after grinding —otherwise the flour becomes rancid.

The bran and wheat germ are removed when white flour is made.

I don't say you must eat only whole-wheat bread. Eat some white bread, too, but be sure it is of high quality, made of unbleached flour and other good ingredients, and firm to the touch. For children, I think, it is important that at least half of the bread they eat should be whole-wheat bread made of fresh stone-ground flour.

MAKING BREAD

There are many recipes for yeast breads—white, whole-wheat, cornmeal, French bread, sour rye and sweet rye, raisin breads and spicy sweet breads.

A basic recipe for white bread or whole-wheat bread can have as many variations as you can find time to try.

There are a few simple rules to follow:

Wheat flour is best for bread making because of the gluten content of wheat. Gluten makes the dough elastic and allows it to expand as the gas bubbles are formed by the action of yeast.

Flour for bread is made from hard wheat, and flour for cake is made from soft wheat. Flour from most other grains should be mixed with some wheat flour in order to get the action of the gluten.

All ingredients should be of the best quality.

Flour for white bread should be unbleached.

Flour for whole-wheat bread should be 100-percent fresh stone-ground hard-wheat flour used not more than two weeks after grinding and kept in a cool place, preferably in a refrigerator.

Originally housewives made their own yeast by fermenting potatoes or by using hops, but nowadays the packaged, dry, granulated yeast made by the various yeast companies is an excellent product and can be kept in your supply

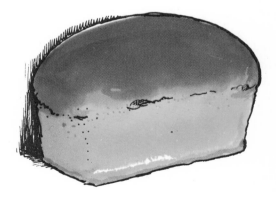

closet for at least a month. The amount of yeast to be used depends upon the length of time you want the dough to rise. A small amount of yeast will require a longer rising time. The directions on the yeast packages are very clear and easy to follow.

Water for dissolving dry yeast should feel very warm but not hot when tested on the inside of the wrist—about 105° F.

If you cannot buy dry yeast, use compressed yeast, which comes in one-ounce cakes. Water for compressed yeast need be only lukewarm—about 90° F.

All other ingredients and utensils should be at room temperature or even warmer.

Mixing bowls should be warmed by rinsing with hot water.

Stone-ground whole-wheat flour, when taken from a cool place, should be warmed slightly in a warm oven before mixing.

Butter or shortening should be melted and cooled before it is added to the mix.

Sugar and salt should be well dissolved in the warm liquid before flour is added to the mix.

Liquid can be all water or all milk or part of each.

After mixing and kneading, the dough should be covered with a damp cloth to prevent the surface from drying out and left to rise in a warm place, about 85° F., until double in bulk.

If it is difficult to find a place which is warm enough for dough to rise in the designated time, one of the following methods may be used.

1. Place the covered bowl of dough in a pan of warm water (about 87° F.); or

2. Heat water to the boiling point in a saucepan and remove from the heat. Place a rack, pie tin or cookie sheet over the pan. Place the covered bowl of dough on this support.

3. Experiment with your stove. Although stoves vary, a slightly warmed oven may be used to raise the dough. Use a

thermometer to check the temperature, keeping the oven not over 85° F.

The proper size for a bread pan is about 9 inches long, 5 inches wide and 3 inches deep.

The pan can be greased with butter or any other shortening.

Pans should be cleaned thoroughly of grease after each baking.

When you start mixing the flour into the liquid, use a strong, long-handled mixing spoon so you can really beat the batter while it is soft.

As you add the last of the flour, the batter becomes a thick dough and then you can use your hands to knead in all of the flour.

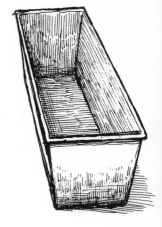

KNEADING

The purpose of kneading is to distribute evenly by pressure all the air holes which are formed in the dough by the gas-producing action of yeast.

Kneading is not difficult.

For the first kneading after the ingredients have been well mixed, place the mixed ball of dough on a lightly floured board, flatten it into a circle with your hands to a thickness of about one inch and fold the top one third of the dough toward you.

On the doubled-over dough, press down and push away from you with the heels of your hands.

Give the dough a quarter-turn to the right and fold the next top in toward you, pressing down and pushing the folded dough away from you.

Continue turning, folding and kneading for at least five minutes until the dough feels smooth and elastic.

Form into a ball and replace in the bowl to rise in a warm place. Keep the bowl covered.

For the second kneading, after the dough has risen to double in bulk, divide the dough according to the number of loaves you are making. Knead each piece about three minutes and then shape into loaves to fit your pans.

Most recipes make two loaves, but with a bread-mixing pail you can easily make six or eight at one mixing and put the extra loaves, properly wrapped, in your freezer. This is a great time saver.

WHITE BREAD
(Makes 1 loaf)

Preheat oven to 400° F., 20 minutes before loaf is ready to bake.

½ cup milk
1 tablespoon sugar
1 teaspoon salt
4 teaspoons shortening or butter
½ cup warm water
1 package or cake yeast, dry or compressed
3 cups sifted white flour

Scald the milk.
Add and stir in the sugar, salt and shortening or butter.
Cool to lukewarm.
Measure into a large mixing bowl the warm (not hot) water.
(Cool to lukewarm for compressed yeast.)
Sprinkle or crumble in the yeast.
Stir until dissolved.
Add the lukewarm milk mixture.
Add and stir in 1½ cups sifted flour.
Beat until smooth.
Add and stir in an additional 1½ cups sifted flour (about).
Turn out on a lightly floured board.
Knead quickly and lightly until smooth and elastic.
Place in a greased bowl; brush lightly with melted shortening or butter.
Cover with a clean damp towel.
Let rise in a warm place, free from draft, until doubled in bulk, about 50 minutes.
Punch down.

Shape into a loaf and place in a greased bread pan, 9 by 5 by 3 inches.

Cover with a clean damp towel.

Let rise in a warm place, free from draft, until doubled in bulk, about 50 minutes.

Bake in a hot oven (400° F.) for about 50 minutes.

WHITE BATTER BREAD
(Makes 2 loaves)

Preheat oven to 375° F., 20 minutes before loaves are ready to bake.

> *1 cup milk*
> *3 tablespoons sugar*
> *1 tablespoon salt*
> *2 tablespoons butter or margarine*
> *1 cup very warm water*
> *2 packages or cakes yeast, dry or compressed*
> *4¼ cups unsifted flour*

Scald the milk; stir in the sugar, salt and butter or margarine.

Cool to lukewarm.

Measure the very warm water into a large warm bowl.

Sprinkle or crumble in the yeast; stir until dissolved.

Add the lukewarm milk mixture.

Stir in the flour; the batter will be fairly stiff.

Beat until well blended, about 2 minutes.

Cover with a clean damp towel.

Let rise in a warm place, free from draft, until more than doubled in bulk, about 40 minutes.

Stir the batter down.

Beat vigorously, about ½ minute.

Turn into 2 greased loaf pans, 9 by 5 by 3 inches.

Bake in a moderate oven (375° F.) for about 50 minutes.

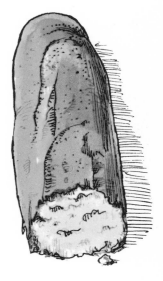

WHITE BREAD (Sponge Method)
(Makes 2 loaves)

Preheat oven to 400° F., 20 minutes before loaves are ready
to bake.

1½ cups very warm water
2 tablespoons sugar
2 packages or cakes yeast, dry or compressed
7 cups unsifted *flour or 7½ cups sifted flour*
1 cup milk
2 tablespoons sugar
1 tablespoon salt
3 tablespoons butter or margarine

Measure the very warm water and sugar into a large bowl.
Sprinkle or crumble in the yeast.
Stir until dissolved.
Add 1½ cups *unsifted* flour or 2 cups sifted flour.
Beat until smooth.
Cover; let rise in a warm place, free from draft, until light
and spongy, about 30 minutes.
Scald the milk; stir in the sugar, salt and butter or margarine;
cool to lukewarm.
Stir the sponge down.
Stir in the lukewarm milk mixture and enough remaining
flour to form a soft dough.
Turn out on a lightly floured board and knead until smooth
and elastic, about 8 to 10 minutes.
Place in a greased bowl, turning to grease all sides.
Cover; let rise in a warm place, free from draft, until doubled
in bulk, about 30 minutes.
Punch down.
Divide in half.
Shape into loaves.
Place in 2 greased bread pans, 9 by 5 by 3 inches.
Cover; let rise in a warm place, free from draft, until dou-
bled in bulk, about 30 minutes.
Bake in a hot oven (400° F.) for about 50 minutes.
Remove from the pans and place on wire racks to cool.

[*214*]

STANDARD WHITE BREAD

(Makes 2 loaves)

Preheat oven to 400° F., 20 minutes before loaves are ready
to bake.

½ cup milk
3 tablespoons sugar
2 teaspoons salt
3 tablespoons butter or margarine
1½ cups warm water
1 package or cake yeast, dry or compressed
5½ cups unsifted *flour (about) or 6¼ cups sifted*
    flour (about)

Scald the milk; stir in the sugar, salt and butter or margarine.
Cool to lukewarm.

Measure the warm water into a large bowl; sprinkle or crumble in the yeast.

Stir until dissolved.

Add the lukewarm milk mixture and 3 cups flour; beat until
smooth.

Add enough additional flour to make a soft dough.

Turn out onto a lightly floured board.

Knead until smooth and elastic, about 8 to 10 minutes.

Form into a smooth ball.

Place in a greased bowl, turning to grease all sides.

Cover; let rise in a warm place, free from draft, until doubled
in bulk, about 1 hour.

Punch down.

Let rest for 15 minutes.

Divide the dough in half.

Shape each half into a loaf.

Place each loaf in a greased bread pan, 9 by 5 by 3 inches.

Cover; let rise in a warm place, free from draft, until doubled
in bulk, about 1 hour.

Bake in a hot oven (400° F.) for about 50 minutes.

WHITE BREAD (QUICK METHOD)

(Makes 4 loaves)

Preheat oven to 400° F., 20 minutes before loaves are ready to bake.

> 2 cups milk
> 5 tablespoons sugar
> 2 tablespoons salt
> 2 packages dry yeast
> 2 cups warm water
> 12–13 cups sifted flour
> 5 tablespoons melted shortening or butter

Scald the milk; add the sugar and salt; cool to lukewarm.

Dissolve the yeast in warm (not hot) water and add to the lukewarm milk.

Add half the flour and beat until smooth.

Add the melted shortening or butter and the remaining flour, or enough to make an easily handled dough.

Knead the dough quickly and lightly until smooth and elastic.

Place the dough in a greased bowl.

Cover and let rise in a warm place, free from draft, until doubled in bulk, about 1½ hours.

When light, divide into 4 equal portions and shape into loaves.

Place in greased loaf pans.

Cover and let rise again until doubled in bulk, about 1 hour.

Bake in a hot oven (400° F.) for 15 minutes; then reduce heat to moderate (375° F.) and bake for about 30 minutes longer.

SALT-FREE WHITE BREAD

(Makes 1 loaf)

Preheat oven to 400° F., 20 minutes before loaf is ready to bake.

> ½ cup milk
> 1½ tablespoons sugar
> 4 teaspoons shortening or butter

½ cup warm water
1 package or cake yeast, dry or compressed
3 cups sifted white flour

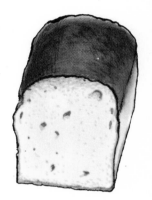

Scald the milk.
Add and stir in the sugar and shortening or butter.
Cool to lukewarm.
Measure into a bowl the warm (not hot) water.
(Cool to lukewarm for compressed yeast.)
Sprinkle or crumble in the yeast.
Stir until dissolved.
Add the lukewarm milk mixture.
Add and stir in the flour.
Turn out on a lightly floured board.
Knead quickly and lightly until smooth and elastic.
Place in a well-greased bowl.
Brush lightly with melted shortening or butter.
Cover with a clean damp towel.
Let rise in a warm place, free from draft, until doubled in
bulk, about 35 minutes.
Punch down.
Shape into a loaf.
Place in a well-greased bread pan, 9 by 5 by 3 inches.
Cover with a clean damp towel.
Let rise in a warm place, free from draft, until doubled in
bulk, about 45 minutes.
Bake in a hot oven (400° F.) for about 50 minutes.

CASSEROLE WHITE BREAD
(Makes 2 loaves)

Preheat oven to 375° F., 20 minutes before loaves are ready
to bake.

1 cup milk
3 tablespoons sugar
1 tablespoon salt
1½ tablespoons shortening or butter
1 cup very warm water
2 packages dry yeast
4½ cups sifted flour

Scald the milk; stir in the sugar, salt and shortening or butter.

Cool to lukewarm.

Measure the very warm water into a bowl.

Sprinkle in the yeast; stir until dissolved.

Add the lukewarm milk mixture and flour.

Stir until well blended, about 2 minutes.

Cover.

Let rise in a warm place, free from draft, until more than doubled in bulk, about 40 minutes.

Stir the batter down.

Beat vigorously for about ½ minute.

Turn into a greased 1½-quart casserole or 2 greased loaf pans, 9 by 5 by 3 inches.

Bake uncovered in a moderate oven (375° F.) for about 1 hour.

BUTTERMILK BREAD

(Makes 2 loaves)

Preheat oven to 375° F., 20 minutes before loaves are ready to bake.

1 cup buttermilk
3 tablespoons sugar
2½ teaspoons salt
⅓ cup margarine or butter
1 cup very warm water .
1 package or cake yeast, dry or compressed
5¾ cups sifted flour (about)
¼ teaspoon baking soda

Scald the buttermilk (it will appear curdled); stir in the sugar, salt and margarine or butter.

Cool to lukewarm.

Measure the very warm water into a large bowl.

Sprinkle or crumble in the yeast.

Stir until dissolved.

Add the lukewarm milk mixture.

Stir in 3 cups sifted flour and the baking soda.

Beat until smooth.

Add the remaining 2¾ cups flour; use a little more or less,

depending on the flour, to make a dough that has a rough, dull appearance and is a bit sticky.

Turn the dough out on a lightly floured board and knead until smooth and elastic (about 8 to 10 minutes).

Form into a ball and put into a greased bowl, turning to grease all sides.

Cover with a clean damp cloth and let rise in a warm place, free from draft, for about 1 hour, or until doubled in bulk.

Punch down, turn out on a lightly floured board and let rest for about 15 minutes.

Divide the dough in half.

Shape into loaves and place in 2 greased bread pans, 9 by 5 by 3 inches.

Cover and let rise in a warm place, free from draft, for about 1 hour, until doubled in bulk.

Bake in a moderate oven (375° F.) for about 35 minutes.

CORN BREAD

(Makes 2 loaves)

Preheat oven to 375° F., 20 minutes before loaves are ready to bake.

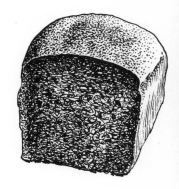

1 cup milk
6 tablespoons sugar
2 teaspoons salt
½ cup (1 stick) margarine or butter
½ cup warm water
2 packages or cakes yeast, dry or compressed
2 eggs, beaten
3½ cups unsifted *flour or 4¼ cups* sifted *flour*
1¾ cups yellow cornmeal

Scald the milk; stir in the sugar, salt and margarine or butter. Cool to lukewarm.

Measure the warm water into a large bowl.

Sprinkle or crumble in the yeast; stir until dissolved.

Stir in the lukewarm milk mixture, beaten eggs, flour and cornmeal.

Beat until well blended, about 2 minutes.

The batter will be stiff.

Turn into 2 greased 8-inch round cake-layer pans or 2 greased loaf pans, 9 by 5 by 3 inches.

Cover and let rise in a warm place, free from draft, until doubled in bulk, about 1 hour.

Bake in a moderate oven (375° F.) for 30 to 35 minutes. Serve warm.

WHEAT-GERM BREAD

(Makes 2 loaves)

Preheat oven to 400° F., 20 minutes before loaves are ready to bake.

> 1¼ *cups water*
> 3 *tablespoons sugar*
> 4 *teaspoons salt*
> ⅓ *cup shortening or butter*
> ⅓ *cup molasses*
> ¾ *cup milk*
> 1 *cup wheat germ*
> ¼ *cup warm water*
> 2 *packages or cakes yeast, dry or compressed*
> 4 *cups unsifted whole-wheat flour*
> 2 *cups sifted white flour*

In a saucepan combine 1¼ cups water and the sugar, salt, shortening or butter, and molasses.

Heat until the shortening melts.

Cool to lukewarm.

Scald the milk.

Pour the scalded milk over the wheat germ.

Let stand until the liquid is absorbed and the mixture has cooled to lukewarm.

Measure into a bowl ¼ cup warm (not hot) water.

(Cool to lukewarm for compressed yeast.)

Sprinkle or crumble in the yeast.

Stir until dissolved.

Add and stir in the lukewarm molasses mixture and the lukewarm wheat-germ mixture.

Add and stir in half of the mixed whole-wheat and white flour.

Beat until smooth.

[220]

Add and stir in the remaining flour mixture.

Turn the dough out on a lightly floured board.

Knead quickly and lightly until smooth and elastic.

Place in a greased bowl and brush the top lightly with melted shortening or butter.

Cover with a clean damp towel.

Let rise in a warm place, free from draft, until doubled in bulk, about 1½ hours; punch down and divide into 2 equal portions.

Shape into loaves and place in 2 greased bread pans, 9 by 5 by 3 inches.

Cover with a clean damp towel.

Let rise in a warm place, free from draft, until doubled in bulk, about 1¼ hours.

Bake at 400° F. for about 50 minutes.

HUNGARIAN CHRISTMAS BREAD

(Makes 4 loaves)

Preheat oven to 350° F., 20 minutes before loaves are ready to bake.

1 cup milk
½ cup sugar
1 teaspoon salt
1 cup (2 sticks) butter or margarine
⅓ cup very warm water
2 packages or cakes yeast, dry or compressed
5½ cups sifted flour (about)
grated rind of 2 lemons (2 tablespoons)

For the filling

2 cups ground poppy seeds
2 cups sugar
1 cup raisins
1 cup milk
grated rind of 2 lemons (2 tablespoons)
⅛ teaspoon powdered saffron (optional)
1 egg, beaten

Scald the milk; stir in the sugar, salt and butter or margarine. Cool to lukewarm.

Measure the very warm water into a large bowl and sprinkle or crumble in the yeast.

Stir in the lukewarm milk mixture.

Add 3 cups flour and the lemon rind.

Beat until smooth.

Add enough remaining flour to form a soft dough.

Turn out onto a lightly floured board and knead until smooth and elastic, about 8 to 10 minutes.

Put in a greased bowl, turning to grease all sides.

Cover and let rise in a warm place, free from draft, for about 1 hour, or until doubled in bulk.

Meanwhile prepare the filling.

Combine the ground poppy seeds, sugar, raisins, milk, lemon rind and saffron.

Mix well.

Cook this mixture, stirring constantly, over medium heat for about 10 minutes, or until thick enough to spread.

The mixture will thicken on standing.

Punch down the dough and divide into 4 equal parts.

Roll out each part into a rectangle ¼ inch thick.

Spread each rectangle with ⅔ cup filling and roll up like a jelly roll.

Place on greased baking sheets, seam side down, and brush with ½ the beaten egg.

Cover and let rise in a warm place, free from draft, for 30 minutes.

Brush with the remaining beaten egg.

Bake in a moderate oven (350° F.) for about 35 minutes, or until golden brown.

Remove from the baking sheets and cool.

OLD-FASHIONED POTATO LOAVES

(Makes 2 loaves)

Preheat oven to 400° F., 20 minutes before loaves are ready to bake.

1 medium potato
1 cup milk
2 tablespoons sugar
2 teaspoons salt

2 tablespoons butter or margarine
½ cup very warm water
2 packages or cakes yeast, dry or compressed
6 cups sifted flour (about)

Peel and dice the potato; boil in water to cover until tender, about 15 minutes.

Drain, reserving ½ cup liquid; mash and cool.

Scald the milk; stir in the sugar, salt, butter or margarine and reserved potato water; cool to lukewarm.

Measure the very warm water into a large bowl.

Sprinkle or crumble in the yeast; stir until dissolved.

Stir in the mashed potato, the lukewarm milk mixture and 3 cups flour; beat until smooth.

Stir in remaining flour to make a soft dough.

Turn out onto a lightly floured board.

Knead until smooth and elastic, about 8 minutes.

Place in a greased bowl, turning to grease all sides.

Cover; let rise in a warm place, free from draft, until doubled in bulk, about 35 minutes.

Punch down; turn the dough over in the bowl; cover and let rise again for about 20 minutes.

Punch down.

Turn out onto a lightly floured board; divide in half.

Shape each half into a loaf; place in 2 greased pans, 9 by 5 by 3 inches.

Cover; let rise in a warm place, free from draft, until the centers of the loaves are slightly higher than the sides of the pans, about 25 minutes.

Dust the loaves with flour.

Bake in a hot oven (400° F.) for 15 minutes; reduce the temperature to moderate (350° F.) and continue baking for about 30 minutes, or until done.

Remove from the pans; cool on wire racks or across the tops of the pans.

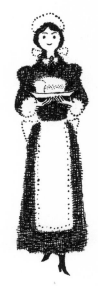

SALLY LUNN
(Makes 2 8-inch squares)

Preheat oven to 400° F., 20 minutes before squares are ready to bake.

1 cup milk
¼ cup sugar
2 teaspoons salt
½ cup (1 stick) butter or margarine
½ cup very warm water
1 cake or package yeast, dry or compressed
3 eggs, well beaten
5 cups sifted or 4½ cups unsifted flour
¼ cup sugar to sprinkle on surface

Scald the milk; add ¼ cup sugar, the salt and the butter or margarine.

Cool to lukewarm.

Measure the very warm water into a large bowl.

Sprinkle or crumble in the yeast.

Stir to dissolve.

Add the lukewarm milk mixture, eggs and flour; beat until smooth.

Cover; let rise in a warm place, free from draft, until doubled in bulk, about 1 hour.

Stir down, pour into 2 well-greased 8-inch-square cake pans.

Cover, let rise in a warm place, free from draft, until doubled in bulk, about 30 minutes.

Sprinkle each bread with 2 tablespoons sugar.

Bake in a hot oven (400° F.) for 25 minutes.

SOUPER-DOOPER BREAD

(Serves 8–10)

Preheat oven to 400° F., 20 minutes before bread is ready to bake.

2 packages or cakes yeast, dry or compressed
⅓ cup very warm water
1 can (10½ ounces) condensed onion soup
1 teaspoon salt ·
½ cup margarine or butter, softened
3½ cups sifted flour
grated cheese or sesame seeds

Sprinkle or crumble the yeast into the very warm water.
Stir until dissolved.

Stir in the onion soup.

Add the salt, the softened margarine or butter and 2 cups flour.

Beat until well blended.

Add the remaining flour and stir until blended.

Cover.

Let rise in a warm place, free from draft, for 1 hour.

Stir down.

Put into a greased 9-inch-square pan.

Spread the batter evenly.

Sprinkle the top with grated cheese or sesame seeds.

Cover.

Let rise in a warm place, free from draft, for 30 minutes.

Bake in a hot oven (400° F.) for 30 to 35 minutes.

QUICK-RISING SWEET DOUGH

¾ cup milk
½ cup sugar
1½ teaspoons salt
½ cup (1 stick) margarine or butter
¾ cup very warm water
3 packages or cakes yeast, dry or compressed
2 eggs, beaten
5½ cups unsifted flour (about)

Scald the milk; stir in the sugar, salt and butter or margarine; cool to lukewarm.

Measure the very warm water into a large bowl.

Sprinkle or crumble in the yeast; stir until dissolved.

Stir in the lukewarm milk mixture, the eggs and 3 cups flour; beat until smooth.

Stir in additional flour to make a soft dough.

Turn dough out onto a floured board; knead until smooth and elastic, about 8 minutes.

Place the dough in a greased bowl; turn the dough to grease it on all sides.

Cover; let rise in a warm place, free from draft, until doubled in bulk, about 30 minutes.

Punch the dough down and turn out onto a lightly floured board.

Proceed according to directions for the desired shapes (p. 245).

COCONUT COFFEE CAKE
(Makes 2 cakes)

Preheat oven to 350° F., 20 minutes before cakes are ready to bake.

Prepare 1 recipe Basic Sweet Dough (below).

½ cup margarine or butter
2 cups confectioner's sugar
2 tablespoons water
1 cup flaked coconut
1 egg yolk
2 tablespoons milk

When doubled in bulk, punch down and turn out on a lightly floured board; divide into 2 equal pieces.

Roll out each piece into a square of dough 14 by 14 by ⅛ inches.

Cream in a bowl the margarine or butter.

Beat in until smooth the sugar and the water.

Spread half of the mixture evenly on each square of dough.

Sprinkle evenly over each square ½ cup flaked coconut.

Roll up each piece as for a jelly roll.

Place on large greased baking sheets.

Shape into circles and seal the ends together firmly.

Flatten each slightly with the palm of your hand.

In each circle, with a sharp knife, make 2 circular cuts around the top about ¾ inch apart, penetrating to, but not through, the bottom layer of dough.

Cover with a clean damp towel.

Let rise in a warm place, free from draft, until doubled in bulk.

Beat together the egg yolk and the milk.

Brush the rings with the egg-and-milk mixture.

Bake in a moderate oven (350° F.) for about 30 minutes.

Sprinkle the tops while hot with confectioner's sugar.

BASIC SWEET DOUGH—NO KNEAD
(Yield: According to shape or shapes selected)

> ¾ cup milk
> ⅓ cup sugar
> 1 teaspoon salt
> ⅓ cup margarine or butter
> ½ cup very warm water
> 2 packages or cakes yeast, dry or
>   compressed
> 3 eggs, beaten
> 5½ cups sifted *flour* or 4½ cups
>   unsifted *flour*

Scald the milk.
Stir in the sugar, salt and margarine or butter.
Cool to lukewarm.
Measure the very warm water into a large bowl.
Sprinkle or crumble in the yeast.
Stir until dissolved.
Add the lukewarm milk mixture, eggs and flour.
Stir until well blended.
Cover.
Chill in the refrigerator for 2 hours or overnight.
Turn out onto a lightly floured board.
Proceed according to directions for the shapes selected (p.
245).

APPLE ORCHARD DELIGHT

Preheat oven to 375° F., 20 minutes before cake is ready to
bake.

> 1 package dry yeast or 1 cake compressed
>   yeast
> ¼ cup warm (not hot) water
> 1 cup milk, scalded
> 2 tablespoons shortening or butter
> 2 tablespoons sugar
> 1 teaspoon salt
> 1 egg, beaten
> 3½ cups sifted flour

½ cup sugar
2 teaspoons cinnamon
1½ cups canned drained apple slices
½ cup broken walnuts or pecans
½ cup raisins
1 egg yolk, beaten
1 tablespoon water

Dissolve the yeast in the warm water.

Combine the milk, shortening or butter, 2 tablespoons sugar and the salt; cool to lukewarm.

Add the yeast and the beaten egg.

Mix well.

Gradually stir in flour to make a soft dough.

Beat vigorously until the dough forms a smooth, satiny ball.

Place in a greased bowl, turn once, cover and let rise until double in size in a warm place (about 1 hour).

Remove the dough, place on a lightly floured board and roll to an oblong shape 12 by 18 inches.

Sprinkle with a mixture of ½ cup sugar and the cinnamon.

Now place the apple slices in rows parallel to the 12-inch edges.

Sprinkle the raisins and nuts evenly to cover the dough.

Roll lengthwise as for a jelly roll.

Place on a greased baking sheet and shape into a ring.

Brush the ring with a mixture of the egg yolk and 1 tablespoon water.

Cover and let rise in a warm place 1 hour.

Bake at 375° F. for 30 minutes.

Decorate with Confectioner's-Sugar Icing (see below), candied cherries and nuts.

Confectioner's-Sugar Icing

Blend together 1½ cups sifted confectioner's sugar, ½ teaspoon flavoring (vanilla, lemon or almond) and about 1½ tablespoons water.

DOUBLE CHOICE CAKES

Preheat oven to 375° F., 20 minutes before cakes are ready to bake.

> *⅓ cup milk*
> *½ cup sugar*
> *1 teaspoon salt*
> *2 packages or cakes yeast, dry or*
>   *compressed*
> *½ cup very warm water*
> *3½ cups sifted flour*
> *½ cup margarine or butter*
> *2 eggs, beaten*
> *1½ teaspoons grated orange rind*

Scald the milk; add ¼ cup sugar and the salt; cool to luke-warm.

Sprinkle or crumble the yeast into the very warm water; stir until dissolved.

Add the milk mixture and 1 cup flour; beat until smooth.

Cover; let rise in a warm place, free from draft, until light, about 20 minutes.

Cream the margarine or butter until light and fluffy.

When the yeast mixture is light, beat in the margarine or but-ter, ¼ cup sugar, the eggs and the orange rind with a wooden spoon.

Stir in the remaining 2½ cups flour; beat hard.

Divide the batter in half.

Orange Loaf

Turn half the batter into a well-greased loaf pan, 9 by 5 by 3 inches.

Cover.

Let rise in a warm place, free from draft, about 1 hour.

Bake in a moderately hot oven (375° F.) for 30 minutes.

When cool, top with an Orange Glaze (below).

Orange Glaze

Add 1 teaspoon grated orange rind and 2 tablespoons orange juice to 1 cup confectioner's sugar.

Beat thoroughly.

Fruit Cake

Toss together ½ cup raisins, ½ cup chopped walnuts, ½ cup chopped candied fruit, ½ teaspoon cinnamon, ½ teaspoon ginger and ¼ teaspoon nutmeg.

Add to the remaining batter and blend well.

Turn into a well-greased mold.

Cover.

Let rise in a warm place, free from draft, about 1½ hours.

Bake in a moderately hot oven (375° F.) for 30 to 35 minutes.

If desired, frost with Confectioner's-Sugar Icing (p. 228).

FRESH PEACH KUCHEN

(Makes 1 9-inch cake)

Preheat oven to 350° F., 20 minutes before cake is ready to bake.

½ cup milk
½ cup warm water
¼ cup margarine or butter
2 packages dry yeast or 2 cakes
    compressed yeast
3½ cups sifted flour
⅓ cup sugar
1½ teaspoons salt
1 egg

For the topping:
½ cup flour
⅓ cup sugar
½ cup chopped pecans
¼ cup margarine or butter
1½ teaspoons cinnamon
2 large peaches, pared and sliced

Scald the milk; remove from heat.

Add the warm water, margarine or butter, and yeast. Stir until dissolved.

Measure the flour, sugar and salt into a large mixing bowl.

Add the beaten egg and the milk mixture.

Stir until well blended.

Cover; let rise in a warm place, free from draft, until doubled in bulk, about 1 hour.

Meanwhile rub together the flour, sugar, chopped pecans, margarine or butter and cinnamon until crumbly.

Stir the dough down and spread evenly in a greased 9-inch-square pan.

Arrange the peach slices on top and sprinkle with the crumbly mixture.

Let rise in a warm place, free from draft, until doubled in bulk, about 40 minutes.

Bake in a moderate oven (350° F.) for 35 minutes.

FRESH APPLE KUCHEN

(Makes 1 9-inch cake)

Preheat oven to 375° F., 20 minutes before cake is ready to bake.

> *¼ cup very warm water*
> *1 package or cake yeast, dry or compressed*
> *½ cup (1 stick) margarine or butter*
> *½ cup sugar*
> *½ teaspoon salt*
> *3 eggs*
> *¼ cup milk*
> *2¾ cups sifted flour*

Measure the very warm water into a small bowl.

Sprinkle or crumble in the yeast; stir until dissolved.

Cream the margarine or butter thoroughly in a large electric-mixer bowl.

Gradually add the sugar and salt; cream together.

Add the dissolved yeast, eggs and milk; beat at medium speed until well blended.

Gradually add and blend in the flour while beating at medium speed; beat until the mixture is well blended.

Spread the dough in a well-greased square pan, 9 by 9 by 2 inches.

Arrange Apple Topping (below) on top.

Cover.

Let rise in a warm place, free from draft, until doubled in bulk, about 1 hour.

[*231*]

Bake in a moderate oven (375° F.) for about 40 minutes.
Turn out of the pan and cool on a wire rack.
Serve warm.

For the topping:
2 cups fresh apple slices
⅔ cup sugar
6 tablespoons butter or margarine
½ cup flour
2 tablespoons cinnamon

Arrange the fresh apple slices on top of the batter.

Mix together until crumbly the sugar, butter or margarine, flour and cinnamon.

Sprinkle over the apples.

APPLE CAKE

(Makes 2 8-by-12-inch cakes)

Preheat oven to 400° F., 20 minutes before cakes are ready to bake.

½ cup milk
½ cup sugar
¼ teaspoon salt
¼ cup (½ stick) butter or margarine
½ cup very warm water
2 packages or cakes yeast, dry or compressed
2 eggs, beaten
4¾ cups sifted flour (about) or 3¾ cups
    unsifted flour (about)
melted margarine or butter
1¼ cup sugar
8 to 10 medium-size apples
1½ teaspoons cinnamon

Scald the milk; stir in the salt, butter or margarine and ½ cup sugar.

Cool to lukewarm.

Measure the very warm water into a large bowl.

Sprinkle or crumble in the yeast; stir until dissolved.

Add the lukewarm milk mixture, the eggs and about half of the flour; beat until smooth.

[232]

Add enough additional flour to make a soft dough.

Turn out onto a lightly floured board; knead until smooth and elastic, about 10 minutes.

Place in a greased bowl, turning to grease all sides.

Cover.

Let rise in a warm place, free from draft, until doubled in bulk, about 1 hour.

Punch down.

Turn out onto a lightly floured board; divide the dough in half.

Roll each half out into an 8-by-12-inch rectangle.

Press each rectangle of dough evenly into a well-greased pan, 13 by 9 by 2 inches.

Brush each cake lightly with melted butter or margarine; sprinkle each with 2 tablespoons sugar.

Peel, core and slice the apples.

Press the apple slices into the dough, sharp edges down and about ¼ inch apart.

Mix together 1 cup sugar and the cinnamon; sprinkle the top of each cake with half of the sugar mixture.

Cover.

Let rise in a warm place, free from draft, until doubled in bulk, about 45 minutes.

Bake in a hot oven (400° F.) for about 40 minutes.

Remove from the pans; cool on wire racks.

CHOCOLATE YEAST CAKE

(Makes 1 10-inch tube cake)

Preheat oven to 350° F., 20 minutes before cake is ready to bake.

¾ cup milk
2 packages or cakes yeast, dry or compressed
¼ cup very warm water
3 cups sifted flour
½ cup margarine or butter
2 cups sugar
3 eggs
6 ounces semi-sweet chocolate, melted
1 teaspoon baking soda

½ *teaspoon salt*
½ *teaspoon vanilla*

Scald the milk; cool to lukewarm.

Sprinkle or crumble the yeast into the very warm water in a small mixer bowl.

Stir until dissolved.

Add the milk and 1½ cups flour.

Beat at medium speed until smooth, about 30 seconds.

Cover; let rise in a warm place, free from draft, until light and spongy, about 30 minutes.

Meanwhile place the margarine or butter and sugar in a large mixer bowl.

Cream well at medium speed.

Add the eggs, one at a time, beating well after each addition.

Add the yeast mixture and remaining ingredients; beat until well blended, about 1 minute.

Turn into a well-greased 10-inch tube pan.

Cover; let rise in a warm place, free from draft, until light and bubbly, about 1 hour.

Bake in a moderate oven (350° F.) for about 50 minutes.

APPLE CRISP CAKE

(Makes 1 9-inch cake)

Preheat oven to 400° F., 20 minutes before cake is ready to bake.

⅓ *cup milk*
¼ *cup sugar*
6 *tablespoons butter or margarine*
¼ *cup very warm water*
1 *package or cake yeast, dry or compressed*
1 *egg, well beaten*
2½ *cups sifted flour*
3 *tart green apples, peeled and sliced*
½ *cup brown sugar*
1 *teaspoon cinnamon*
½ *teaspoon nutmeg*

Scald the milk; stir in the sugar and 2 tablespoons butter or margarine.

Cool to lukewarm.

Measure the very warm water into a large bowl.

Sprinkle or crumble in the yeast; stir until dissolved.

Add the lukewarm milk mixture, the egg and 2 cups flour.

Beat until smooth.

Spread the batter evenly in a well-greased 9-inch-square pan.

Arrange the apple slices on top.

Sprinkle with a combination of the brown sugar, remaining flour, cinnamon, nutmeg and remaining ¼ cup butter or margarine.

Cover; let rise in a warm place about 1 hour, free from draft, until doubled in bulk.

Bake in a hot oven (400° F.) for 30 minutes.

Serve warm, topped with vanilla ice cream.

COFFEE LACE

Preheat oven to 375° F., 20 minutes before lace is ready to bake.

For the batter
2 packages or cakes yeast, dry or compressed
⅓ cup very warm water
¾ cup sugar
2 teaspoons salt
1 cup butter or margarine
2 cups milk, scalded
7 cups sifted flour
2 eggs

To fill one braid
½ cup brown sugar
1 teaspoon cinnamon
½ cup apricot preserves
slivered almonds

Dissolve the yeast in the very warm water.

In a mixing bowl combine the sugar, salt and butter or margarine.

Add the scalded milk.

Stir until the shortening melts.

Cool to lukewarm.

Add 4 cups flour to the lukewarm milk mixture and, with the electric mixer on medium speed, beat for 2 minutes.

Add the eggs and the yeast mixture.

With the electric mixer on medium speed, beat ½ minute.

With a spoon blend in the remaining 3 cups flour and beat until smooth, about 2 minutes.

The batter will be stiff.

Cover.

Let rise in a warm place, free from draft, until doubled in bulk, about 50 minutes.

Stir down and turn out onto a floured board.

Cover; let rest for 5 minutes.

For 1 braid, roll ⅓ of the dough into a 14-by-8-inch rectangle.

Brush generously with melted margarine or butter.

Place on a well-greased baking sheet.

Combine the brown sugar and cinnamon and sprinkle down the center of the rectangle in a strip 3 inches wide.

Top with the apricot preserves and almonds.

At each side of the filling make cuts 2 inches apart (2 inches into the dough), making 7 strips on each side.

Cross the strips over the filling.

Cover.

Let rise in a warm place, free from draft, until doubled in bulk, about 30 to 40 minutes.

Bake in a moderate oven (375° F.) until golden brown, 20 to 30 minutes.

Brush with Sugar Glaze (below).

If desired, repeat twice with the remaining dough or shape as desired into rolls or coffee cakes.

Sugar Glaze

1 tablespoon butter or margarine
3 tablespoons top milk
½ teaspoon lemon extract
confectioner's sugar

Melt 1 tablespoon margarine or butter.

Add 3 tablespoons top milk.

Heat but do not boil.

Add enough confectioner's sugar to make a thin creamy glaze.

Blend in ½ teaspoon lemon extract.

QUICK 'N' EASY COFFEE CAKE
(Makes 1 cake and 9 muffins)

Preheat oven to 400° F., 20 minutes before cake is ready to bake.

> *1 cup milk*
> *⅔ cup granulated sugar*
> *1½ teaspoons salt*
> *8 tablespoons butter or margarine*
> *½ cup warm water*
> *2 packages or cakes yeast, dry or compressed*
> *2 eggs*
> *4 cups sifted white flour*
> *½ cup brown sugar*
> *¼ cup chopped nuts*

Scald the milk.

Stir in the granulated sugar, the salt and 6 tablespoons butter or margarine.

Cool to lukewarm.

Measure into a bowl the warm (not hot) water.

(Cool to lukewarm for compressed yeast.)

Sprinkle or crumble in the yeast.

Stir until dissolved.

Add the lukewarm milk mixture.

Stir in the eggs, well beaten.

Stir in the flour.

Stir only enough to dampen the flour.

Fill well-greased muffin pans half full.

Pour the remaining batter into a well-greased 8-inch-square pan.

Mix together the brown sugar, 2 tablespoons butter or margarine, and the chopped nuts.

Sprinkle on top of the muffins and coffee cake.

Cover.

Let rise in a warm place, free from draft, until doubled in bulk, about 50 minutes.

Bake at 400° F. for about 20 to 25 minutes.

DUTCH APPLE CAKE
(Makes 1 9-inch cake)

Preheat oven to 400° F., 20 minutes before cake is ready to bake.

> 1/3 cup milk
> 1/4 cup granulated sugar
> 1/2 teaspoon salt
> 4 tablespoons butter or margarine
> 1/4 cup warm water
> 1 package or cake yeast, dry or compressed
> 1 egg
> 1 1/3 cups sifted flour
> 1 1/2 cups canned apple slices, drained
> 2 tablespoons brown sugar
> 1/4 teaspoon cinnamon
> 1/4 teaspoon nutmeg

Scald the milk.

Stir in the granulated sugar, the salt and 2 tablespoons butter or margarine.

Cool to lukewarm.

Measure into a bowl the warm (not hot) water.

(Cool to lukewarm for compressed yeast.)

Sprinkle or crumble in the yeast.

Stir until dissolved.

Stir in the lukewarm milk mixture.

Add the egg, well beaten, and the flour.

Beat until smooth.

Spread the dough evenly in a greased pan, 9 by 9 by 2 inches.

Arrange on top the canned apple slices.

Sprinkle with a mixture of the brown sugar, cinnamon and nutmeg.

Dot with 2 tablespoons butter or margarine.

Cover and let rise in a warm place, free from draft, until doubled in bulk, about 40 minutes.

Bake in a hot oven (400° F.) for 25 minutes.

CINNAMON APPLE LOAF
(Makes 2 loaves)

Preheat oven to 375° F., 20 minutes before loaves are ready
to bake.

> ⅓ *cup milk*
> ⅓ *cup sugar*
> ¾ *teaspoon salt*
> 3 *tablespoons butter or margarine*
> ⅓ *cup very warm water*
> 1 *package or cake yeast, dry or compressed*
> 2 *eggs*
> 3½ *cups* sifted *flour (about)* or 3 *cups*
>   unsifted *flour (about)*
> *melted butter or margarine*
> 1 *cup sugar*
> 1 *teaspoon cinnamon*
> ½ *teaspoon nutmeg*
> 2 *medium-to-large apples*

Scald the milk; stir in ⅓ cup sugar, the salt and the butter
or margarine.

Cool to lukewarm.

Measure the very warm water into a large bowl.

Sprinkle or crumble in the yeast; stir until dissolved.

Add the lukewarm milk mixture, eggs and half the flour;
beat until smooth.

Add enough additional flour to make a soft dough.

Turn out onto a lightly floured board; knead until smooth and
elastic, about 10 minutes.

Place in a greased bowl, turning to grease all sides.

Cover.

Let rise in a warm place, free from draft, until doubled in
bulk, about 1 hour.

Punch down.

Turn out onto a lightly floured board; divide the dough in
half.

Roll one half out into an 8-by-12-inch rectangle.

Brush lightly with melted butter or margarine.

Mix together the cinnamon, nutmeg and 1 cup sugar.

Sprinkle ⅓ of the sugar mixture on the dough.

Roll the dough up tightly from each 8-inch side toward the center to form a scroll-shaped loaf.

Make 7 slashes about 1 inch apart across both rolls of dough, going about halfway down into the dough.

Place the loaf in a well-greased bread pan, 9 by 5 by 3 inches.

Pare, core and slice 1 apple.

Press the apple slices, sharp edge down, into the slashes in the dough.

Brush lightly with melted butter or margarine.

Repeat with the remaining half of the dough and the other apple.

Sprinkle each loaf with half of the remaining sugar mixture. Cover.

Let rise in a warm place, free from draft, until doubled in bulk, about 1 hour.

Bake in a moderate oven (375° F.) for about 35 minutes.

Serve warm.

APPLE CRUMB COFFEE CAKE

(Makes 1 9-inch cake)

Preheat oven to 375° F., 20 minutes before cake is ready to bake.

> *¼ cup very warm water*
> *1 package or cake yeast, dry or compressed*
> *½ cup (1 stick) margarine or butter,*
>   *softened*
> *½ cup sugar*
> *½ teaspoon salt*
> *3 eggs*
> *¼ cup milk*
> *2⅓ cups unsifted flour*

Measure the very warm water into a small warm bowl.

Sprinkle or crumble in the yeast.

Stir until dissolved.

Cream the butter or margarine thoroughly in a large electric-mixer bowl.

Gradually add the sugar and salt.

Cream together.

Add the yeast mixture, eggs and milk.

Beat at medium speed until well blended.

Gradually add and blend in the flour while beating at medium speed; beat until the mixture is well blended.

Spread the batter in a well-greased pan, 9 by 9 by 2 inches.

Arrange Apple Crumb Topping (below) over the dough.

Cover and let rise in a warm place, free from draft, until doubled in bulk, about 1 hour.

Bake in a moderate oven (375° F.) for about 35 to 40 minutes.

Turn out of the pan and cool on a wire rack.

Apple Crumb Topping

2 or 3 large apples
⅔ cup sugar
½ cup flour
2 teaspoons cinnamon
6 tablespoons butter or margarine

Core, peel and slice the apples and arrange on the dough.

Combine the remaining ingredients and mix until crumbly.

Sprinkle over the apples.

SWEDISH CARDAMOM BRAID

(Makes 1 large braid)

Preheat oven to 350° F., 20 minutes before braid is ready to bake.

½ cup milk
½ cup sugar plus 2 tablespoons
1½ teaspoons salt
¼ cup butter or margarine
½ cup warm water
2 packages or cakes yeast, dry or compressed
2 eggs, beaten
5 cups sifted white flour
1½ teaspoons ground cardamom
½ cup seedless raisins
1 egg white

Scald the milk.

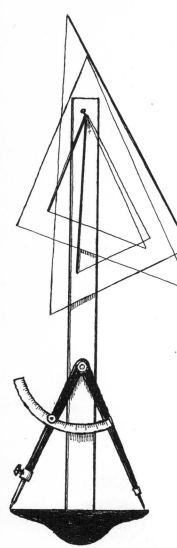

Stir in ½ cup sugar, the salt and the butter or margarine.
Cool to lukewarm.
Measure into a bowl the warm (not hot) water.
(Cool to lukewarm for compressed yeast.)
Sprinkle or crumble in the yeast.
Stir until dissolved.
Stir in the lukewarm milk mixture.
Add the beaten eggs, 3 cups flour, and the cardamom and raisins.
Beat until smooth.
Stir in an additional 2 cups sifted enriched flour (about).
Turn the dough out on a lightly floured board.
Knead until smooth and elastic.
Place in a greased bowl; brush the top with soft shortening.
Cover.
Let rise in a warm place, free from draft, until doubled in bulk, about 1 hour.
Punch down and turn out on a lightly floured board.
Divide the dough into thirds.
Roll each part into a strand 10 inches long, tapering the ends.
Braid loosely.
Place on a greased baking sheet.
Cover.
Let rise in a warm place, free from draft, until doubled in bulk, about 1 hour.
Before baking, brush with the egg white and 2 tablespoons sugar.
Bake at 350° F. for about 35 minutes.

GOLDEN TWIST RINGS

PEANUT TWIST

CINNAMON CRESCENTS

Makes: 1 Golden Twist Ring
1 Peanut Twist
12 Cinnamon Crescents

Preheat oven to 400° F., 20 minutes before ready to bake.

Basic Dough

¾ cup milk
¼ cup sugar
1½ teaspoons salt
1 cup (2 sticks) butter or margarine
½ cup very warm water
2 packages or cakes yeast, dry or compressed
3 egg yolks, beaten
4½ cups sifted or 3½ cups unsifted
  flour

Scald the milk; stir in ¼ cup sugar, the salt and the butter or margarine; cool to lukewarm.

Measure the very warm water into a large bowl.

Sprinkle or crumble in the yeast; stir until dissolved.

Add the lukewarm milk mixture and beaten egg yolks; stir to blend.

Add the flour and beat until well blended.

Cover tightly with aluminum foil.

Refrigerate at least 4 hours or overnight.

Golden Twist Rings

Divide the dough into 3 parts.

Divide ⅓ of the dough in half.

Roll each half into a strip 18 inches long.

Twist the 2 strips around each other.

Place on a greased baking sheet.

Form into a ring; tuck the end pieces under the ring and seal.

Cover; let rise in a warm place, free from draft, until doubled in bulk and light, about 1 hour.

Bake in a hot oven (400° F.) for about 15 minutes.

Cool.

Frost with Confectioner's-Sugar Icing (p. 228) and sprinkle with finely chopped nuts.

Peanut Twist

This takes ½ cup peanuts.

Knead ½ cup chopped peanuts into ⅓ of the dough and divide this dough in half.

Roll each half into a strip 18 inches long.

Twist the 2 strips around each other.

Place on a greased baking sheet.

Seal the ends of the twist and tuck under.

Cover; let rise in a warm place, free from draft, until doubled in bulk, about 1 hour.

Bake in a hot oven (400° F.) for about 20 minutes.

Cool.

Frost with Confectioner's-Sugar Icing (p. 228).

Cinnamon Crescents

This takes ½ cup sugar and 1 teaspoon cinnamon.

Roll the remaining ⅓ of the dough into a 12-inch circle.

Brush with melted butter or margarine.

Cut into 12 pie-shaped pieces.

Sprinkle with ¾ of a mixture of ½ cup sugar and 1 teaspoon cinnamon.

Beginning at the rounded edge, roll up.

Place on a greased baking sheet, with the point underneath. Curve in half circles.

Brush with melted butter or margarine.

Sprinkle with the remaining ¼ of the sugar-cinnamon mixture.

Bake in a hot oven (400° F.) for 12 to 15 minutes.

TO SHAPE ROLLS

Pan Rolls

Form the dough into small balls about 1 ounce each and set close together in a round pan.

Crescents

Roll a piece of dough into a 12-inch circle ¼ inch thick.
Cut into wedge-shaped pieces.
Brush with butter and roll up from the wide end.
Put on a baking sheet with the pointed end underneath.

Cloverleaf

Use muffin tins to bake these.
Make tiny balls of dough and put 3 into each buttered muffin cup.

Twists and Circles

Roll the dough to ¼-inch thickness.
Spread with butter.
Cut in ½-inch strips and twist the strips into circles or knots.

Parker House Rolls

Roll dough to ¼-inch thickness.
Cut into 1½-inch squares.
Brush well with soft butter and fold in half.
Place close together in a buttered pan.

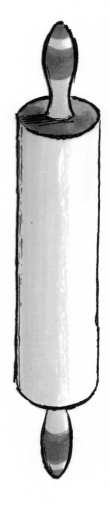

AMBROSIA ROLLS

(Makes 28 rolls)

Preheat oven to 350° F., 20 minutes before rolls are ready to bake.

> ¾ cup milk
> ½ cup sugar
> 1½ teaspoons salt
> ½ cup (1 stick) butter or margarine
> ¾ cup very warm water
> 3 packages yeast, dry or compressed

2 eggs, beaten
6 cups sifted flour (about)
½ cup butter, melted
1½ cups brown sugar
grated rind of 2 oranges
1½ cups flaked coconut

Scald the milk; remove from heat.

Stir in ½ cup sugar, the salt and ½ cup butter or margarine; cool to lukewarm.

Measure the very warm water into a large bowl.

Sprinkle or crumble in the yeast; stir until dissolved.

Stir in the lukewarm milk mixture and eggs.

Add 3 cups flour; beat until smooth.

Stir in additional flour to make a soft dough.

Turn the dough out onto a floured board; knead until smooth and elastic, about 8 to 10 minutes, sprinkling additional flour on the board as needed to keep the dough from sticking.

Place the dough in a greased bowl twice the size of the dough; turn the dough to grease it on all sides.

Cover.

Let rise in a warm place, free from draft, until doubled in bulk, about 25 minutes.

Punch the dough down and turn it out on a lightly floured board.

Cut the dough in half.

Roll out each half into an oblong about 12 by 16 inches.

Brush each with half of the melted butter.

Mix the brown sugar, grated orange rind and coconut together; sprinkle half over each oblong.

Roll up from the long side, as for a jelly roll, to make a roll 16 inches long.

Seal the sides.

Cut into 14 equal pieces.

Place, cut side up, in 2 greased 9-inch layer-cake pans.

Cover.

Let rise in a warm place, free from draft, until doubled in bulk, about 20 minutes.

Bake in a moderate oven (350° F.) for about 30 minutes, or until done.

APRICOT PEANUT SQUARES
(Makes 24 squares)

Preheat oven to 350° F., 20 minutes before squares are ready to bake.

> ½ cup very warm water
> 2 packages or cakes yeast, dry or compressed
> 2 tablespoons sugar
> 1 teaspoon salt
> ¼ cup (½ stick) melted butter or margarine
> 2 eggs
> 2 cups sifted flour or 1½ cups unsifted flour
> ¾ cup chopped cocktail peanuts
> 1 cup apricot preserves
> ¼ cup (½ stick) melted butter or margarine
> 1 teaspoon vanilla

Measure the very warm water into a large bowl.

Sprinkle or crumble in the yeast; stir until dissolved.

Stir in the sugar, salt, ¼ cup melted butter or margarine, eggs and 1 cup flour.

Beat until smooth.

Add the balance of the flour.

Cover.

Let rise in a warm place, free from draft, until doubled in bulk, about 45 minutes.

Meanwhile mix together the cocktail peanuts, apricot preserves, ¼ cup melted butter or margarine and the vanilla.

Blend well.

When the batter has doubled in bulk, stir down.

Spread in a well-greased jelly-roll pan (10 by 15 inches).

Spread the apricot-peanut mixture over the batter.

Let rise in a warm place, free from draft, until doubled in bulk, about 25 minutes.

Bake in a moderate oven (350° F.) until done, about 30 to 35 minutes.

Turn out on a wire rack to cool.

Cut into squares to serve.

SHAPED BATTER ROLLS
(Makes 24 rolls)

Preheat oven to 400° F., 20 minutes before rolls are ready to bake.

¾ cup milk
¼ cup sugar
1 teaspoon salt
¼ cup (½ stick) butter or margarine
½ cup very warm water
2 packages yeast, dry or compressed
1 egg
3½ cups unsifted *flour (about)*

Scald the milk; stir in the sugar, salt and butter or margarine; cool to lukewarm.

Measure the very warm water into a large bowl.

Sprinkle or crumble in the yeast; stir until dissolved.

Add the lukewarm milk mixture, the egg and 2 cups unsifted flour; beat until smooth.

Stir in the remaining flour to make a soft dough.

Cover; let rise in a warm place, free from draft, until doubled in bulk, about 30 minutes.

Punch down.

Turn out onto a lightly floured board and shape into rolls of various shapes.

Cover; let rise in a warm place, free from draft, until doubled in bulk, about 30 minutes.

Bake in a hot oven (400° F.) for 15 minutes.

EASY REFRIGERATOR ROLLS
(Makes about 48 medium rolls)

Preheat oven to 400° F., 20 minutes before rolls are ready to bake.

2 packages or cakes yeast, dry or compressed
2 cups very warm water
½ cup sugar
2 teaspoons salt
¼ cup soft shortening or butter

[248]

1 egg
6½ to 7 cups sifted *flour*

In a mixing bowl, dissolve the yeast in the very warm water.
Stir in the remaining ingredients except the flour.
Mix in flour by hand until the dough is easy to handle.
Place in a greased bowl, turning once to grease the top.
Cover with a cloth; place in the refrigerator.   (The dough keeps for about 5 days.)
About 2 hours before baking, shape the dough into the desired rolls and coffee cakes.
Cover and let rise until doubled in bulk (1½ to 2 hours).
Bake in a hot oven (400° F.) for 12 to 15 minutes.

ENGLISH BATH BUNS

(Makes 24 buns)

Preheat oven to 350° F., 20 minutes before buns are ready to bake.

½ cup milk
1½ cups sugar
1 teaspoon salt
¾ cup (1½ sticks) butter or margarine
½ cup very warm water
2 packages or cakes yeast, dry or compressed
4 egg yolks
3 eggs
4½ cups sifted flour
½ teaspoon lemon extract
½ cup chopped candied fruit
¼ cup sliced blanched almonds

Scald the milk; stir in ½ cup sugar, the salt and butter or margarine.
Cool to lukewarm.
Measure the very warm water into a large bowl.
Sprinkle or crumble the yeast into the very warm water and stir until dissolved.
Add the lukewarm milk mixture, egg yolks, eggs, sifted flour and lemon extract.

Beat thoroughly until smooth, about 5 minutes.

Cover and let rise in a warm place, free from draft, until doubled in bulk, about 1¼ hours.

Stir down, cover well and chill in the refrigerator overnight.

Divide into small pieces; shape into balls and place on greased baking sheets.

Cover and let rise in a warm place, free from draft, until doubled in bulk, about 50 minutes.

Before baking, press candied fruit and almonds into the tops.

Brush with an egg mixed with milk.

Sprinkle the remaining 1 cup sugar over the tops.

Bake in a moderate oven (350° F.) for 15 to 20 minutes.

Remove from the baking sheets and serve warm.

HERB BREAD STICKS

(Makes 24 sticks)

Preheat oven to 400° F., 20 minutes before sticks are ready to bake.

> 1¼ cups warm (not hot) water
> 1 package or cake yeast, dry or compressed
> 3 tablespoons sugar
> 1½ teaspoons salt
> 1 tablespoon margarine or butter
> 3½ cups sifted flour (about)

3 teaspoons caraway seeds
1 teaspoon sage

Measure the water into a large bowl (warm, not hot, water for active dry yeast; lukewarm water for compressed yeast).

Sprinkle or crumble in the yeast.

Stir until dissolved.

Add the sugar, salt and margarine or butter.

Add and stir in 2 teaspoons caraway seeds, the sage and the flour.

Turn the dough out on a lightly floured board; knead until smooth and elastic, about 10 minutes.

Place in a greased bowl, turning once to grease the top.

Cover; let rise in a warm place, free from draft, until doubled in bulk, about 1 hour.

Punch down, turn out on a floured board and cut into 2 equal portions.

Roll each half into a roll 12 inches long; cut each into 12 even pieces.

Roll each piece on the board with the palms of your hands to form a rope about ⅓ inch thick and 12 inches long.

Place the sticks on a greased baking sheet.

Sprinkle lightly with the remaining caraway seeds.

Cover.

Let rise in a warm place, free from draft, until doubled, about 1 hour.

Bake in a hot oven (400° F.) for 15 to 20 minutes.

LIGHT ROLLS

(Makes about 36 rolls)

Preheat oven to 400° F., 20 minutes before rolls are ready to bake.

2 cups milk
½ cup sugar
2 teaspoons salt
½ cup shortening or butter
2 packages dry yeast
¼ cup warm water
1 egg
1 teaspoon baking powder

¼ *teaspoon soda*
7 *to* 8 *cups sifted flour*

Scald the milk.

Stir in the sugar, salt and shortening or butter.

Cool to lukewarm.

Dissolve the yeast in the warm (not hot) water.

Stir in the egg.

Add the lukewarm milk mixture, baking powder, soda and half the flour.

Beat until smooth.

Stir in enough remaining flour to make a soft dough.

Beat hard for several minutes.

Cover and let rise in a warm place, free from draft, until doubled in bulk, about 1 hour.

Punch down and shape into rolls of various shapes.

Cover and let rise again until doubled in bulk, about 30 to 45 minutes.

Bake in a hot oven (400° F.) for 15 minutes.

SAFFRON BUNS
(Makes 16 buns)

Preheat oven to 375° F., 20 minutes before buns are ready to bake.

¾ *cup milk*
⅓ *cup sugar*
1 *teaspoon salt*
¼ *cup (½ stick) margarine or butter*
1 *teaspoon saffron*
2 *tablespoons boiling water*
½ *cup very warm water*
2 *packages or cakes yeast, dry or compressed*
1 *egg, beaten*
4 *cups sifted flour (about)*
¼ *cup currants or seedless raisins*

Scald the milk; stir in the sugar, salt and margarine; cool to lukewarm.

Meanwhile add the saffron to the boiling water; let stand.

Measure the very warm water into a large bowl.

Sprinkle or crumble in the yeast; stir until dissolved.

Stir in the lukewarm milk mixture, beaten egg, saffron and 2 cups flour; beat until smooth.

Stir in the currants, then enough remaining flour to make a soft dough.

Turn out onto a floured surface; knead until smooth and elastic, about 8 minutes.

Place in a greased bowl, turning to grease all sides.

Cover; let rise in a warm place, free from draft, until doubled in bulk, about 1 hour.

Punch down; turn out onto a floured board; cover and let rest for 10 minutes.

Cut off a piece of dough about 2 inches in diameter.

Divide the rest of the dough into 16 equal pieces.

Shape each piece into a ball; place in a well-greased small brioche mold or muffin cup.

Divide the 2-inch piece of dough into 16 pieces; shape each into a small ball.

Make a deep indentation in each bun; press a small ball into each indentation.

Cover; let rise in a warm place, free from draft, until doubled in bulk, about 30 minutes.

Bake in a moderate oven (375° F.) for about 15 minutes, or until done.

REFRIGERATOR WHOLE-WHEAT ROLLS
(Makes 48 rolls)

Preheat oven to 375° F., or as required, 20 minutes before rolls are ready to bake.

> *1 cup hot water*
> *⅔ cup sugar*
> *1 tablespoon salt*
> *¼ cup (½ stick) margarine or butter*
> *1 cup very warm water*
> *2 packages or cakes yeast, dry or compressed*
> *2 eggs, beaten*
> *1 cup whole-wheat flour*
> *6 cups sifted flour (about)*

Combine the hot water with the sugar, salt and margarine or butter; cool to lukewarm.

Measure the very warm water into a large bowl.

Sprinkle or crumble in the yeast; stir until dissolved.

Stir in the lukewarm mixture, beaten eggs, whole-wheat flour and 3 cups sifted flour; beat until smooth.

Stir in enough remaining flour to make a soft dough; mix well.

Place in a greased bowl, turning to grease all sides of the dough.

Cover closely with waxed paper or aluminum foil.

Store in the refrigerator until needed.

To use, punch the dough down and cut off the amount needed. The dough may be kept 4 days in the refrigerator.

Strip Rolls

Use ¼ of the dough.

Roll out on a floured board to make an oblong 10 by 5 inches.

Let rest for 5 minutes.

Meanwhile melt 2 tablespoons margarine or butter in a 10-by-6-inch pan.

Cut the dough into 8 strips 5 inches long.

Dip each strip into melted margarine or butter, coating all sides.

Arrange the strips in a baking pan.

Cover; let rise in a warm place, free from draft, until doubled in bulk, about 1 hour.

Bake in a moderate oven (375° F.) for about 30 minutes, or until done.

Makes 8.

Pan Ring

Use ¼ of the dough.

On a floured board, roll out to make a 12-inch roll.

Cut into 12 equal pieces.

Shape each piece into a ball; roll in melted margarine or butter.

Place in a 9-inch greased ring mold.

Cover; let rise in a warm place, free from draft, until doubled in bulk, about 1 hour.

Bake in a moderate oven (375° F.) for about 30 minutes.
Makes 12.

Figure 8's

Use ¼ of the dough.
Roll out to ¼-inch thickness.
Cut with a doughnut cutter.
Twist once to make a figure 8.
Place on a greased baking sheet about 2 inches apart.
Cover; let rise in a warm place, free from draft, until doubled
in bulk, about 1 hour.
Bake in a hot oven (400° F.) for about 12 to 15 minutes, or
until done.
Makes 12.

Whole-Wheat English Muffins

Roll ¼ of the dough out to ¼-inch thickness.
Cut into 3-inch squares or rounds and place on a greased
baking sheet.
Cover; let rise in a warm place, free from draft, until doubled
in bulk, about 1 hour.
Bake on an ungreased griddle over low heat for about 10 min-
utes; turn and bake 10 minutes longer.
Or bake in an electric skillet with the temperature control at
325° F.
To serve, split and toast under the broiler.
Makes 12.

RAISED CORN ROLLS
(Makes 30–36 rolls)

Preheat oven to 400° F., 20 minutes before rolls are ready to
bake.

> ½ cup yellow cornmeal
> 2 tablespoons sugar
> 1 teaspoon salt
> 2 tablespoons margarine or butter
> ¾ cup boiling water
> ¼ cup very warm water
> 1 package or cake yeast, dry or compressed

1 egg, beaten
3 cups sifted flour (about)

Combine the cornmeal, sugar and salt in a large bowl.

Add the margarine or butter.

Pour in the boiling water, stirring.

Cool to lukewarm.

Measure the very warm water into a small bowl.

Sprinkle or crumble in the yeast; stir until dissolved.

Stir yeast into the lukewarm cornmeal mixture; stir in the egg and 2 cups flour; beat until smooth.

Stir in remaining flour to make a soft dough.

Turn out onto a floured board; knead until smooth and elastic, about 10 minutes.

Place in a greased bowl, turning to grease all sides.

Cover; let rise in a warm place, free from draft, until doubled in bulk, about 1 hour.

Punch the dough down.

Turn out on a lightly floured board.

Divide the dough in half.

Cut each half into 9 to 12 equal parts and shape each into a ball.

Place about 3 inches apart on a greased baking sheet and pat to form a round of dough about ¾ inch thick.

Brush lightly with melted margarine or butter.

Cover; let rise in a warm place, free from draft, until doubled in bulk, about 1 hour.

Bake in a hot oven (400° F.) for about 20 minutes.

RICH GOLDEN ROLLS

(Makes 32 rolls)

Preheat oven to 400° F., 20 minutes before rolls are ready to bake.

½ cup milk
⅓ cup sugar
1 teaspoon salt
1 cup (2 sticks) margarine or butter
3 packages yeast, dry or compressed
½ cup warm (not hot) water

2 eggs
4¼ cups sifted flour (about)

Scald the milk; add the sugar, salt and margarine or butter. Cool to lukewarm.

In a large bowl dissolve the yeast in water (warm, not hot, water for dry yeast, lukewarm water for compressed yeast).

Add the lukewarm milk mixture, eggs and half the flour; beat until smooth.

Stir in enough remaining flour to make a soft dough.

Turn out onto a lightly floured board; knead until smooth and elastic, about 10 minutes.

Place in a greased bowl; brush the top with soft shortening.

Cover; let rise in a warm place, free from draft, until doubled in bulk, about 1 hour.

Punch down; divide into quarters.

Roll each quarter out on a lightly floured board to make a circle ⅛ inch thick; cut the circle into 8 wedges.

Roll up each wedge, starting at the wide end.

Place the rolls, with the point underneath, on a lightly greased cookie sheet; if desired, turn the ends in to make crescent shapes.

Cover; let rise in a warm place, free from draft, until doubled in bulk, about 1 hour.

Bake in a hot oven (400° F.) for about 20 minutes, or until golden.

SUNDAY BREAKFAST ROLLS
(Makes 36 rolls)

Preheat oven to 400° F., 20 minutes before rolls are ready to bake.

4 cups sifted flour
¼ cup sugar
1 teaspoon salt
1 teaspoon grated lemon rind
1 cup (2 sticks) margarine or butter
1 package or cake yeast, dry or compressed
¼ cup very warm water
1 cup milk, lukewarm
2 eggs, beaten

1 cup sugar
1 tablespoon cinnamon

In a large bowl, combine the flour, ¼ cup sugar, the salt and grated lemon rind.

With a pastry blender or 2 knives cut the shortening into the flour mixture.

Sprinkle or crumble the yeast into the very warm water; stir until dissolved.

Scald the milk and cool to lukewarm.

Add the dissolved yeast, lukewarm milk and eggs to the flour mixture.

Toss lightly until thoroughly combined.

Cover tightly and refrigerate overnight.

Divide the dough in half.

Roll half on a well-floured board into a rectangle 18 by 12 inches.

Sprinkle with half the mixture of 1 cup sugar and the cinnamon.

Roll up tightly, beginning at the wide side.

Cut each roll into 1-inch slices.

Place, cut side up, on a greased baking sheet.

Flatten with the palm of your hand.

Repeat with the remaining dough and sugar-cinnamon mixture.

Bake immediately in a hot oven (400° F.) for about 12 minutes.

APPLE DANISH

(Makes 24 pastries)

Preheat oven to 375° F., 20 minutes before pastries are ready to bake.

¾ cup milk
⅓ cup sugar
2 teaspoons salt
⅓ cup butter or margarine
2 packages or cakes yeast, dry or compressed
¼ cup warm (not hot) water (cool to
*   lukewarm for compressed yeast)*
½ teaspoon lemon extract

3 eggs, beaten
4½ cups sifted flour
1 cup (2 sticks) butter or margarine
1 no. 2 can (2½ cups) sliced apples
1 cup sugar mixed with 2 tablespoons
  cinnamon

Scald the milk; stir in the sugar, salt and ⅓ cup butter or margarine.

Cool to lukewarm.

In a large bowl dissolve the yeast in warm water.

Add the lukewarm milk mixture.

Stir in the lemon extract and eggs.

Add the flour gradually.

Place the dough in a greased 9-by-13-inch pan.

Chill in the refrigerator for 1 to 2 hours.

Turn the chilled dough out onto a floured board.

Roll into a rectangle 12 by 16 inches.

Spread ⅓ cup butter or margarine over ⅔ of the dough.

Fold the unspread portion of the dough over half the covered portion.

Fold the third section over the first two.

Roll the dough to its original size and repeat this process twice, using the remaining butter or margarine.

Return the dough to the refrigerator and chill overnight.

When ready to make, divide the dough in half.

Roll into a rectangle 14 by 9 inches.

Cut into strips 14 by ¾ inches.

Twist and form each strip into a special roll, building up the sides.

Fill the shells with drained apple slices.

Sprinkle with the cinnamon-sugar combination.

Cover.

Let rise in a warm place, free from draft, until doubled in bulk.

Bake in a moderate oven (375° F.) for about 12 minutes.

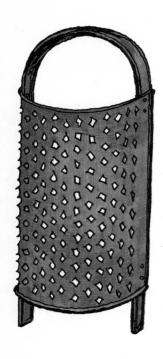

CHEESE CRESCENTS
(Makes 24 crescents)

Preheat oven to 400° F., 20 minutes before crescents are ready to bake.

> *1¼ cups milk*
> *2½ tablespoons sugar*
> *1½ teaspoons salt*
> *¼ cup butter or margarine*
> *¼ cup warm water*
> *1 package or cake yeast, dry or compressed*
> *4¼ cups sifted white flour (about)*
> *1 cup Cheddar cheese, grated*

Scald the milk.

Add and stir the sugar, salt and butter or margarine.

Cool to lukewarm.

Measure into a bowl the warm (not hot) water.

(Cool to lukewarm for compressed yeast.)

Sprinkle or crumble in the yeast.

Stir until dissolved.

Add the lukewarm milk mixture.

Add the flour.

Add and stir in the cheese.

Turn the dough out on a lightly floured board; divide into 3 equal pieces.

Roll out each piece into a circle about 9½ inches in diameter and ¼ inch thick.

Cut with a sharp knife into 8 pie-shaped pieces.

Brush lightly with melted margarine or butter.

Roll up, beginning at the wide end, and seal ends firmly.

Place on a greased baking sheet about 2 inches apart.

Curve in half-circles.

Cover with a clean damp towel.

Let rise in a warm place, free from draft, until doubled in bulk, about 45 minutes.

Bake at 400° F. for about 15 minutes.

[260]

BRIOCHE
(Makes 24 individual brioches)

Preheat oven to 375° F., 20 minutes before brioches are ready to bake.

> *½ cup milk*
> *½ cup (1 stick) butter or margarine*
> *⅓ cup sugar*
> *1 teaspoon salt*
> *¼ cup very warm water*
> *1 package or cake yeast, dry or compressed*
> *3 whole eggs*
> *1 egg yolk*
> *3½ cups unsifted flour or*
> > *4 cups sifted flour*
> *1 egg white*
> *1 tablespoon sugar*

Scald the milk; cool to lukewarm.

Cream the butter or margarine in a large bowl.

Gradually add ⅓ cup sugar and the salt, and cream together.

Measure the very warm water into a small bowl; sprinkle or crumble in the yeast; stir until dissolved.

Add the dissolved yeast and lukewarm milk to the creamed mixture; then add the eggs, egg yolk and flour.

Beat vigorously for 2 minutes.

Cover.

Let rise in a warm place, free from draft, until more than doubled in bulk, about 2 hours.

Stir down and beat vigorously for 2 minutes.

Cover tightly with aluminum foil and refrigerate overnight.

Beat down; turn the soft dough out onto a lightly floured board.

Divide into 2 pieces, one about ¾ the weight of the dough and the other about ¼ the weight of the dough.

Cut the larger piece into 24 equal pieces.

Form into smooth balls.

Place in well-greased muffin pans, 2¾ by 1¼ inches.

Cut the smaller piece into 24 equal pieces.

Form into smooth balls.

Make a deep indentation in the center of each large ball; dampen slightly with cold water.

Press a small ball into each indentation.

Let rise in a warm place, free from draft, until doubled in bulk, about 50 minutes.

Brush with a mixture of 1 egg white and 1 tablespoon sugar.

Bake in a moderate oven (375° F.) for about 15 to 20 minutes.

QUICK CELERY CRESCENTS
(Makes 12 crescents)

Preheat oven to 425° F., 20 minutes before crescents are ready to bake.

½ cup milk
2 tablespoons sugar
1½ teaspoons salt
1 cake yeast or 1 package
  dry yeast
½ cup lukewarm water
3 cups sifted flour
3 tablespoons melted shortening
  or butter
½ teaspoon salt
1 teaspoon celery seeds

Scald the milk, add the sugar and 1½ teaspoons salt; cool to lukewarm.

Dissolve the yeast in the lukewarm water and add to the lukewarm milk.

Add 1½ cups flour and beat until perfectly smooth.

Add the melted shortening and remaining flour, or enough to make an easily handled dough, and knead well.

Roll the dough into a circular shape about ¼ inch thick.

Cut into 12 pie-shaped pieces.

Brush lightly with melted butter or margarine and, beginning at the wide end, roll up to the pointed end.

Shape into crescents and place on a well-greased baking sheet with the pointed end underneath.

Brush with melted butter or margarine; sprinkle with ½ teaspoon salt and the celery seeds.

Cover and set in a warm place, free from draft.

Let rise until light, about 1 hour.

Bake in a hot oven (425° F.) for 20 minutes.

CHOCOLATE STICKY BUNS

(Makes 18 buns)

Preheat oven to 350° F., 20 minutes before buns are ready to bake.

For the batter

1 package or cake yeast, dry or compressed
⅓ cup very warm water (105° F.)
⅓ cup sugar
1 teaspoon salt
½ cup (1 stick) butter or margarine
¾ cup milk, scalded
3½ cups sifted flour
1 egg

For the topping

½ cup (1 stick) margarine or butter
1 cup brown sugar
¼ cup corn syrup
3 tablespoons cocoa
1 cup whole pecans

For the filling

1 cup sugar
2 tablespoons cocoa
2 teaspoons cinnamon

In a small bowl, dissolve the yeast in the very warm water.

In a mixing bowl, combine the sugar, salt and butter or margarine.

Add the scalded milk.

Stir until the shortening melts.

Cool to lukewarm.

Add 1½ cups flour to the lukewarm milk mixture.

Blend with an electric mixer at medium speed; beat for 2 minutes.

Add the egg and the yeast mixture.

Beat at medium speed for ½ minute.

With a spoon, blend in the remaining 2 cups flour and beat until smooth, about 2 minutes.

The batter will be stiff.

Cover.

Let rise in a warm place, free from draft, until doubled in bulk, about 50 minutes.

Meanwhile prepare the topping.

In a saucepan melt ½ cup butter or margarine; add the brown sugar, corn syrup and cocoa.

Bring to a boil and cook for 1 minute.

Divide the syrup into 2 9-inch cake pans.

Arrange the pecans in the syrup.

When the batter has doubled, stir down and turn out onto a well-floured board.

Cover; let rest for 5 minutes.

Divide the dough in half.

Roll out 1 piece of dough into an oblong about 14 by 9 inches.

Brush lightly with melted margarine or butter.

Combine 1 cup sugar and the cocoa and cinnamon for the filling.

Sprinkle the oblong with half of the sugar filling.

Roll up as for a jelly roll to make a roll 9 inches long.

Seal the edges firmly.

Cut into 9 equal pieces.

Place in the prepared 9-inch cake pan.

Repeat with the remaining dough.

Cover.

Let rise in a warm place, free from draft, until doubled in bulk, about 1 hour.

Bake in a moderate oven (350° F.) for 35 minutes.

Turn out of the pan immediately.

STUFFING

Stuffing isn't just for turkeys! You can do lots of things with it.

In a bakery you never know exactly how many loaves to bake, so you are almost sure to have some left over after the orders are filled.

I remembered how much I loved stuffing, so I decided to make some from the extra bread.

But fresh bread crumbs have a certain amount of moisture and will not keep long without molding.

A dried product which could be packaged seemed to be the answer, but there were problems galore. We had to find a way of drying the product and still keeping the aroma and flavor of the herbs. We finally solved it by making a special machine for our Pepperidge Farm Stuffing.

ASPARAGUS WITH CHEESE
(Serves 4)

Preheat oven to 450° F.

> *1 package frozen or 1 can whole asparagus*
> *3 tablespoons butter*
> *2 tablespoons flour*
> *1½ cups milk, scalded*
> *½ cup Pepperidge Farm Stuffing*
> *½ cup grated Parmesan cheese*

Prepare the asparagus according to the directions on the package or can.

Make a cream sauce by melting the butter and adding the flour slowly while stirring.

Add the milk and cook until thick, stirring constantly.

Mix the stuffing and cheese together.

For each serving, arrange 3 cooked asparagus on a thin slice of freshly made toast in an earthenware dish.

Pour over each portion some well-seasoned cream sauce and sprinkle with the stuffing mixture.

Dot generously with butter or margarine and bake in a hot oven (450° F.) for 5 to 10 minutes until delicately browned.

GREEN PEPPER SURPRISE
(Serves 4)

Preheat oven to 350° F.

4 green peppers
½ cup chopped celery
2 tablespoons chopped onion
½ cup butter
1 cup Pepperidge Farm Stuffing
½ cup water
1 cup fresh or canned crabmeat
1 can (6 ounces) tomato sauce

Cut the green peppers in half; remove the stems and seeds.
Cook for 5 minutes in boiling salted water and drain.
Sauté the celery and onion in butter until golden.
Add the stuffing, water and crabmeat; mix thoroughly.
Fill the pepper halves with the crabmeat mixture.
Place in a greased shallow baking dish and bake in a moderate oven (350° F.) for about 30 minutes.
Heat the tomato sauce just to the boiling point and serve separately to pour over the peppers.

STUFFED FISH FILLETS
(Serves 4)

Preheat oven to 350° F.

4 fillets of sole (about 1 pound)
*   fresh or frozen*
2 tablespoons sherry wine
¼ teaspoon salt
⅓ cup chopped celery
1 tablespoon chopped onion
1½ cups Pepperidge Farm Stuffing
¼ cup water

For the sauce

2 tablespoons lemon juice
4 tablespoons melted butter
2 tablespoons sherry wine (optional)

If the fillets are frozen, thaw them and wipe with a damp paper towel.

Marinate the fillets in 2 tablespoons sherry and ¼ teaspoon salt for 5 minutes.

In melted butter, sauté the celery and onion over low heat until soft and golden.

Add the stuffing and water; mix well.

Spread ¼ of the mixture on each fillet.

Roll up (as for a jelly roll) and secure with toothpicks or skewers if necessary.

Place in a greased shallow baking dish, cover and bake in a moderate oven (350° F.) for about 25 minutes.

Serve with lemon wedges or lemon butter sauce.

For the sauce, mix together the lemon juice, butter and sherry and serve over the fish.

SALMON TIMBALES

(Serves 4)

Preheat oven to 350° F.

1 can (1 pound) salmon
⅔ cup milk (approximately)
1 tablespoon lemon juice
2 tablespoons butter or margarine
2 tablespoons flour
⅛ teaspoon pepper
1 cup Pepperidge Farm Stuffing
½ cup finely chopped celery
1 tablespoon minced parsley
1 teaspoon minced onion
1 egg, slightly beaten

Drain the salmon, reserving the liquid and adding enough milk to make 1 cup liquid.

Remove the bones and skin from the salmon and flake with a fork.

Sprinkle with the lemon juice.

Melt the butter in a saucepan over low heat; add the flour and mix well.

Gradually pour in the milk mixture and stir constantly over low heat until thickened.

Add the remaining ingredients and stir lightly.

Spoon into greased custard cups, place in a pan of hot water and bake in a moderate oven (350° F.) for about 30 minutes.

After baking, turn out of the custard cups and serve with Cream Soup Sauce (below).

Garnish with parsley.

CREAM SOUP SAUCE

Blend 1 can (10½ ounces) condensed cream of celery or cream of mushroom soup with ⅓ to ½ cup milk.

Simmer in a heavy saucepan for about 2 minutes.

TURKEY PIE
(Serves 6)

Preheat oven to 425° F.

1¼ cups Pepperidge Farm Stuffing
¼ cup melted butter or margarine
½ cup milk
1 can (10½ ounces) condensed cream of celery soup
1½ cups cooked turkey, in large pieces
¾ cup cooked peas
1 tablespoon instant minced onion
⅛ teaspoon pepper

For the topping
¾ cup Pepperidge Farm Stuffing
¼ cup melted butter or margarine

Mix 1¼ cups stuffing with ¼ cup melted butter or margarine; press firmly to the bottom and sides of a 9-inch pie plate.

In a saucepan, over low heat, gradually stir the milk into the soup and mix until smooth.

Add the turkey, peas, onion and pepper, and spoon into the pie shell.

Roll ¾ cup stuffing into fine crumbs between two pieces of waxed paper and mix with ¼ cup melted butter or margarine.

Make a border of this mixture around the rim of the pie and bake in a hot oven (425° F.) for about 10 minutes, or until browned and bubbly.

CORN AND CHEESE FONDUE

(Serves 6)

Preheat oven to 350° F.

> 1 cup milk
> 1 cup canned cream-style corn
> 1½ cups Pepperidge Farm Stuffing
> 1 cup grated cheese
> 1 tablespoon butter or margarine, melted
> 3 eggs, separated

Combine all the ingredients, except the eggs, and mix thoroughly.

In a deep bowl beat the egg whites until stiff, and set aside.

Beat the egg yolks until thick and lemon-colored and add to the corn mixture.

Slowly pour onto the beaten egg whites and, with a rubber spatula, gently fold the mixture into the egg whites.

Pour into a casserole of about 2 quarts capacity, and place in a pan of water (water about 1 inch deep).

Bake in a moderate oven (350° F.) for 1 hour.

STUFFED CABBAGE ROLLS

(Serves 6)

Preheat oven to 375° F.

> 1 head cabbage
> 1 cup Pepperidge Farm Stuffing
> ¼ cup instant minced onion
> ½ cup water
> 1 pound ground beef

1 teaspoon salt
¼ teaspoon pepper

For the sauce
1 can (10½ ounces) condensed tomato soup
½ cup water
¼ teaspoon pepper
1 teaspoon oregano

Gently remove 6 perfect leaves from the cabbage.
Let stand in boiling water for about 5 minutes.
Combine the stuffing, instant minced onion and water in a large bowl.
Set aside for 5 minutes.
Add the meat, salt and pepper and mix lightly but thoroughly.
Divide the mixture evenly into 6 portions and place a mound in the center of each cabbage leaf.
Carefully fold over the sides of each leaf and roll up.
Arrange the rolls in a shallow oblong baking dish.
Mix the tomato soup with the remaining ingredients and pour over the rolls.
Cover the dish and bake in a moderate oven (375° F.) for about 1½ hours.

ITALIAN MEAT LOAF
(Serves 4–6)

Preheat oven to 375° F.

1 medium onion, chopped
2 tablespoons butter or margarine
1 egg
½ cup milk
½ cup Pepperidge Farm Stuffing
1 teaspoon salt
2 tablespoons chopped parsley
1 pound ground beef
¼ teaspoon pepper
1 can (6 ounces) tomato sauce
¼ teaspoon oregano

Sauté the onion in butter over low heat until golden.

In a large bowl beat the egg slightly; add the milk and stuffing.

Let stand for 5 minutes.

Add the beef, parsley, salt and pepper, and mix lightly but thoroughly.

In a shallow baking dish, shape the meat into a loaf.

Bake in a moderate oven (375° F.) for 30 minutes.

Pour the tomato sauce over the meat, sprinkle with oregano and bake for 20 minutes longer.

GALA STUFFINGS

Celery Stuffing

Mix Pepperidge Farm Stuffing and add ½ cup diced celery per package.

Mushroom Stuffing

Mix Pepperidge Farm Stuffing and add 1 cup drained, sliced, cooked or canned mushrooms per package.

Cranberry Stuffing

Mix Pepperidge Farm Stuffing and add 1 cup chopped raw cranberries per package.

Oyster Stuffing

Mix Pepperidge Farm Stuffing and add ½ pint (1 cup) drained, chopped, fresh or frozen oysters per package.

Giblet Stuffing

Simmer turkey giblets with a celery stalk, an onion and a sprig of parsley for about 4 hours, or till tender.

Drain, chop and add to mixed Pepperidge Farm Stuffing.

TURKEY LOAF
(Serves 6–8)

Preheat oven to 375° F.

2 eggs, slightly beaten
4 tablespoons melted butter or margarine
1 package Pepperidge Farm Stuffing
1½ cups turkey or chicken broth
2 cups cooked turkey or chicken, cut up
2 tablespoons parsley
1 tablespoon minced onion
2 tablespoons minced green pepper

For the sauce
1 can (10½ ounces) condensed cream of celery soup
¾ cup milk

Mix together all the ingredients in order as listed.
Turn into a greased loaf pan, 9 by 5 by 3 inches.
Bake at 375° F. for 30 to 40 minutes or until firm.
For the sauce: Blend the cream of celery soup with the milk
in a saucepan.
Simmer for about 2 minutes.
Pour over the loaf.

TURKEY SUPREME
(Serves 6)

Preheat oven to 400° F.

1 cup Pepperidge Farm Stuffing
1 package frozen string beans, thawed
¼ cup slivered, blanched almonds
2 cups cooked turkey, cut in large pieces
1 can (10½ ounces) condensed cream of mushroom soup
½ cup milk

For the topping
1 cup Pepperidge Farm Stuffing
2 tablespoons melted butter or margarine
¼ cup water

[272]

Arrange a layer of stuffing crumbs in the bottom of a buttered baking dish; cover with a layer of beans, almonds and turkey.

Blend the soup with the milk; pour over the casserole.

Top with 1 cup stuffing which has been mixed with the butter or margarine and water.

Bake in a hot oven (400° F.) for 20 to 30 minutes until browned and bubbly.

TURKEY CROQUETTES

(Serves 8)

1½ cups cooked turkey, finely chopped
1 can (10½ ounces) condensed cream of
    chicken soup, undiluted
1 cup Pepperidge Farm Stuffing
2 eggs, slightly beaten
1 tablespoon instant minced onion
flour

For the sauce
1 can condensed cream of mushroom soup
⅓ to ½ cup milk

Mix the first 5 ingredients until well blended.

Turn the mixture into a shallow dish and place in the refrigerator for 2 or 3 hours until firm and well chilled.

Divide the mixture into 8 equal parts and form into log shapes.

Dust lightly with flour and fry in deep fat until golden brown.

For the sauce: Blend the cream of mushroom soup with the milk, in a saucepan.

Simmer for about 2 minutes.

Serve over the croquettes.

BAKED FISH, PEPPERIDGE STYLE
(Serves 6)

Preheat oven to 375° F.

1 5-pound fish, such as red snapper, sea trout or bass
juice of 3 limes, lightly salted
¾ cup Pepperidge Farm Stuffing
¼ pound butter or margarine
1 cup dry white wine
½ cup almonds or cashews, chopped
2 limes, cut in wedges

For the stuffing

1 clove garlic, crushed
6 tablespoons butter or margarine
1 small onion, finely chopped
2 stalks celery, finely chopped
1¼ cups Pepperidge Farm Stuffing
1½ cups almonds or cashews, blanched and chopped
1 cup mild cheese, grated
¼ cup chopped parsley
½ to 1 cup milk
2 bay leaves, finely crumbled
½ teaspoon nutmeg
salt
cayenne

Rub the fish inside and out with the lightly salted lime juice and chill it for at least 4 hours.

Meanwhile prepare a stuffing as follows:

In a saucepan place the crushed garlic in 6 tablespoons butter or margarine, and in the garlic-seasoned butter or margarine sauté the chopped onion and celery.

Add 1¼ cups Pepperidge Farm Stuffing, 1½ cups almonds or cashews, the cheese and parsley, and moisten the mixture to the consistency of a stiff paste with the milk.

Add the bay leaves, nutmeg, salt and cayenne to taste, and blend well.

Wipe the chilled fish dry, arrange it in a well-greased baking dish and fill the cavity with the stuffing.

Sprinkle the top with ¾ cup Pepperidge Farm Stuffing and dot generously with butter or margarine.

Bake the fish in a moderately hot oven (375° F.) for 15 to 20 minutes per pound, basting frequently with a mixture of the wine and 4 tablespoons melted butter or margarine.

Just before serving, sprinkle the fish with ½ cup chopped almonds or cashews tossed in melted butter or margarine and place it under the broiler for a few moments to brown the nuts.

Serve with wedges of lime.

PIONEER BREAD
(Serves 12)

Preheat oven to 350° F.

> *½ package Pepperidge Farm Stuffing*
> *½ cup flour*
> *½ cup yellow cornmeal*
> *1 tablespoon sugar*
> *1 tablespoon baking powder*
> *1 egg*
> *¾ cup milk*
> *2 tablespoons chopped onions*
> *1 tablespoon salad oil*

Run the Pepperidge Farm Stuffing through the fine blade of the food chopper, or crush it in a blender, to make ½ cup fine crumbs.

Combine the crumbs with the flour, cornmeal, sugar and baking powder.

Beat the egg and add the milk; add the onions, which have been sautéed until light brown in the salad oil (include the oil when adding the onions).

Stir the dry ingredients into the egg mixture, blending well.

Pour the batter into a well-greased heavy skillet and bake slowly on top of the stove for about 25 minutes, or until puffed and set.

Or bake in a greased square pan, 8 by 8 inches, in a moderate oven (350° F.) for 25 to 30 minutes.

MEAT LOAF ROYALE
(Serves 8)

Preheat oven to 400° F.

1¾ pounds beef, ground
½ pound pork, ground
1 cup red wine
2 bay leaves, crumbled
¼ teaspoon freshly ground pepper
Worcestershire sauce
2 cups Pepperidge Farm Stuffing
1 egg
1 onion (or 3 scallions), chopped
2 cloves garlic, pressed or chopped
2 stalks celery, chopped with leaves
¼ pound mushrooms, sliced and sautéed
¼ cup grated Parmesan cheese
¼ cup chopped parsley
1 teaspoon salt
¼ teaspoon oregano
½ cup Provolone cheese, cubed
3 hard-boiled eggs
4 strips bacon

Marinate the ground beef and pork for several hours in a mixture of the wine, the bay leaves, the pepper, and Worcestershire sauce to taste.

When the meat is well marinated, leave it in the marinade and add the Pepperidge Farm Stuffing, 1 egg, the onion or scallions, garlic, celery, mushrooms, Parmesan cheese, parsley, salt and oregano, and mix until thoroughly blended.

Place the meat mixture in a baking pan and form it into an oblong loaf with a well down the center.

Into the well put the cubed Provolone and make a line of the hard-boiled eggs.

Cover the cheese and eggs with meat and finish shaping the loaf.

Sprinkle with Pepperidge Farm Stuffing, place the bacon strips across the top and bake in a hot oven (400° F.) for 7 minutes.

[276]

Reduce the oven temperature to 350° F. and continue baking the meat loaf for about 1 hour, or until it is cooked through but still juicy.

BOMBAY CHICKEN
(Serves 6)

Preheat oven to 300° F.

6 chicken breasts
2 tablespoons butter or margarine
1 medium onion, chopped
½ cup chopped celery
1 large carrot, finely shredded
1 small can chopped mushrooms
1 tablespoon chopped parsley
1 bouillon cube
1 cup water
1 package Pepperidge Farm Stuffing
1 cup flour
1 teaspoon paprika
½ teaspoon celery salt
dash pepper
2 teaspoons sesame seed
1 tablespoon soy sauce
2 tablespoons brown sugar
2 tablespoons cooking oil
½ teaspoon ground ginger
½ cup pineapple juice
½ cup sherry or white wine

In a saucepan, melt the butter or margarine, add the chopped onion and celery, and cook slowly until the vegetables are just tender.

Cool the vegetables and add the carrot, mushrooms and parsley.

Dissolve the bouillon cube in the water and add to the vegetables.

Add the Pepperidge Farm Stuffing, tossing all the ingredients lightly with a fork until well blended.

Fill the chicken breasts with this mixture, tie the pieces securely with string to keep the stuffing in place and dredge them with the flour seasoned with the paprika, celery salt and pepper.

Sauté the stuffed chicken breasts in hot fat until brown, then arrange them in a flat baking dish.

Spread the sesame seed in a pie plate and brown in a slow oven (300° F.).

Combine the soy sauce, brown sugar, cooking oil, ginger, pineapple juice, and sherry or white wine; add the sesame seeds and mix well.

Pour the sauce evenly over the chicken breasts, cover the baking dish tightly with aluminum foil and bake in a moderately hot oven (375° F.) for about 45 minutes.

SPICY BAKED APPLES

(Serves 6)

6 large baking apples
1 cup Pepperidge Farm Stuffing
2 tablespoons butter or margarine
¼ cup water
1 cup sweetened cranberry juice
granulated sugar

Core and wipe the apples and remove a strip of peel from the stem end of each.

Combine the Pepperidge Farm Stuffing with the butter or margarine and water, and prepare according to directions on the package for crumbly stuffing.

Fill the apple cavities with the stuffing.

Place the stuffed apples in a skillet and pour over them the cranberry juice.

Cover the skillet and simmer the apples over low heat until tender, about 8 to 10 minutes.

Sprinkle the peeled surface of the apples with a little sugar, glaze them quickly under the broiler and serve as a garnish for chicken or pork.

RHUBARB SCALLOP
(Serves 6)

Preheat oven to 350° F.

> *2 packages frozen rhubarb*
> *1 package Pepperidge Farm Stuffing*
> *¼ cup brown sugar*
> *1 medium onion, chopped*
> *2 tablespoons butter*

Cook the frozen rhubarb, using the amount of water called for in the directions on the packages, and remove the rhubarb from the fire as soon as the liquid is well colored.

Sweeten with the brown sugar.

Prepare the Pepperidge Farm Stuffing according to the directions for crumbly stuffing, substituting the rhubarb juice for water.

Toss the stuffing with the onion, chopped and sautéed in the butter, and brown it lightly.

Place rhubarb and stuffing in a buttered casserole in alternate layers, using stuffing for the top layer, and bake for 30 minutes in a moderate oven (350° F.).

Serve with duck or lamb.

CALICO CRAB

(Serves 4–6)

Preheat oven to 425° F.

1½ cups Pepperidge Farm Stuffing
¾ cup butter or margarine
3 tablespoons minced green onion tops
¼ cup flour
1½ cups milk
1½ cups frozen or canned crabmeat
2 tablespoons chopped pimiento
¼ teaspoon dry mustard
½ cup sour cream
salt and pepper
minced parsley

Roll the Pepperidge Farm Stuffing to make fine crumbs, and mix the crumbs with ½ cup butter or margarine.

Press this mixture firmly against the bottom and sides of a deep 8-inch pie plate.

Sauté the minced onion tops in ¼ cup butter or margarine, add the flour and cook for a few minutes, stirring constantly.

Add gradually the milk and cook, stirring, until the sauce is smooth and thick.

Add the crabmeat, pimiento, mustard, and salt and pepper to taste.

Stir in the sour cream.

Turn the mixture into the prepared pie shell and bake in a hot oven (425° F.) for about 10 minutes.

Garnish with minced parsley.

STUFFING CROQUETTES

(Makes about 12 croquettes)

1 package Pepperidge Farm Stuffing
1 cup boiling water
3 tablespoons chicken or turkey fat
1 egg, beaten
1 teaspoon Worcestershire sauce
½ cup toasted chopped pecans

Combine all the ingredients, spread the mixture on a shallow platter and chill it well in the refrigerator.

Shape the mixture into pointed croquettes.

Brown the croquettes a few at a time in hot deep fat (390° F.), drain them on paper toweling and keep them hot in the oven.

Serve hot with cold sliced turkey and hot leftover turkey gravy, or with fried chicken or pot roast.

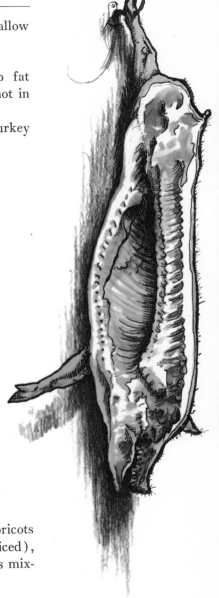

APRICOT SWEET-SOUR SPARERIBS

(Serves 4)

Preheat oven to 350° F.

> *4 pounds spareribs*
> *1 package Pepperidge Farm Stuffing*
> *1 cup dried apricots*
> *½ cup diced celery*
> *2 cups water*
> *¼ cup vinegar*
> *2 white onions, sliced thin*
> *½ cup maple syrup*
> *1 teaspoon allspice*
> *½ cup gingersnap crumbs*
> *½ cup raisins*
> *1 lemon, sliced thin*

Lay a strip of cracked spareribs in a baking dish.

Combine the Pepperidge Farm Stuffing with the apricots (cooked until tender in water to cover, then drained and diced), ½ cup apricot liquid and the diced celery, and spread this mixture on the ribs.

Cover with a second strip.

Combine the water, vinegar, sliced onions, raisins, sliced lemon, maple syrup, allspice and gingersnap crumbs.

Boil for about 10 minutes, until the sauce is thick.

Bake the ribs for about 1½ hours in a moderate oven (350° F.), basting them every 20 minutes with the sauce.

Any leftover sauce may be served with the roasted ribs.

STUFFED ACORN SQUASH
(Serves 6)

Preheat oven to 350° F.

> *3 acorn squash*
> *½ pound lean beef, ground*
> *½ pound fresh pork, ground*
> *1 cup Pepperidge Farm Stuffing*
> *1 cup consommé*
> *melted butter or margarine*

Combine the ground beef, ground pork, stuffing and consommé, and mix well.

Cut the squash in half and discard the seeds.

Parboil the squash, cut side down, in a little boiling water for about 5 minutes and brush it generously with melted butter or margarine.

Divide the stuffing mixture among the squash shells and bake in a moderate oven (350° F.) for about 1 hour, or until the squash is tender.

ROLLED STEAK AND SPAGHETTI
(Serves 4)

> *1 flank steak*
> *salt and pepper*
> *1 package Pepperidge Farm Stuffing*
> *1 cup grated Parmesan cheese*
> *3 tablespoons chopped parsley*
> *1 small sweet onion, minced*
> *olive oil*
> *½ pound pork shoulder, ground*
> *1 no. 3 can Italian-style plum tomatoes*
> *2 tablespoons sweet basil, chopped*
> *½ teaspoon oregano, chopped*
> *1 clove garlic, crushed*
> *1 bay leaf*
> *1 6-ounce can concentrated tomato paste*
> *1 pound spaghetti*

Flatten the flank steak on a board and season with salt and pepper.

Combine the stuffing with ½ cup grated Parmesan cheese and the chopped parsley and minced onion.

Spread this stuffing on the flank steak and roll it tightly, beginning at the narrow end; tie the roll firmly with kitchen string.

Brown the roll on all sides in hot olive oil in a Dutch oven.

At the same time, brown the ground pork shoulder.

Add the plum tomatoes (forced through a strainer to eliminate the seeds), basil, oregano, garlic and bay leaf.

Cook gently, stirring from time to time, for about 25 minutes.

Add the tomato paste, mixed with ½ cup water, and cover the pot.

Cook very slowly for about 2 hours, until the sauce is thick and the meat is tender.

Transfer the meat to a serving platter and carve in slices 1½ inches thick.

Pour a little of the sauce over the meat and sprinkle generously with grated Parmesan cheese.

Serve the rest of the sauce with spaghetti cooked until barely tender and still firm.

HAM TIMBALES

(Serves 6)

Preheat oven to 375° F.

> ¼ cup butter or margarine
> ½ cup Pepperidge Farm Stuffing
> 2 cups milk
> 2 cups ground cooked ham
> 2 teaspoons finely minced green pepper
> 2 teaspoons finely minced onion
> 4 eggs, slightly beaten
> 1 teaspoon prepared mustard
> ¼ teaspoon pepper
> ½ teaspoon salt (about)

For the sauce
1 teaspoon dry mustard
1 teaspoon sugar
1 egg, beaten
2 tablespoons melted butter or margarine
2 tablespoons vinegar
½ cup cream, whipped (or more)

Combine the stuffing, milk and ¼ cup butter and cook together for 5 minutes, stirring constantly.

Add the ground ham, green pepper, onion and 4 eggs slightly beaten, and season to taste with the prepared mustard, pepper and salt.

Turn the mixture into 6 well-buttered custard cups or molds and set the molds in a shallow pan of hot water.

Bake in a moderately hot oven (375° F.) for about 1 hour, or until a silver knife inserted near the center comes out clean.

Remove the pan from the oven and let the timbales stand for 5 minutes before unmolding them on a serving dish.

Combine the dry mustard, sugar, melted butter or margarine, vinegar and 1 beaten egg.

Cook, stirring, until the mixture is thick enough to coat a spoon; cool it.

Just before serving, fold in the whipped cream (additional whipped cream will make a milder sauce).

Serve with the timbales.

CAESAR SALAD
(Serves 4)

2 cups Pepperidge Farm Stuffing
9 tablespoons olive oil
1 clove garlic, split
2 heads romaine, chilled
¼ teaspoon dry mustard
¼ teaspoon black pepper
½ teaspoon salt (about)
½ cup grated Parmesan cheese
juice of 2 lemons
2 eggs
4 or 5 fillets of anchovy (optional)
4 slices bacon (optional)
dash Worcestershire sauce (optional)

Prepare croutons by frying the Pepperidge Farm Stuffing over a low flame in 3 tablespoons olive oil flavored with the garlic.

Into a garlic-rubbed wooden bowl tear the chilled romaine heads into medium-size pieces and sprinkle with the dry mustard, black pepper, salt (to taste) and grated Parmesan cheese.

Add 6 tablespoons olive oil and the lemon juice.

Break 2 eggs (some chefs prefer to coddle them for 1½ minutes) on the greens and toss enough to mix thoroughly, but not so vigorously as to bruise the greens, and until no trace of egg can be seen; the leaves should be coated, but there must not be excess liquid in the bowl.

Taste for seasoning.

An instant before serving, add the croutons, tossing the salad briefly to mix in the croutons without making them soggy.

Fillets of anchovy, cut into small pieces, are sometimes added to this salad; or bacon slices cut into small pieces and fried until crisp may be added with the croutons.

A dash of Worcestershire sauce may also be added.

APPLE STUFFING (for Poultry)

8 large tart apples
½ cup cold water
2 cups Pepperidge Farm Stuffing
1½ tablespoons sugar
2 tablespoons melted butter
1 egg

Pare, quarter and core the apples.

Place them in a saucepan, add the cold water, cover and cook until the apples are tender but not broken.

Cool.

Add the Pepperidge Farm Stuffing, sugar, melted butter and egg.

Toss the stuffing thoroughly but gently.

CRANBERRY STUFFING (for Pork)

1½ cups raw cranberries
3 to 4 tablespoons sugar
⅔ cup melted butter or margarine
4 cups Pepperidge Farm Stuffing
½ teaspoon sweet marjoram
1 teaspoon salt
pinch black pepper
pinch mace
pinch thyme
pinch dill
2 tablespoons grated onion
1 clove garlic, mashed

Put the raw cranberries through the food chopper, using the coarsest blade.

Mix them in a saucepan with 3 to 4 tablespoons sugar (depending on the sweetness desired) and the Pepperidge Farm Stuffing, marjoram, salt, pepper, mace, thyme, dill, onion and garlic.

Mix well and cook over a medium flame for about 10 minutes, stirring constantly.

Cool the stuffing before filling a crown roast of pork.

MUSHROOM STUFFING (for Fish)

1 small onion, finely chopped
4 tablespoons butter or margarine
2 to 3 cups Pepperidge Farm Stuffing
2 tablespoons chopped parsley
lemon juice
¼ pound raw mushrooms, sliced thin
¼ cup light cream
salt and pepper

Sauté the chopped onion in the butter or margarine for 5 minutes over a low flame.

Remove from the fire and blend with the Pepperidge Farm Stuffing, parsley, mushrooms and a few drops of lemon juice.

Add the light cream—just enough to moisten the stuffing.

Season with salt and pepper and blend well.

PART FOUR

COOKING FROM ANTIQUE COOKBOOKS

UNTIL I became active in the food business, I had never thought much about what food was eaten in past ages or how it was prepared. I was content to think the twentieth century was new in everything.

But one day, browsing in a bookstore, I found a dusty old book entitled *The Ladies Cabinet, Containing Many Rare Secrets*. It was a cookbook by Lord Ruthven, published in London in 1658, and, like all early cookbooks, it offered first-aid advice and medical hints. In fact, all the recipes were prepared from a medical standpoint, for Lord Ruthven was a "learned chymist."

That book aroused my interest in the history of food and cooking. I woke up to the fact that there is very little which is really new in food and cooking since the time of the Bible stories, where foods familiar to us are mentioned many times —bread, almonds, anise, beans, butter, cinnamon, cucumbers, most of the grains, dates, figs, fish, honey, melons, olives, nuts, partridges, sheep, vinegar, wine and many others.

Meat was not mentioned very often, for it was not an article of ordinary diet. Few animals were slaughtered except for purposes of hospitality or festivity.

Food markets have not changed much either. Today's elegant supermarkets have grown from the simple street bazaars that existed in Jerusalem two thousand years ago. Everything for eating and housekeeping was for sale in one place, and that's just about what we have in a supermarket today. Most of the foods mentioned in the Bible are here now, wrapped in pretty packages with colored pictures, and they are picked off the shelves of the markets by hurrying housewives who push carts along the aisles instead of being followed by a slave carrying a basket. These girls wear shorts or slacks instead of figure-concealing voluminous robes, but the Arab girls pinched the pomegranates to find the ripest just as American housewives pinch melons today.

Precooked food is not new, for nuts were roasted and flat cakes of unleavened bread were toasted on charcoal braziers in the bazaars. Even freezing of food is not new, for the Eskimos froze food centuries ago.

I began a search for old cookbooks. Reading cookbooks must have been an indoor sport in the past as well as the present, for I found some fascinating ones dating from the seventeenth and eighteenth centuries, and even earlier. The Ten Books of Apicius were handwritten during the time of Imperial Rome, and some medieval manuscripts are in great collections today.

The old books I found were lovely to look at and to hold in my hands. The faded, worn leather bindings, the soft gold lettering of the titles, almost obliterated by age, the dry, stiff paper, the names of former owners written in careful Spencerian script with ink now faded to the brown of withered leaves, the marginal notes in many of them—all tell of books treasured by lovers of home and family. As I read them, I found myself fascinated by the fun of tracing back to early dates the food and cooking methods of today.

The pride of my collection of antique books is a copy of the world's first printed cookbook, DE HONESTA VOLUPTATE by Bartholomaeus de Platina, written in medieval Latin and printed in Venice in 1475. This rare volume was given to me by the Pepperidge Farm employees in 1957 when we were celebrating the twentieth anniversary of the founding of the business. We had a great ceremony when it was presented to me together with a hand-illuminated scroll which contained the signature of every employee—over one thousand!

As far as I know, Platina's book has never been translated in its entirety, but I found an enthusiastic young Latin professor who was willing to tackle the job of translating part of the book.

The results gave me the idea for this chapter on cooking from old cookbooks.

mus. Equitatem: pudicitiam: bonam rationem : pudorem:
fidem: pietatem: constantiam: honestatem: sanam mentem
et bonam spem amittentes ab integra uoluptate : quam et
bone ualitudini coniunctam dicimus: cum dedecore decli
nabimus.   FINIS.
                Laus Deo trino.

Habes splendidissime lector uiri doctissimi Platinæ opu
sculum de obsoniis: de honesta uoluptate ac nalitudine di
ligenterqʒ Bononiæ Impressum per Ioannẽ antonium pla
tonidem Benedictorum bibliopolam necnõ ciuem Bono
niensem sub Anno domini. Mccccxcix. die uero. xi. mensis
Maii. Ioanne Bentiuolo fœliciter illustrante.

DE HONESTA VOLUPTATE ET VALETUDINE

(OF HONEST VOLUPTUOUSNESS AND HEALTH)

OR

(VIRTUOUS ENJOYMENT AND GOOD HEALTH)

BY BARTHOLOMAEUS DE PLATINA

PRINTED IN ROMAN TYPE IN VENICE *13* JUNE *1475*

THE title of Platina's work, as is true of many books of the period, appears in various forms. One variant, *De obsoniis ac honesta voluptate*, can be freely translated as: "On meat dishes and their virtuous enjoyment." Platina stresses that his recipes do not lead to the sin of gluttony. So you can enjoy your three-inch charcoal-broiled steaks and still feel virtuous.

This book is important not only as the first printed cookery text, but also as an excellent source of knowledge of daily life in the mid-fifteenth century, and particularly for insights into dietary customs of the time.

Platina, I discovered, was not a cook. He is recorded first as a soldier and later as a distinguished scholar. In 1474 he presented the handwritten manuscript of his now famous *Lives of the Popes* to Pope Sixtus IV. The original is still in the Vatican Library. His reward was an appointment to the extremely important post of Librarian to the Vatican.

How did this scholar come to write a cookbook? The clue may be found in the book itself, where he mentions his "good friend Martino," the chef of one of the Chamberlains

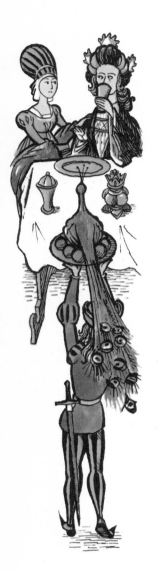

to the Pope. They must have become acquainted at the Vatican. A manuscript treatise on food and cookery written by Martino is in the Library of Congress. It is quite evident that Martino's manuscript formed the basis for Platina's book, for he says of his friend in Chapter VI, "which cook, by the immortals, could compare with my companion Martino of Como, by whom these things I write have for the most part been considered? You will call him another Carneades if you hear him discussing extemporaneously the things put forth here."

Platina's book is rather casual in its approach to actual cooking, and the entries in the long table of contents may not guide the reader to any hint of a recipe. For instance, the chapter on edible birds deals with swans and storks, but only relates their living habits.

It must be remembered, however, that in the fifteenth century the common people could neither read nor write. Books were commissioned by rich patrons who collected handwritten books with elaborate hand-painted illuminations. Any cookery manuscript would have been a carefully guarded secret, available only to professionals. I suppose the student apprentices who had to pay for their training were sworn to secrecy and learned not by reading but by working with their masters, who probably couldn't write out directions anyway. But Platina, a trained scholar and experienced writer, turned out a well-written book by the standards of his time, even though the recipes lack specific information.

What fascinates me is that so many of the same foods we use today were being used then in practically the same way. Platina refers to eggs, pastry, bread and grains, cheese, all the vegetables, practically all the fruits, including cherries, grapes and figs, chicken, frogs, salted meat, squid, octopus and all our modern spices.

And his chapters of advice concerning healthful habits seem amazingly timely today, when exercise and recreation are considered of vital importance for good health.

From Book I, Chapter 2

Concerning the Exercise of the Body

BECAUSE leisure weakens the body and because health aids life, liberal exercise must be used, and the limbs become stronger and readier for what must be done; and the stomach in which the vital heat resides is quickened by the motion for a good appetite; and the mind with its aiding senses is rendered quicker and sharper for learning things occult and admirable.

But this is not to be done before eating nor with a hungry or famished body. Wait for the first meal after no indigestion is to be feared.

Walking and shopping exercise a man well, as do walking up and down hills, the carrying of a thing not too heavy from place to place when we are at home, hoeing, harrowing, planting and pruning while we are cultivating gardens and orchards for the sake of our souls.

Some exercise by throwing the javelin, some harder, some more easily in the horse and foot contests or in gladiatorial contests, but these are lower class. However, to contend in jumping, to throw darts, to bend the bow, to wrestle, to pursue the hunt do not seem alien to a well-born and civil man, since, if it were necessary to fight for one's country, arms would be taken up with strength. These things are better for health and indeed more pleasurable in the open air and sunlight than under a roof or in the shade.

These exercises are especially to be praised, as Celsus says, of which the end product is a good sweat or at least weariness which is close to fatigue. But this especially ought to be guarded against: that all the limbs are exercised equally according to their strength lest we spare one and harm the rest with excessive work. Indeed, they are endangered from excessive leisure as well as from excessive fatigue. A middle course ought to be held lest we exchange pleasure for sorrow.

And today we are told the very same thing—moderate but constant exercise is better than thirty-six holes of golf every other Saturday and nothing in between.

From Book J, Chapter 5

Concerning Sleep

EXCESSIVE exercise, moreover, and long watches sap the vigor of the body, they impede digestion, weaken the vital spirits and irritate the brain.

Thus, temperate sleep, and not that which comes from drunkenness and inebriation, restores limbs worn out with toil, administers the vital heat to the stomach, cleanses the mind and indeed renews the whole body for honest action from which the habits of virtue are prepared.

As in winter a mattress of feathers is better, so in summer one of wool or bombazine is healthier.

But excessive sleep is to be guarded against, whence the body grows lean, and the senses are weakened, the stomach is vexed by diarrhea and the head and brain are made heavy and stupefied. What is quiet, dark, cool and moist invites us mortals to sleep.

Now, bedbugs are the most disturbing, which you will bear most easily in this manner. Pickle a cucumber in water and sprinkle this where you will on the bed. Or pour bovine gall mixed with vinegar; none will come. The flea will likewise leave the bedroom if you spread around water from coriander.

To siesta, that is to sleep at noon, is unhealthy and pestiferous unless in a sitting position while vapors are smoking. For the head is weakened, the fluids are increased, the phlegm grows, the natural heat is weakened, all in all the body is rendered lazy, slothful, lean and languid.

From Book I, Chapter 13

About Bread

AMONG the fruits discovered for the use of man the most useful is grain, of which the species according to Celsus are considered *halica*, rice, *tissana* (millet?), *hamilum* (sorghum?), wheat, winter wheat, and spelt (*far*), which the ancients called *adoreum*, whence it is said "to adore" because sacred offerings are made to the gods with *adoreum*.

Nothing is more fertile or pleasant than wheat nor nourishes more, especially if it is the hill and not the field variety.

Barley fruit is the most noble of all, because it can be sown in dry and broken earth, because it grows quickly and is cut before all grain because of the slimness of its reed. From this, peeled barley and water mixed are better for the sick than bread.

African winter wheat whose bread the ancients used to praise I do not believe to be similar to that which our age eats, since no kind of bread making is more distressing nor less useful for satisfying the appetite.

Who therefore follows the trade of baker, let him take meal well ground up from wheat (although called *farina* from *far*), by putting it through a meal sieve, let the bran be separated from the fine meal, which is placed on a bread-making table closed on the sides with hot water and also salt as the people of Ferrara do, if you live in a wet climate; and when the yeast has been added it should be kneaded with the help of associates even to that thickness at which a good bread can be made.

Let the baker beware lest he put in more or less yeast than is right; for in the former case the bread is sour, and in the latter is heavier in digestion and less healthy since it binds the bowels.

Bread should be well cooked in the oven and eaten not of the same day, and it does not nourish well from recently harvested wheat even if digested slowly.

From Book II, Chapter 6

About Citrus Fruit *

CITRUS or citreus Cloanthius called the Persian apple from its place of origin. And Virgil, imitating Homer, wrote of the citrus in a long periphrasis: "Happy fruit, than which nothing is more helpful, if ever the savage witches pour cups, or mix herbs or incant harmful spells."

No one doubts this to be said about citrus, of which there are various kinds. For some there are which the woods in the territory of Mauretania produce; others which grow in Italy or Media. All of these, differing more in size than in kind, have the same or almost the same quality.

Some are most odoriferous and kill moths living in clothing. Whence clothes are said by Naevius to smell of citrus. They are grown artificially in any season; some are picked before they are ripe; others ripen on the tree.

It is thought also to be an antidote for poison, since those drinking a purgation mixed with wine guard against their own weaknesses.

There is not, however, one and the same virtue in all parts of the citrus. The peels are not edible. Within is the seed case, by which it is clear the stem holds the vine. They go with roasted or hot food at any season but especially in the summer, since they repress bile and extinguish thirst and bring on a desire for eating. . . .

The citrus is a medicine for many sick people, for it even keeps pregnant women from nausea. Given mixed with a drink of wine, it cures a weak and pained body. There are those who eat citrus cut up in pieces with salt, oil and vinegar.

---

* Platina apparently thought that the citrus described by ancient authors was similar to citrus as he knew it and as it is understood today—oranges, lemons, etc. But the citrus of the ancient world was what we call the pear. This has caused a certain confusion in Platina's account.

Concerning the citrus or Persian apple which we commonly call the orange, almost the same things can be said. But some are sweet and some are sour. The method of eating may be sought from the prior instructions. The sweet ones eaten at any time you wish before a meal are agreeable to the stomach. So are the sour ones if eaten with sugar. Let the core be taken out and the membranes cut.

𝔉rom 𝔅ook 𝔛, 𝔠hapter 63

𝔚hat 𝔍s to 𝔅e 𝔈aten at the 𝔗hird 𝔠ourse

IT ought to be said here and shortly what ought to be taken in the third course at the end of the meal as a seal for the stomach.

If there were meats either broiled or boiled, according to the time of the year, you should eat either apples or sour pears, which drive out the exhalations of previously eaten food from the head.

There are those who wondrously approve the radish, among whom is Nicander, which taken after a meal aids digestion by penetrating to the bottom of the stomach, it thins the pip, depresses vapors raised to the head and cleanses the kidneys and bladder; it is considered healthful against the poison of fungi, against the bites of vipers and scorpions. So strong is the wild variety especially that it is said that, put on the back of a scorpion with the skin removed, it kills it immediately.

Taken at the first course, the doctors do not approve, since, because of its strength and heat, it does not allow the force of the food in the stomach to be quiet. It causes belching and impedes digestion by bringing on vomiting.

A small amount of cheese is thought to seal the stomach and keep back the exhalations which seek the head and brain. It easily brings about, moreover, an aversion for oily or sweet food.

Those fastidious at the table eat anise or coriander rolled in sugar to clear the head and mouth, the vulgar eat fennel.

There is great dispute about the chestnut, whose nature is cold and dry. Some think it an almond, as Virgil "chestnut almonds," and others, as the Sardians who call it an acorn, think it to be numbered among the walnuts.

Horse chestnuts with the burr removed and the membrane also are considered a delicacy, especially those which are called Tarentine acorns. They used to praise those from Naples as they now do those from Milan. Chestnuts are easy on the teeth, and, eaten by a good stomach, they are nourishing and filling and are thought to increase the appetite. They are considered better cooked among twigs and ashes than boiled; or they should be toasted at the fire in a perforated dish. For in this way the excessive turgidity is cooked out.

Pomegranates of Cotona are good at this, as are all which are stringent, as calob and pistachios.

After fish either almonds or hazelnuts or walnuts should be eaten because they are thought to repress the cold and wet by their dryness.

From Book II, Chapter 16

Cheese

AND if we eat cheese at the third course, this is the place to explain its nature, since it is made from milk. For making a great deal, it is frequently cooked this way:

Place coagulated milk (not greatly coagulated lest the cheese, as often happens, get sour at the hand of the maker) not runny and hot but thick and warm, made into a ball and taken from the pan into forms of reed or straw.

Let it be squeezed for a long time until the liquid within runs out.

Salt cheese is rendered somewhat distasteful by the smoke from which it gets the salt, but it improves with age and will be given not unrightly to eat.

Quality comes to cheese from its origin and from the herds, as I said about milk. There are two today which contend for first place: Marceolinus, for so the Etruscans call what is made in the month of March in Etruria, and Permensis in the Cisalpine region, which is called Maialem from the month of May.

Cheese gets character from its age. Fresh it is cold and wet; salt cheese is hard, hot and dry. Fresh cheese nourishes well and greatly. It represses heat in the stomach, aids the creation of blood and harms phlegm.

Old cheese is difficult to digest; it nourishes hardly at all, it churns up the stomach and bowels, it causes bile, podager, sore side and generates sand and stones.

From Book III, Chapter 9

Cinnamon

WHAT Herodotus tells about cinnamon is fantastic and false. Moreover, it grows in Ethiopia.

Its trunk is short, with low branches, since it never grows above two urns. It has a thickness of four digits. Moreover, it grows in swamps and bogs and for this reason is not gathered without difficulty.

Cinnamon is the bark of the branch. The goodness of which is found in the top parts for a length of two palms. Second best are the parts nearest to the top, but they are of shorter measure. The worst is the part next to the roots.

Pliny asserts that he saw a root of great weight dedicated in the temple of Capitoline Jove and Peace by the Emperor Vespasian.

Cinnamon is by nature hot and dry; it helps digestion and aids the stomach and liver. Cinnamon I believe to be the same as Cinnamomum, for in my judgment the former word was made by metrical syncope.

From Book III, Chapter 10

Ginger

GINGER is white and dry, although it tends to go bad in part when it rots. It aids a cold stomach by drying the excessive moisture in cooked green vegetables. A bite is considered an antidote against poison.

From Book III, Chapter 32

Savory

THYMBRA, by Pliny's testimony, is called by us savory. It is an aromatic herb and has a strong odor, as even Virgil explains in a verse: "Smelling heavily from the abundance of savory."

This herb is sown as a rival to oregano in the month of January. Savory moves the urine and in a drink made of wine stirs up those sleeping weakly near death.

Against beasts who sting it is considered not unuseful.

This herb makes a love potion, whence it well takes its name from *saturitas*, which means desire.

All of Platina's recipes are frustrating, for no quantities are given and no definite cooking directions appear. You were just supposed to be a "born cook" in those days.

Have a look at these old recipes, but, for goodness' sake, don't try them unless you are the gambling type.

Use the modern versions—I can guarantee them, for we have eaten them one and all.

[*304*]

1475
Chicken in a Pungent Sauce

Cook chicken with salted meat. When it is half cooked, put seeded grapes in the pot. Throw in parsley and a pinch of mint. Crush together pepper and saffron. Put all the ingredients in the pot when the chicken is cooked and serve immediately.

Platina says

"There is nothing more healthful than this food, which Poggio frequently eats when I have been invited. It is nourishing, easily cooked, agrees with the stomach, heart, liver, kidneys and checks the bile."

MODERN VERSION
CHICKEN IN A PUNGENT SAUCE
(Serves 4–6)

2 2-pound broilers
8 slices bacon
2 cups seedless grapes
2 tablespoons parsley, chopped fine
1 sprig fresh mint, or 1½ teaspoons dried
½ teaspoon pepper
1 teaspoon salt
½ teaspoon saffron (powdered variety)
2 cups chicken broth made from necks,
     gizzards and livers

Fry the bacon until crisp in a large iron frying pan.

Remove from the pan, drain on paper toweling, break into small pieces and set aside.

Brown slowly in the bacon fat the broilers which have been quartered, necks removed.

When nicely browned, transfer the chicken to a large earthenware casserole and keep warm.

Crush together 1 tablespoon chopped parsley, the dried powdered mint or leaves of fresh mint chopped fine, the salt, freshly ground pepper and saffron.

Sprinkle over the chicken.

Add to the brown residue in the frying pan the chicken broth.

Bring to a boil, stir well and pour over the chicken.

Place the casserole on a flame tamer over low heat, cover tightly and cook gently until the chicken is tender, or for about 30 minutes.

Drain off most of the juice into a small saucepan and reduce to a syrupy consistency by boiling rapidly, for about 5 minutes.

Pour back over the chicken, sprinkle with another tablespoon of chopped parsley and the pieces of bacon, and add the grapes.

A macedoine of cooked chopped carrots, string beans, lima beans and peas, well buttered, would be good with this dish.

Platina mentions several odd fishes not usually used today as food, such as cuttlefish, scorpions, lampreys and sea-lion. But most of his fish are still favorites—eels, lobsters, crabs, oysters, sturgeon and sturgeon eggs (which he calls caviar), salmon, sole, etc., and he gives a recipe for a Squid Dish for Days of Abstinence.

Although squid is eaten today in the South of France and Greece, and can be found in special fish shops here, I would prefer salmon or halibut. But if you hanker for squid, just go ahead with it if you can find some, and be sure to have the fish man prepare it for you by removing the black liquid from the backbone.

1475
A Squid Dish for Days of Abstinence

Boil the squid. Crush what is good in a mortar. Prepare a paste of almonds with rosewater strained through a sieve; or, if you can't provide this, use the juice of peas or white chickpeas. Crush together small grapes and five figs. Mix a little rock parsley and a little fresh marjoram leaves. Add as much cinnamon, ginger and sugar as is necessary. Mix these well with whites of eggs so that they will stick together and cook better.

With the mixture well greased, and with a crust above and beneath, set it on the hearth at a little distance from the flame. Sprinkle sugar and rosewater on the cooked mixture.

This dish assails all the members.

MODERN VERSION
FISH PIE
(Serves 4–6)

Preheat oven to 450° F.

> 1¾ *pounds salmon*
> *Plain Pastry with Butter for a 2-crust pie (p. 154)*
> 1 *cup white wine* ⎫
> 3 *cups cold water* ⎪
> 1 *onion, peeled and sliced* ⎪ *for court bouillon*
> 1 *carrot, peeled* ⎬
> 1 *teaspoon salt* ⎪
> 3 *peppercorns* ⎭
> 1 *cup seedless grapes*
> ½ *teaspoon powdered marjoram*
> ½ *teaspoon powdered ginger*
> ½ *teaspoon powdered cinnamon*
> ½ *cup grated, ground or chopped almonds*
> 2 *teaspoons rosewater*
> 5 *small fresh black figs or dried figs*
> 2 *teaspoons sugar*
> 1½ *teaspoons salt*
> ⅛ *pound butter*
> 1 *tablespoon chopped parsley*
> 1 *egg white*

Wrap the salmon in a piece of cheesecloth, tie securely with string and cook gently for about 30 minutes in a court bouillon made of water, white wine, salt, onion, peppercorns and carrot.

Remove from the bouillon, unwrap, and remove all skin, bones and the black part of the flesh.

When cool enough to handle, flake it with your fingers to be sure you feel and extract all the bones.

Peel the figs and add to them the washed and stemmed grapes.

Crush the fruits together, using a wooden spoon, and season them with the marjoram, cinnamon, ginger, sugar and 1½ teaspoons salt.

Grate or grind the blanched almonds, moisten them with the rosewater and add to the fruit.

Now stir in the flaked salmon, chopped parsley and 4 tablespoons melted butter.

Beat the egg white with a fork until frothy, then stir it into the whole mixture.

Line a 9-inch pie dish with pastry and fill it with the salmon mixture.

Cover with more pastry.

Trim, roll under and crimp the edges.

Make 5 or 6 generous slits in the top crust and place in a 450° F. oven.

Bake for about 20 minutes, turn the regulator to 400° F. and continue baking until it looks done, or for about 45 minutes in all.

Serve at once with white wine.

1475
𝔉rogs' 𝔏egs

Frogs, which are on no account to be numbered among the fishes, shall properly at this point come to the kitchen. I am rejecting as harmful toads and those living under the earth. It is the water variety about which I am speaking.

Frogs which have been caught in a net are considered better to eat than those which have been speared. For the latter have been damaged by the fluke of the spear. Damaged frogs are not thought to approach the net.

We allow the skinned legs of the captured frogs to soak overnight, or else a day, in fresh water.

We fry them in oil after they have been covered with meal. When they have been fried and are put on a plate, my friend

Palellus pours on salsa verde [green sauce—such as minced parsley sauce] and sprinkles them with fennel and aromatic herbs.

MODERN VERSION #1
FROGS' LEGS
(Serves 4)

12 pairs frogs' legs
¾ cup olive oil
6 shallots, chopped and blanched
¼ to ½ pound Clarified Butter (p. 152)
3 tablespoons chopped fennel tops
salt and pepper to taste
1 cup water-ground white cornmeal
1 tablespoon cut dill
1 tablespoon cut chives
3 tablespoons chopped parsley
2 lemons

Soak the frogs' legs in cold water acidulated with the juice of ½ lemon for at least 2 hours.

Prepare 3 tablespoons chopped fennel greens.

Peel and chop fine 6 shallots, cover with cold water, bring to a boil, strain and allow cold water to run over them.

Prepare and mix together 1 tablespoon cut chives, 1 tablespoon cut dill and 3 tablespoons chopped parsley.

Clarify ¼ to ½ pound butter and add to this, while hot, the blanched shallots.

Keep warm over hot water.

Drain the frogs' legs and dry them well on paper toweling.

Salt and pepper them lightly and roll in white cornmeal.

Heat about ¾ cup olive oil in a large frying pan, and place the frogs' legs in the pan one by one so that they do not lie one on top of another.

Cook over moderate heat until lightly browned and until the meat is opaque through, or for 7 to 10 minutes.

Turn them over carefully as they brown.

When done, place on a hot serving platter.

Add the mixture of chives, parsley and dill to the hot butter and shallots and pour over the frogs' legs.

Sprinkle with the prepared chopped fennel tops and garnish with lemon.

Serve at once with French bread, white wine and a green salad lightly treated with French dressing and chopped dill.

MODERN VERSION #2
FROGS' LEGS
(Serves 4)

Soak 12 pairs of frogs' legs in 1 cup water and 1 cup milk for 3 hours.

Dry well on paper towels.

Shake in a paper bag with flour seasoned with salt and pepper, or roll in corn meal.

Fry in hot butter or olive oil until golden brown on all sides, for 7 to 10 minutes.

Remove from the pan to a hot platter, sprinkle with chopped parsley and serve with wedges of lemon and mayonnaise sauce.

To 2 cups Mayonnaise add 2 tablespoons chopped chives, 4 tablespoons chopped parsley and 3 tablespoons finely chopped garlic dill pickles.

Platina hardly mentions eggs. Perhaps they were somewhat of a delicacy, or perhaps too plebeian for eminent chefs.

1475
Boiled or Poached Eggs

In boiling water put fresh eggs with shells removed. Take them out when they are firm; it is best to eat them while tender. Add sugar, rosewater, aromatic sweets, vinegar or orange juice.

There are those who sprinkle on grated cheese, but neither Phosphoros nor I like this—we very often eat such food. It is very good without the cheese and very agreeable to eat.

Or else, cook eggs in milk or sweet wine with the same method as above. Let no other mention be made of cheese; this method is more nourishing, although it leads to sluggishness of the blood.

Eggs can be poached in a number of ways in various liquids, just as they were done in the fifteenth century.

The basic liquid can be water, milk, wine or bouillon flavored with anything you like.

For each egg use one cup of liquid.

To my mind, there is really nothing better than a fresh egg poached in boiling salted water for three minutes and served on hot buttered toast with nothing but salt and freshly ground pepper.

It seems foolish to make a fancy poaching base with milk or wine if it can't be served with the eggs, so if I do make a fancy base I make one that can be used as a sauce.

MODERN VERSION #1
BOILED OR POACHED EGGS

6 eggs
6 slices white bread
1 cup white wine
1 cup chicken broth
¼ bay leaf
1 tablespoon chopped parsley
⅛ teaspoon thyme
½ clove garlic (peeled)
pinch cayenne
¼ teaspoon freshly ground pepper
½ teaspoon salt
¾ tablespoon butter creamed with
1 tablespoon flour
3 tablespoons additional butter
1 tablespoon finely chopped parsley

Have ready ¾ tablespoon butter creamed with 1 tablespoon flour.

Toast 6 slices white bread and butter them with 2 tablespoons butter.

Place side by side on a serving platter.

Keep very warm.

Butter a medium-size frying pan (preferably enamel-lined) and heat together in it 1 cup white wine and 1 cup clear chicken broth.

Bring to a boil, break 6 fresh eggs one at a time into a saucer and slip the eggs very carefully into the pan.

Poach the eggs until almost done, or for about 3 minutes, basting them constantly with the broth so as to form a white film over the yolks.

Carefully lift each egg with a slotted spoon out of the liquid and place each egg on a slice of toast.

Now add to the wine and chicken broth the bay leaf, thyme, garlic and other seasonings and reduce to about ¾ cup by boiling it rapidly.

Stir in the flour and butter.

Bring to a boil, stirring constantly until just thickened, then remove from the fire and stir in another tablespoon of butter.

Pour the sauce over the eggs, sprinkle with chopped parsley and serve at once with white wine, well chilled.

MODERN VERSION #2
ANOTHER WAY TO POACH EGGS WITH A SAUCE

In a saucepan cook 1 sliced onion in 2 tablespoons butter until clear but not browned, stirring constantly.

Add ½ cup thinly sliced mushrooms and 2 chicken livers sliced thin, and cook for 5 minutes.

Add   *2 cups consommé*
2 cups canned tomatoes
½ teaspoon salt
1 teaspoon sugar
¼ teaspoon oregano

Cover and simmer for 20 minutes.

Drop in 4 eggs, one at a time.

Cover tightly again and poach for 4 minutes.

Serve immediately with the sauce from the pan on hot buttered toast.

1475
Cherry Tart

Grind sour cherries in a mortar after they have been stoned. When these are ground, add red roses, finely chopped, a little fresh cheese and a little old cheese, ground, a little pepper, a little ginger, a little sugar; mix in four broken eggs.

After the mixture has been lined with a crust, cook it in a well-greased pan over a slow fire.

When it has been removed from the fire, pour over it sugar and rosewater.

MODERN VERSION
CHERRY TART
(Serves 6)

Preheat oven to 450° F.

Plain Pastry with Butter (p. 154)
2 cups cooked and sweetened fresh sour cherries or
    1 can (1 pound 4 ounces) sour cherries, drained of juice
¼ teaspoon salt
¼ teaspoon ground ginger
½ cup granulated sugar
3 eggs
2 cups milk
3 tablespoons rosewater
½ pint sour cream
8 ounces creamed cottage cheese
pink candied red rose petals

Prepare Plain Pastry with Butter for 1 pastry shell.
Line a 9-inch pie pan with the plain pastry crust.
Brush the inside bottom of the crust with beaten egg white and chill in the refrigerator while preparing the cherry custard filling.
Wash 2 cups fresh sour cherries and remove stems and pits.
Sweeten to taste and cook for a few minutes.

Or use 2 cups drained canned sour cherries.

Sprinkle the cherries with 2 tablespoons rosewater and let stand while preparing the custard mix.

Beat together the eggs, sugar, salt, ginger and milk.

Add the cherries to the custard mix, stir well and pour into the chilled pastry shell.

Bake for 10 minutes in a hot (450° F.) oven; turn the indicator down to 350° F. and bake about 30 minutes longer, or until a silver knife blade inserted in the center comes out clean.

Cool before serving.

In the meantime beat together the creamed cottage cheese and sour cream.

When ready to serve, sprinkle 1 tablespoon rosewater over the tart and cover the surface with the cheese.

Garnish to your heart's delight with pink candied rose petals (obtainable at food specialty shops).

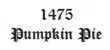

1475
Pumpkin Pie

Shred well-cleaned pumpkins and, as with cheese, let them cook a little either in heavy juice or in milk. When partially cooked, pass it through a sieve into a pan, as, I said first, for cheese.

Mix together a half-pound of sow's belly or rich fat boiled and beaten with a knife, or in place of these, if you wish, the same amount of butter or liquamen; a half-pound of sugar, a little ginger, some cinnamon, six eggs and two cups of milk with a little saffron.

This dessert will be rich with a good crust only if cooked above or below a slow fire.

There are those who add pieces of leaves in place of the upper crust and call the dish *lagana*. When cooked and put in a dish, sprinkle on it sugar and rosewater.

Cassius, who was bothered by colic and stones, did not eat this. It is difficult to digest and nourishes badly.

[*314*]

MODERN VERSION
PUMPKIN PIE
(Serves 6)

Preheat oven to 450° F.

> *Plain Pastry (p. 153)*
> *1½ cups canned pumpkin*
> *⅔ cup brown sugar*
> *1 teaspoon cinnamon*
> *½ teaspoon ginger*
> *½ teaspoon salt*
> *2 eggs*
> *1 cup milk*
> *1 cup cream*

Line a 9-inch pie pan with pastry, making a high edge.

Brush the pastry all over with egg white.

Place in the refrigerator while preparing the filling.

Mix together the pumpkin and the spices.

Sift the brown sugar onto the pumpkin and mix well.

Beat the eggs and add them.

Then add the milk and cream and mix well.

Pull out the shelf of the oven, set the prepared pie pan on the shelf and carefully pour the filling into the crust.

Don't pour all onto one spot, but take a cupful at a time and spread the filling around to avoid breaking the crust. Filling the crust this way avoids spilling.

Bake at 450° F. for 10 minutes, then reduce heat to 350° and bake 45 minutes more until the custard is set.

1475
𝔅𝔩'𝔐𝔞𝔫𝔤𝔢

Bl'Mange, which is more properly called white food, is made for twelve servings in this way. Pound well in a mortar two pounds of almonds soaked in water the night before and shelled. Sprinkle on water, very little lest oil be made. Then grind up in the same mortar a deboned breast of chicken. Put in bread sauce fortified with lean broth. Add an ounce of ginger and a half-pound of sugar. When all these are mixed up, pour them through a meal sieve into a clean pan. Let it boil over a slow flame. Stir often so that it does not get lumpy. When cooked pour in three ounces of rosewater. Serve in the dishes where the meat was or separately, but in small dishes. But if you wish to, pour it into a large dish where it will seem more noteworthy; sprinkle over it pomegranate seeds. But if you wish to divide the dessert in two parts, color one part with a sauce made from egg yolk mixed with a small amount of saffron. The other part is white, and serve it as I said. This I prefer always to Apician desserts. Nor is there any reason why the tastes of our ancestors should be preferred.

MODERN VERSION
PLAIN BLANC MANGE
(Serves 4)

1 pint milk
1 envelope plain gelatin
3 tablespoons sugar
¼ cup cold water
1 teaspoon vanilla
8 pitted stewed plums

Soak the gelatin in the cold water.

Scald the milk with the sugar.

Stir in the gelatin and cool, stirring occasionally.

Flavor with the vanilla when cold, and pour into 4 ½-cup-size custard molds.

Chill until set, run a knife around the edge and turn out on a dessert dish.

Garnish with 8 pitted stewed plums, fresh or canned, and serve.

THE
LADIES CABINET
ENLARGED and OPENED:

Containing,
Many Rare SECRETS, and Rich
ORNAMENTS, of several kinds,
and different Uses.

Comprized
Under three General Heads,

Viz. of
1. Preserving, Conserving, Candying, &c.
2. Physick and Chirurgery.
3. Cookery and Houswifery.

Whereunto is added,
Sundry Experiments, and Choice Ex-
tractions of Waters, Oyls, &c.

Collected and practised,
By
The late Right Honourable and
Learned Chymist,
The Lord RUTHUEN.

The third Edit. with Additions;
AND
A particular Table to each Part.

LONDON, Printed for *G. Bedel* and *T. Collins*
at the Middle Temple Gate Fleet-street, 1658.

To the Industrious impro-
vers of Nature by Art; espe-
cially the vertuons Ladies
and Gentlewomen
of this Land.

Courteous Ladies, &c:

THe first Edition of
this-- (call it what you
please) having recei-
ved a kind entertain-
ment from your Ladiships
hands, for reasons best known
to your selves, notwithstanding
the disorderly and confused
jumbling together of things
of different kinds, hath made
me (who am not a little concerned

A

This book, for its size (3 inches by 5 inches), is a treasure trove of information—most of it useless today but interesting and amusing. Like all cookbooks of its period, it has medical and surgical advice and recipes for what seem like magic potions supposed to cure a multitude of very odd ailments.

1658
A SPECIAL REMEMBRANCE FOR PRESERVING

When you preserve quinces or make marmalade, take the kernels out of the raw quinces and wash off the Jellie (that groweth about them) in fair water; Then strain the water and jelly from the kernels through some fine Cobweb Lawn, put the same into the Marmalade or Preserved Quinces—but put not so much for it will jelly the quinces too much.

MODERN VERSION

Today prepared pectin syrup, usually made from apples, is used in making jelly and marmalade, and the rule mentioned above still applies—don't use too much or your jelly will be stiff and tough.

1658
TO PRESERVE PEARES

Take peares new gathered from the tree, and Sound, let them be pretty mellow, then take an Earthen pot, and lay in the bottome of it some dryed vine leaves, and so lay Peares, and leaves until the pot be full, then filling the pot with old wine, lay some heavy thing on it, that the Peares may not swim, you may also take whole ginger, and cut the same small, and strew it between each rowe.

MODERN VERSION
PRESERVED PEARS

ripe pears
granulated sugar
brandy

Weigh as many pears as you want to preserve and then weigh out half their weight in sugar.

Core and stem but do not peel the pears.

Put alternate layers of pears and sugar in an earthenware jar or crock.

Add brandy to cover the fruit.

Cover the jar closely and keep in the refrigerator or in a cool place for at least 2 weeks.

For 8 quarts pears, 1 quart brandy will suffice.

1658
TO PRESERVE ORANGES AND LEMMONS

Take your Oranges or Lemmons, Lay them in water three days and three nights to take away their bitterness, then boile them in fair water til they be tender, make as much Syrup for them as will make them swimme about the Pan, let them not boil too long therein, for it will make the skinnes tough; then let them lie all night in the syrup and make them take the syrup; in the morning boil your syrup to this thickness and put them in Gallipots or glasses, to keep all the yeare: And this is the best way to preserve Oranges, Lemmons or Citrons.

MODERN VERSION
THREE-DAY ORANGE MARMALADE

12 oranges
6 lemons
3 grapefruit
sugar

Wash and slice the fruit as thin as possible, discarding all seeds.

For each quart of fruit and juice add 3 quarts cool water and let stand overnight.

Next day bring to the boil and cook for 2 hours, then let stand again overnight.

Next day measure and add ¾ cup sugar for each cup of fruit and juice and boil until thick (about 2 hours).

Pour into hot sterilized jars, seal with hot wax and protect with jar covers.

[*319*]

1658
THE BEST WAY TO PRESERVE APRICOCKS

Take the weight of your Apricocks (what quantity soever you mind to use) in sugar finely beaten, pare and stone your Apricocks, and lay them in the sugar in your preserving Pan all night, and in the morning set them upon the embers till the sugar be all melted, and then let them stand and scald an hour; then take them off the fire, and let them stand in that syrup two days, and then boile them softly, till they be tender and well coloured and after that, when they are cold, put them up in glasses or pots, which you please.

MODERN VERSION
APRICOT JAM

For every pound of apricots without the pits, use ¾ pound granulated sugar and ¼ cup water.

Cut the apricots in quarters; do not peel, but remove the pits.

Add the sugar and water, mix well, bring to a boil and cook rapidly, stirring constantly, until the jelly stage is reached, or 235° F. on a jelly thermometer.

Fill sterilized jars or jelly glasses and seal with wax.

1658
TO PRESERVE BULLASSES AS GREEN AS GRASS

Take your Bullasses as new gathered as you can, wipe them with a cloth, and prick them with a knife, and quaddle them in two waters close covered: then take a pound of clarified sugar, and a pint of Apple water, boile them well together (keeping them well scummed) unto a syrup, and when your Bullasses are well dript from the water, put them into the syrup, and warm them three or four times at the least; at the last warming, take them up and let them adropping from the syrup, and boil the syrup a little by itself, till it come to a jellie, and then between hot and cold put them up to keep for all the year.

MODERN VERSION
PRESERVED GREENGAGE PLUMS

6 pounds greengage plums
3 pounds sugar
3 cups water

Wash the plums and prick each plum several times with a large needle to prevent bursting.

Bring the sugar and water to a boil.

Add the plums a few at a time and cook until soft, but without breaking the skins.

Remove the plums from the syrup.

Pack into hot sterilized jars and fill the jars to within ½ inch of the top with boiling syrup.

Place covers on the jars, but do not seal.

For processing instructions, see below.

TO PROCESS FRUIT IN SYRUP

Place a wooden or metal rack in the bottom of a large kettle.

Fill with sufficient water to cover the jars to be processed, to a depth of 1 to 2 inches above their tops.

Bring to a boil.

The jars should be filled with fruit and syrup to within ½ inch of the top, and their covers and rubbers properly adjusted.

(If the jars have screw tops, screw tight and turn back ½ inch. If they are glass-topped jars, snap the top clamp into place and leave the side clamp up. If self-sealing jars, adjust the screw band tightly or adjust the clamps.)

With jar tongs, lower the jars into the boiling water, placing them far enough apart so that the water can circulate freely around them.

Cover the kettle tightly and begin to count the called-for processing time from the time the water boils vigorously.

In the case of plums (see recipe above), 5 minutes of processing is required.

1658
HOW TO MAKE FINE BISKET BREAD, CALLED IN SOME PLACES NORSSE CAKES AND COMMONLY CALLED DIET BREAD

Take all the yolkes, and half the whites of fifteen eggs, beat them well together; then put to them a pound of the finest wheat flower, as much as the best loafe sugar, very finely beaten and fearced, with a quarter of a pint of rosewater and half a quarter of a pint of Sacke (if you please), beating them thus compounded together about two hours very well, then throwing upon it two spoonsful of Coriander seeds, and as much Annis-seed finely beaten and then working them well into Paste, bake it in boxes or upon plates well buttered, keeping a little Sugar in a piece of Cobweb Lawne, to fearce upon it, and ice it. If you make it for some physical use, then use the Sack, and put in a quarter of a pound of Annis-seed and as much Liquorice beaten into fine powder.

How do you like this! Diet bread in 1658! Well, it is just rusks or zwieback. You could have fun making some on a cold rainy day when you can't get out for a game of golf, or else you could just buy a package of rusks.

MODERN VERSION
RUSKS
(Makes 4 dozen)

Preheat oven to 350° F.

Make 1 recipe of Basic Sweet Dough (p. 227).

After the first rising, punch it down and weigh it off into 8-ounce pieces and shape into small, long, narrow loaves.

Set to rise in a warm place until doubled in bulk.

Bake in a medium hot oven (350° F.) until light brown; do not overbake.

Cool and keep in a covered container overnight.

On the following day, cut into slices ½ inch thick.

Lay the slices close together on a baking sheet and bake in a slow oven (300° F.) until light golden brown in color and thoroughly dried.

These will keep for several weeks in a closed container.

1658
A PORK PIE

Boil your leg of Pork, season it with nutmeg, pepper and salt; bake it five houres in a high round Pie.

MODERN VERSION
PORK PIE
(Serves 4)

Preheat oven to 350° F.

> *Plain Pastry (p. 153)*
> *3 thin slices ham*
> *6 strips lean bacon*
> *1 pound sliced fresh pork*
> *2 cups thin-sliced new potatoes*
> *3 hard-boiled eggs, sliced*
> *1 cup chicken broth or water*
> *salt*
> *pepper*
> *thyme*
> *sage*
> *chopped parsley*

Line a deep pie pan with alternate strips of thin-sliced ham and lean bacon.

Place in alternate layers the sliced pork, sprinkled with salt, pepper, thyme, sage, chopped parsley; the sliced raw potatoes and sliced onions; and the sliced eggs.

Moisten with the chicken broth or water.

Cover with a pastry top.

Bake in a moderate oven (350° F.) for 2 hours.

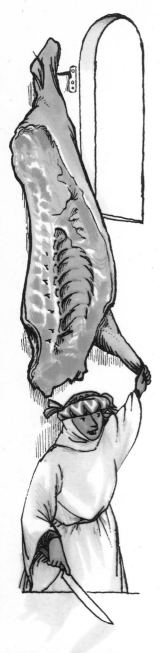

1658
FRICASSEE OF VEAL

Cut your meat in thin slices, beat it well with a rolling pin, season it with nutmeg, lemmon and thyme, fry it slightly in the pan, beat two eggs and one spoonful of verjuice, and put it into the pan, and stir it together, and dish it.

MODERN VERSION
FRICASSEE OF VEAL
(Serves 8)

4 pounds breast of veal
2 medium-size onions, peeled
4 stalks celery
1 large carrot, peeled
salt and pepper to taste
peppercorns
½ teaspoon nutmeg
½ teaspoon thyme
thin rind from 1 lemon
juice of 1 lemon, strained
2 hard-boiled eggs
8 tablespoons butter
flour
1 tablespoon chopped parsley

Buy 4 pounds breast of veal, cut in medium-size pieces.

Wash, and place in a deep large saucepan.

Cover with cold water and bring very slowly to the boiling point.

From time to time skim off the grayish foam that comes to the surface.

When the broth is clear, add the lemon rind, salt to taste, a few peppercorns, the carrot, onions, celery and thyme.

Simmer gently until the meat is tender, or for about 1½ hours.

Drain through a sieve, saving the broth, of which there should be about 4 cups.

Spread the meat out on a platter to cool until it may be handled, at which time take it piece by piece and discard all the bone,

fat and gristle, placing the good meat on a piece of wax paper sprinkled lightly with flour.

When this is accomplished, sprinkle the meat lightly with more flour.

Melt 4 tablespoons butter in a frying pan, and when it is sizzling hot, add the lightly floured meat, cook just long enough to brown lightly on both sides, and set aside.

To make the sauce, melt 4 tablespoons butter in the top of a double boiler, and stir in 4 tablespoons flour.

Cook over low heat without browning for a minute or two, then stir in gradually the veal broth.

Add a little of this to the meat in the frying pan, stir to incorporate the brown residue and add the whole to the sauce.

Add the lemon juice, and season to taste with additional salt and pepper if necessary, and at least ½ teaspoon nutmeg.

Place over boiling water until ready to serve. Garnish with the hard-boiled eggs shelled and cut in thick slices and 1 tablespoon chopped parsley, and serve accompanied by a bowl of flaky rice, lightly buttered.

1658
TO BOIL A MALLARD WITH CABBAGE

Halfe roast your fowle, then take it off and case it down, then put it into a pipkin with the gravie, then pick and wash some cabbage and put to your mallard, with as much fair water as will cover it, then put in a good piece of butter and let it boil an hour, season it with pepper and salt, and serve it upon sops.

MODERN VERSION
DUCK WITH CABBAGE
(Serves 6)

Preheat oven to 350–375° F.

> *2 fresh-killed ducks weighing, when dressed, about*
>   *4 pounds each*
> *1 large head green cabbage*
> *salt and pepper to taste*

¼ pound butter
1½ cups chicken broth
1 teaspoon caraway seeds (optional)
parsley

Wash and dry the ducks thoroughly, inside and out.

Sprinkle the inside of each with ¼ teaspoon pepper and ¾ teaspoon salt.

Melt 4 tablespoons butter in a large heavy iron frying pan and brown the ducks on all sides, slowly, turning them over and over.

This will take at least 30 minutes, so don't try to hurry the process.

Prick the legs and lower part of the ducks with a 2-prong fork as they brown, to draw out the fat as it melts.

Transfer to a large roasting pan and place in a preheated 350–375° F. oven.

Pour off all the fat in the frying pan, and add to the pan 1½ cups chicken broth.

Bring to a boil, stirring well with a wooden spoon to incorporate the brown residue in the pan.

Strain into a small pan and pour over the ducks; cover tightly and continue roasting, basting occasionally, until well done, or for about 1¼ hours longer.

In the meantime remove the outer leaves from the cabbage, quarter and core it and shred fine with sharp knife.

Wash in cold water, place in a large pan, sprinkle with 2 teaspoons salt and cover with boiling water.

Bring to a boil, skim carefully and boil for 5 minutes.

A teaspoon of caraway seeds cooked with the cabbage enhances the flavor, in my opinion, but this is optional.

Drain the cabbage thoroughly.

When the ducks are done, remove them temporarily from the roasting pan and drain off all the juice in the pan into a small saucepan.

Allow the juice to stand for a while, place the ducks back in the roasting pan and continue cooking, uncovered this time, while you skim off all the fat from the gravy.

Put the drained cabbage in a large saucepan, add 4 tablespoons butter and ¼ teaspoon coarsely ground pepper, pour the gravy over the cabbage and heat thoroughly.

Place the ducks on a deep, large, hot platter, garnish with parsley and surround with piping hot cabbage.

Serve at once, to be carved at the table.

Tiny boiled potatoes and buttered fresh green peas would be good with this, likewise a good red wine.

1658
A GAMMON OF BACON BAKED

Take your Gammon, and after you have watered it, that it is pretty fresh, then seethe it until it be very tender, then take off the skin and farce it with parsley, penny-royal, Thyme, Marjoram, Marigolds, Camomile and Sage, let all these be chopped small, and seasoned with salt, pepper, cloves, small raisins, yolks of eggs, hard roasted, cut off the lean of your bacon and mince it small, and taking a handful of farcing, mingle it together with three or four yolks of raw eggs and cast it on the Gammon of Bacon, closing the skin again, put it into paste.

MODERN VERSION
BAKED BACON
(Serves 8)

Preheat oven to 350° F.

> *4-pound piece of good Irish bacon or heavy lean American bacon*
> *⅔ cup chopped parsley*
> *1½ cups Pepperidge Farm Stuffing*
> *2 eggs*
> *¼ teaspoon cloves*
> *¼ teaspoon marjoram*
> *¼ teaspoon sage*
> *¼ teaspoon thyme*
> *¼ teaspoon cracked pepper*
> *½ teaspoon salt*
> *½ cup raisins (seedless)*
> *2 cups broth in which the bacon was simmered*

Wash the bacon in warm water, scrubbing the rind quite well.

Put the bacon into a saucepan and cover with cold water.

Bring very slowly to the boiling point (this will take at least 1¼ hours).

Skim carefully and simmer gently until tender, or for about 1¾ hours.

When cooked, remove from the water and, with the aid of a sharp knife, take off the bacon skin.

Score the underside and stretch the bacon out flat in a baking dish.

Make a mixture of the Pepperidge Farm Stuffing, parsley and raisins (washed in warm water), and increase seasoning by adding the cloves, marjoram, sage, thyme, cracked pepper and salt.

Beat 2 eggs together with ½ cup cold water, and stir into the crumb mixture.

Spread over the bacon.

Add 2 cups broth in which the bacon was cooked, and place in a moderate (350° F.) oven.

Cook, basting occasionally, for about 45 minutes, or until all the juice has evaporated.

Serve on a hot platter, to be cut crosswise in thin slices.

Accompany with plain boiled potatoes, cabbage and sweet gherkin pickles.

1658
HOW TO BOIL A CAPON HANDSOMELY

Take the fat end of a neck of mutton, and cut it into two or three pieces, making one piece of two or three bones; and boil these with your Capon; and of herbs taken an handful of parsley, as much Thime, and half as much Endive, and bind them up in a bunch together and boil them with your Capon; when it is boiled enough, season it with salt and Verjuice; then take a deep dish and cut into it sops of fine stale Manchet, and scald them with the fat which cometh off the Capon and Mutton; you must boil readie in a Pippin or some skillet, half a pound of choice prunes, will they be well and plump, but not overboiled, and when you serve up your Capon, garnish the dish sides with your Prunes, and lay them thick upon your Capon. You may also boil some marrow with your Prunes, and lay it on your Capon.

MODERN VERSION
BOILED CAPON
(Serves 6)

Preheat oven to 450° F.

> 1 good fat capon
> 6 carrots, scraped and cut in half
> 6 stalks celery
> ½ teaspoon thyme
> 2 large onions, peeled
> salt to taste
> 2½ quarts warm water
> 3 dozen plump pitted cooked prunes
> 2 tablespoons butter
> 6 slices white bread, crusts removed
> parsley
> 1 pound endives
> 1 teaspoon sugar
> juice of ½ lemon

For the sauce
> 6 tablespoons butter
> 6 tablespoons flour
> 1 cup heavy cream
> nutmeg
> pepper

Wash, dry and truss the capon.

Place it on a trivet in a roasting pan and pour the warm water over it.

Bring very slowly to the simmering point, skimming it carefully.

Add the onions, celery and carrots.

Stand by and skim again when it comes to the simmering point.

Season to taste with about 2 tablespoons salt and the thyme.

Cover tightly and simmer gently until tender, or for about 2½ to 3 hours, counting from the time you add the salt and thyme.

Turn it over once or twice as it cooks.

Meanwhile wash the endives and cut off a bit of each root end.

Remove the crusts from 6 slices white bread and cut in two, making triangles.

Pit the prunes and place in a little pan with 2 tablespoons butter.

Skim off a bit of the fat from the capon and place it in a saucer.

Dip your bread quickly in and out of the fat and place on flat tins.

Place in the oven and allow to brown lightly.

Keep warm.

Put the endives in a small saucepan, squeeze the juice of half a lemon over them and cover with 1½ cups of the broth from the capon, straining it through a fine sieve.

Cover tightly and cook gently until tender, or for about 45 minutes.

Add the sugar and continue cooking until all the juice has boiled dry and the endives begin to brown slightly on the bottom.

Remove from the heat and keep warm.

Half an hour before you will be serving the capon, remove the cover and turn off the heat.

With the aid of a small knife, remove as much skin from the bird as possible without destroying its shape.

Cover and keep warm over very low heat while you make the sauce.

Melt 6 tablespoons butter in the top of a double boiler, stir in 6 tablespoons flour, cook for 1 minute without browning it, stirring constantly with a wooden spoon, and add gradually about 2½ cups strained broth from the capon, making a thick, smooth sauce.

Season to taste with nutmeg and pepper, and stir in gradually 1 cup heavy cream.

Keep warm over boiling water while you dish up the handsome bird.

Place on a very large hot platter, remove the strings, and cover the bird with part of the sauce.

Garnish with the prunes (which must be heated before using), the toast and the carrots from the broth.

Place a large bunch of parsley in the cavity, and send to the table to be carved and served on hot plates.

Serve with it the endives piping hot, sprinkled with parsley and the remainder of the sauce.

A handsomely boiled capon indeed!

1658
FRICASSEE OF LAMB

Cut your meat in thin slices, season it with nutmeg, pepper and salt, mince some thyme and lemmon, and throw it upon your meat; then fry it slightly in a pan, then throw in two eggs, beaten in verjuice and sugar, into the pan, also a handful of gooseberries, shake it together and dish it.

MODERN VERSION
FRICASSEE OF LAMB
(Serves 8)

4 pounds breast of lamb, cut for stew
2 quarts boiling water
¾ teaspoon thyme
¼ teaspoon nutmeg
1 large onion, peeled
3 slices lemon, including the rind
a few peppercorns
2 teaspoons salt
chopped parsley
4 eggs
6 tablespoons butter
6 tablespoons flour
1 14-ounce jar whole gooseberries

The day before you wish to serve this delicious dish, place the breast of lamb, cut in pieces suitable for stewing, in a saucepan and pour the boiling water over it.

Bring to the simmering point, skim carefully and add the thyme, nutmeg, peppercorns, salt, onion and slices of lemon.

Simmer, tightly covered, for about 2¼ hours, by which time it should be nice and tender.

Remove the meat from the broth and spread out on a platter to cool.

Strain the juice through a fine sieve.

As soon as the meat is cool enough to handle, take it piece by piece and remove all fat, bone, gristle and bits of white membrane you may encounter.

Place the good meat in a saucepan and strain over it the broth.

When cold, place in the refrigerator overnight, or until ready to complete the dish.

The lamb fat will rise to the surface of the broth in the refrigerator and solidify.

Remove the fat, place on low heat to warm and add a cupful of gooseberries (which come preserved in a heavy syrup, but do not include any of the syrup).

In the meantime hard-boil the eggs for 10 to 15 minutes, drop in cold water and immediately remove the shells.

Place back in the warm water while you thicken the juice on the meat by stirring in the flour creamed with the butter.

Stir well but gently, and simmer for 10 to 15 minutes before serving.

Place in a hot serving dish, garnish with the eggs cut in thick slices and a sprinkle of chopped parsley.

Serve on hot plates accompanied by little boiled potatoes (these are a must) and creamed celery (as an extra treat).

1658
TO MAKE VEAL TOOTS OR VEAL OLIVES

Take the kidney of a loyne of Veal roasted, with a good deal of the fat, and a little of the flesh, mince it very small and put to it two eggs, one nutmeg finely grated, a good quantity of sugar, a few currans, a little salt, stir them well together and make them into the form of little pastries, and fry them in a pan with sweet butter.

MODERN VERSION
VEAL-KIDNEY SCRAMBLED EGGS
(Serves 4)

2 veal kidneys
8 eggs
1 teaspoon nutmeg (scant)
½ cup milk
½ teaspoon salt
¼ teaspoon pepper

[*332*]

½ teaspoon sugar
3 tablespoons olive oil
3 tablespoons butter
6 slices hot buttered toast

From the veal kidneys trim off the fat and the thin filament surrounding them.

Split in two and remove the white core.

Slice into small pieces, discarding all the white part encountered.

Break the eggs into a bowl and beat well with a wire whisk, adding the milk.

Place the olive oil and butter in a frying pan and heat until bubbling hot.

Add the kidneys and cook 2 to 3 minutes, stirring constantly.

Season them to taste with the salt, pepper, nutmeg and sugar.

Add the beaten eggs and cook over very low heat, stirring well, until the eggs are soft and creamy.

Serve on hot buttered toast.

1658
FRICASSEE OF CHICKENS

Kill your chickens, pull skin and feathers off together, cut them in thin slices, season them with thime and lemmon minced, nutmeg and salt, and handful of sorrel minced, and then fry it well with six spoonsfuls of water, and some fresh butter; when it is tender, take three spoonsfuls of verjuice, one spoonful of sugar, beat it together, to dish it with sippets about.

MODERN VERSION
FRICASSEE OF CHICKEN
(Serves 6)

1 4¼-pound stewing chicken, cut up for fricassee,
*   the breast cut in 4*
5 cups water
salt and pepper to taste
1 large onion
½ bay leaf

1 leek
4 stalks celery
¼ teaspoon thyme
¼ teaspoon nutmeg
2 slices unpeeled lemon
4 tablespoons flour
4 tablespoons butter
½ cup canned sorrel
½ cup heavy cream
6–8 sippets (large croutons)

Singe, wash and dry the pieces of chicken.

Place the neck, back and giblets in a pan, cover with the water, bring to the boiling point, skim carefully, add the leek, celery, onion, bay leaf and thyme and simmer for about 1 hour.

Strain through a fine sieve.

Place the remainder of the chicken in a large pot, add the lemon slices and pour over it the broth.

Bring gently to the boiling point, skim carefully and simmer gently until tender, or for about 1½ hours.

Drain off the broth and as soon as the chicken is cool enough to handle, pick off as much skin as possible.

Place chicken in an ovenproof casserole, pour about ½ cup broth over all and keep warm on very low heat while you make the sauce.

Melt the butter in a saucepan, add the flour and stir with a wooden spoon; cook for a minute or two without browning, then add gradually 3 cups broth, making a smooth sauce.

Add the sorrel, stir well, season to taste with salt, pepper and about ¼ teaspoon nutmeg.

Simmer for a minute or two, then stir in gradually the heavy cream.

Pour over the chicken and garnish with triangular sippets (croutons) browned in chicken fat or butter.

Serve at once, with fluffy mashed potatoes and buttered carrots.

1658
TO ROAST A SHOULDER OF MUTTON WITH LEMMONS

Take a shoulder of mutton half roasted. Cut off most of the meat thereof in thin slices into a fair dish, with the gravie thereof, put thereto about the quantity of a pint of claret wine, with a spoonful or two at most of the best Wine vinegar, season it with Nutmegs and a little Ginger; then pare off the rindes of one or two good Lemmons, and slice them thin into the Mutton, when it is almost well stewed between two dishes, and so let them stew together two or three walms; when they are enough put them in a clean dish with some slices and rinde of the Lemmons, and so serve it.

MODERN VERSION
ROAST LAMB OR MUTTON
(Serves 6)

Preheat oven to 450° F.

5 pounds boned and rolled shoulder of lamb or mutton
4 tablespoons soft butter
2 cups red Bordeaux wine
2 cups bouillon
salt and pepper to taste
¼ teaspoon nutmeg
¼ teaspoon powdered ginger
4 tablespoons flour
4 tablespoons fat
1 lemon
chopped parsley
½ cup candied ginger slices, chopped fine

Buy a shoulder of lamb or mutton weighing about 5 pounds, and ask your butcher to bone and roll it and trim off the excess fat.

Place the roast in a small roasting pan and rub the top with the butter.

Place in a 450° F. oven and roast until lightly browned, or

for about 20 minutes; reduce the heat to 350° and continue cooking for about 50 to 60 minutes longer.

It should be pink inside when done.

Remove from the pan and prepare for the messy job of slicing the meat in thin slivers, discarding all fat and undesirable bits.

Place in a hot casserole and keep warm while you make the gravy.

Pour off the fat in the roasting pan and measure it.

You should have about 4 tablespoons of it.

If not, make up the difference with butter.

Return to the roasting pan and stir in the flour.

Stir with a wooden spoon until lightly browned, then add the bouillon, stirring constantly until free from lumps; then stir in the red Bordeaux wine.

Season to taste with salt, pepper and the powdered ginger and nutmeg.

Simmer gently while you slice the lemon very thin.

Remove the seeds and add the slices to the sauce.

At this point add the candied ginger, cut into tiny bits.

Pour the sauce over the meat, sprinkle with parsley and serve immediately on hot plates.

Mashed potatoes go well with this dish.

Note: This dish is even better warmed up. Place the covered casserole in a hot (500° F.) oven until bubbling hot and serve.

1658
A RICE PUDDING

Take thin Creame, or good milk of what quantity you please, boil it on the fire with a little Cinnamon in it, and when it hath boiled a while, take out the cinnamon, and put in Rosewater and sugar enough to make it good and sweet; then having your rice ready beaten as fine as flour (and searced as some do it) throw it in, till it be of thickness, of a hasty pudding: then pour it into a dish, and serve it at the Table.

My favorite rice pudding is the old-fashioned creamy pudding, so easy to make.

[*336*]

MODERN VERSION
RICE PUDDING
(Serves 4)

Preheat oven to 300° F.

> *1 quart milk*
> *⅓ cup rice*
> *½ teaspoon salt*
> *½ cup sugar*
> *dash of cinnamon*
> *2 tablespoons rosewater*

Butter a 2-quart casserole.

Put the rice into a strainer and let cold water from the tap run through it for a few minutes.

Put the washed rice in the casserole.

Pour in the milk.

Add the seasonings and stir well.

Bake for 3 hours in a slow oven (300° F.).

Stir every 15 minutes during the first hour to keep the rice from staying in the bottom of the casserole.

When cooked, sprinkle 2 tablespoons rosewater over the top.

Serve hot or cold, with or without cream.

LES DELICES

DE LA CAMPAGNE,

Suitte du JARDINIER FRANÇOIS,

Où est enseigné à preparer pour l'usage de la vie tout ce qui croist sur la Terre, & dans les Eaux.

Dedié aux Dames Mesnageres.

SECONDE EDITION,
augmentée par l'Autheur.

A AMSTERDAM,
Chez IEAN BLAEV.
M. DC. LXI.

EPISTRE AVX DAMES.

MESDAMES,

I'ay toûjours fait tant d'estime de vostre Vertu, qui est particulierement loüable à cause de l'habitude que vous vous estes acquises à perseverer dans le travail, reiglant si bien vostre famille, que vous faites admirer par tout la conduite de vostre gouvernement ; & je suis si fort porté à vous honorer, quand je considere que c'est par vostre œconomie que les maisons non seulement subsistent dans la splendeur de leur lustre, mais encore augmentent de beaucoup, par le bon ordre que vous y apportez ; Car ve-rita-

* 3

This, too, is a book of very small size, being only 2¾ inches wide. It was printed in French in 1661 and modestly proclaims that it "teaches for Life's Use the Preparation of All that grows on the Earth and in the Sea."

The detailed instructions for running a household give the impression of limitless numbers of helpers. If only the author could see our self-service pushbutton life today!

The introduction to this book, which I give here in my own translation, is entitled

An Epistle to the Ladies

MESDAMES, I have always had much esteem for your virtue, which is particularly praiseworthy because you have made it your custom to persevere in the task of regulating your family so well that you are admired everywhere for the conduct of your government, and I am so strongly persuaded to honor you when I consider that it is by your economies that your homes retain their splendor and indeed are greatly increased in their glory by the good order which you maintain. Because truthfully the gentlemen, your husbands, would trouble themselves in vain to acquire much wealth if you did not dispense it usefully.

I have estimated that it was only reasonable to contribute my elegy to your care with all my power and also that my insatiable curiosity which I have had all my life to know a little about everything has led me to know about you, and I address to you this little book entitled *The Delights of the Country*. Pardon any delinquencies which you remark even though I brought all possible curiosity to avoid them. Excuse the faults of him who has always esteemed as the greatest favor all the occasions which have been presented to make known to you the strong passion which he has always had to be esteemed by the ladies.

This book offers much advice for running the household and setting the table. The following table instructions are of interest for their picture of the extreme luxury and lavish service some households enjoyed in the seventeenth century.

For a company of thirty people of high position and who should be treated sumptuously, it was the opinion that one would dress a table with as many places, at a distance one from another of the space of a chair, putting fourteen on each side and one at the head and one at the bottom. The table should be large enough and the tablecloth drop to the ground on all sides; there should be salt cellars and forks and dish holders in the middle to put the platters on.

On going to the table, one would be served from thirty basins, in which there would be soup. Some basins would have soup with meat in pieces and the others hash on soaked bread, to be served alternately, also putting at the top end of the table a good vegetable soup and at the other a queen's soup made of partridge or pheasant, also a hash of mushrooms or artichokes.

The second service was composed of all kinds of ragouts, such as fricassees, roast venison, pâtés in pastry crusts, tongues, sausage, melons and fruits in season, with some little ragouts and salads in the middle.

The third service was large roasts—partridge, pheasant, chicken, hare, whole lambs, putting oranges, lemons, olives and sauceboats in the middle.

The fourth service was small roasts—snipe, larks, ortolans, sweetbreads.

Fifth service was fish—salmon, trout, carp, pike and fish mousse.

Sixth service was all kinds of sweets—eggs and jellies of all colors and "Blanc Manger" (white puddings).

Seventh service was fruit in season with cream and almonds.

[*340*]

Eighth service was conserves, liquid and dry, marzipan, jams and ices. On the plates, branches of fennel powdered with sugar of all colors, with toothpicks. Grapes and chocolate.

For the butler, this author had many suggestions. In the first place, he should serve always from the right side, if he could, for the convenience of the hand which held the platters.

In the second place, he had to have an assistant to take away from the other side as the butler served, and they must leave only four places empty at a time.

In the third place, he must not place a platter of big meat in front of important people, in order not to block the view of the table.

It was necessary for the butler to know what was going on at other entertainments so that he could learn some novelties!

To maintain good order in his spending, he must have the good will of those he would deal with, and his spending must be regulated so that the meat dishes would cost no more than one third of the total expenses of the banquet!

Here are a few gems from this book.

1661
PUMPKIN BREAD

To make pumpkin bread, it is necessary to parboil the pumpkin as you would to fricassee and pass it through a heavy towel to take out the little nerves which are therein, adding the water in which the pumpkin was cooked as much as is necessary to knead in the ordinary way—and governing your dough for two raisings, and thus, as I say, before you will make a good bread which will be a little fat when cooked and yellow which is excellent for those who have need of refreshment and to have a free stomach.

MODERN VERSION
PUMPKIN MUFFINS
(Makes 30 muffins)

Preheat oven to 425–450° F.

> *1 teaspoon baking soda*
> *2 cups white flour*
> *2 cups yellow cornmeal*
> *2 tablespoons baking powder*
> *2 teaspoons salt*
> *½ cup liquid honey*
> *½ cup light molasses*
> *1 cup canned or cooked pumpkin*
> *3 well-beaten eggs*
> *½ cup melted butter (¼ pound)*
> *2 cups buttermilk*

Sift together the flour, cornmeal, baking soda, baking powder and salt.

Beat the eggs well.

Add the pumpkin, honey, molasses and buttermilk, and mix thoroughly.

Add the sifted dry ingredients and beat with a spoon until well mixed; last of all stir in the melted butter.

Fill well-greased muffin tins ⅔ full and bake at 425° to 450° F. until nice and brown, or for about 18 to 20 minutes.

Serve hot with lots of butter.

[*342*]

1661
TO PRESERVE EGGS

To preserve an egg for a long time in all its goodness and that it will appear fresh with the milk within it, it is first necessary that it be quickly taken from the chicken, put it in fresh water well covered and do not take it out until you want to eat it. This is a very easy experience to do and has been well proven. The reason is that, being in the water, the very delicate milk of the egg cannot evaporate. If you keep it a long time it is well to change the water several times.

MODERN VERSION

Eggs can be preserved by protecting them from air. They can be kept for six months in an earthenware crock well covered with a solution of waterglass (p. 101). Have at least 2 inches of the solution over the eggs and keep in a cool place. These eggs are not good for boiling but excellent for other types of cooking.

1661
BOILED EGGS

Everyone has his manner of cooking boiled eggs. One puts them in the pan on the fire with cold water and as soon as the water starts its first boiling take out the egg.

Another wants the water to be boiling before putting in the egg and then count just up to the number of 200, pronouncing distinctly, and then take the egg out of the water.

These two methods are not as certain as one which is much better because it cooks the egg equally just into the middle instead of the other two previous methods, which do nothing but seize the white of the egg and the center is often not even heated.

I would say therefore that the most certain fashion to well cook an egg and the easiest to practice is to put on the fire two pints of water in a saucepan and when it commences its first boiling, put

[*343*]

in the eggs and at the same time take the saucepan off the fire, put it on the ground close to the andirons and when the water has cooled enough to pull the eggs out with your hand without annoying you, they will be cooked perfectly.

Another method is to cook eggs right in the hot ashes, but you must make a little hole in the big end for fear the egg will crack, or else when it commences to heat up put a drop or two of water on the end.

MODERN VERSION

Just about the same today as in 1661—but we can by-pass the hot-ashes method!

1661
VEAL AND BEEF

Of all the animals with four legs, veal is the most natural food for feeble stomachs and is that which doctors order most often for their patients because of its refreshing qualities and good nourishment.

MODERN VERSION

Today's doctors and dietitians prescribe beef as one of the best of high-protein foods.

1661
CALF'S LIVER

Lard the whole liver and cook in a casserole with butter, wine, water, salt, spices, orange or lemon rind, a bay leaf. When cooked, add a little cream to the juices.

MODERN VERSION

I would do just as above and experiment with the same seasonings. I would use 1 cup white wine and 1 cup chicken broth for the liquid, but I shall leave it to my readers to invent their own versions!

1661
SHOULDER OF VEAL

Roast the shoulder, basting with butter while cooking.

The best part of the shoulder is a little fat muscle, found under the skin, which is called the ear of the shoulder.

MODERN VERSION

No change here.

Use a slow oven (300° F.) and allow 30 minutes per pound.

1661
BREAST OF VEAL

The breast is excellent to boil. One can put stuffing between the skin and the little bones, or boil it and then powder it with flour and fry in butter.

MODERN VERSION

This is just about how I do it today.

Drop the pieces of breast of veal into boiling water seasoned with an onion, and simmer for 1 hour. When you remove the pieces from the broth, the little bones will slip out.

A
QUEENS DELIGHT:
OR
The ART
OF
Preserving, *Conserving*, and *Candying* ;

As also
A right Knowledge of
making PERFUMES, and
Diſtilling the moſt
Excellent Waters,

Never before Publiſhed.

Printed by *J. G.* for *Nath. Brooks*, at the
Angel in *Cornhill*, 1663.

This book was printed in 1663 and was "never published be-fore."

Along with the usual medical and surgical "recipes," it spe-cializes in perfumes and distilled waters for cosmetic use.

One chapter is headed "Choice Secrets Made Known," and one daring recipe is entitled quite simply and directly "How to Make Hair Grow."

Another one sounds like a witch's brew: "A Water for a Consumption or for a Brain That Is Weak." This one is made with milk, wine, flowers, herbs and seeds, licorice, a cock that has been chased and beaten before he was killed, and white sugar candy.

Then there is "Water of Time for the Passion of the Heart."

Another intriguing one is "A Receipt to Make Damnable Hum!"

The author tells us that this book hath had a generall Receiption, travelling up and down the Kingdoms, and like the good Samaritane giving comfort to all it met; neither have we known of any that have bought it, who have not certified their high Esteem thereof. And indeed how should it otherwise be, knowing out of what Elaboratories it was produced? Nor is it without its variety, here preserving the Fruits of the Earth with such a curious neatnesse.

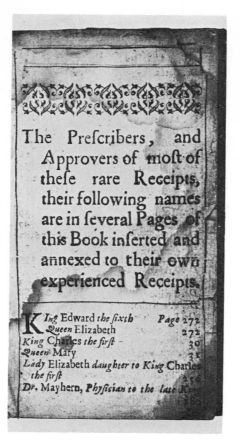

The Prescribers, and Approvers of most of these rare Receipts, their following names are in several Pages of this Book inserted and annexed to their own experienced Receipts.

The Approvers Names.		The Approvers Names.	
Dr. Bates	186	Mr. Phillips *Apothecary*	296
Dr. King	284	Bp. Lawd *Archbishop of* Canterbury	275
Dr. Mountford	290	Bishop of Worcester	19
Dr. Forster	176,177	Earl of *Arundel* CC.	3
Dr. More	178	Lord *Treasurer*	32
Dr. Butler	1,2,293	Lord Bacon *Vic. of* St. Albans	281
Dr. Bassa, *an Italian*	7,8	Lord Vic. Conway CC.	99
Dr. Adrian Gilbert	11	Lord Spencer	283
Dr. Atkinson	17,160	Lord Sheffeld	62
Dr. Goffe	121	Sir Walter Raleigh	274
Dr. Stephens	21,87,140,275	Thomas Mayner	33
Dr. Price	24	Sir Edward Terrel	40
Dr. Read	39	Sir Edward Bolstward	72
Dr. May	47	Sir Edward Spencer	28
Dr. Blacksmith	55,56,83	Sir Kenelm Digby	290
Dr. Brasdale	59	Mr. *Justice* Hutton	191
Dr. Frier	55,173	Countess of Arundel	25,49,168
Dr. Atkins	65,73,74,83	Countess of Worcester	69
Dr. Gifford	3	Countess of Oxford	56
Dr. Twine	82,288	Countess of Kent	274
Dr. Wetherborn	89	Countess of Rutland CC.	109
Dr. Lewkener	134,154	Lady Mounteagle	141
Dr. Eglestone	136	Lady Abergany CC.	42
Dr. Soper	147	Lady Nevel	147,163
Mr. Stepkins *Occulist*	18,130	Lady Spotiwood	286
Mr. Penton *Chyrur.*	24	Lady Drury	44
Mr. Francis Cox *Chyrur.*	66	Lady Gifford	299
Mr. Lumley *Chyrur.*	123	Lady Hobby	11
Mr. Thomas Potter *Chyrur.*	145	Lady Leonard	158
Mr.		*Lady.*	

1663
TO PRESERVE GRAPES

Take Grapes when they be almost through ripe, and cut the
stalks off, and stone them in the side, and as fast as you can stone
them, strew sugar on them; you must take to every pound of
Grapes three quarters of a pound of Sugar, then take some of the
sower Grapes, and wring the juyce of them, and put to every
pound of Grapes two spoonfuls of juyce, then set them on the
fire, and still lift up the pan and shake it round, for fear of burning to, then set them on again, and when the Sugar is melted,
boil them as fast as you can possibly, and when they look very
clear, and the syrup somewhat thick, they are enough.

MODERN VERSION
PRESERVED GRAPES

Take ripe seedless green grapes from the stems, wash them
and for every pound of grapes use ¾ pound sugar.

Make a syrup by boiling each cup of sugar with 1 cup water,
1 tablespoon lemon juice and a little grated lemon rind.

Drop the grapes into the boiling syrup, boil until tender but not
broken, fill into hot sterilized jars and seal.

[*349*]

1663
CANDY ORANGE PEELS AFTER THE ITALIAN WAY

Take Orange peels so often steeped in cold water, as you think convenient for their bitterness, then dry them gently, and candy them with some convenient syrup made with Sugar; some that are more grown, take away that spongious white under the yellow peels, others do both together.

MODERN VERSION
CANDIED ORANGE PEEL

Prepare orange peel in thin strips, removing all the white part inside the skin.

Cover the strips with boiling water and let stand for ½ hour.

Pour off the water and boil in fresh water for 20 minutes.

Prepare a heavy syrup of 2 cups sugar and 1 cup water.

Boil the peel in the syrup until tender and then remove from the syrup.

Cool and sprinkle with granulated sugar.

1663
CONSERVES OF VIOLETS IN THE ITALIAN MANNER

Take the leaves of Blew Violets separated from their stalks and greens, beat them very well in a stone Mortar, with twice their weight of Sugar, and reserve them for your use in a glass vessel.

The heat of Choler it doth mitigate, extinguisheth thirst, asswageth the Belly, and helpeth the Throat of hot hurts, sharp droppings, and dryness, and procureth rest. It will keep one year.

MODERN VERSION

I give up here!

1663
TO PICKLE CUCUMBERS

Put them in an Earthen Vessel, lay first a Lay of Salt and Dill, then a lay of Cucumbers, and so till they be all Layed, put in some Mace and whole pepper, and some Fennel-seed according to direction, then fill it up with Beer-Vinegar, and a clean board and a stone upon it to keep them within the pickle, and so keep them close covered, and if the Vinegar is black, change them into fresh.

MODERN VERSION

See Dill Cucumber Pickles (p. 186).

1663
TO BOYLE A RUMP OF BEEF AFTER THE FRENCH FASHION

Take a rump of beef, or the little end of the Brisket, and parboyle it half an houre, then take it up and put it in a deep Dish, then slash it in the side that the gravy may come out, then throw a little Pepper and Salt between every cut, then fill up the Dish with the best Claret wine, and put to it three or foure pieces of large Mace, and set it on the coales close covered, and boyle it above an houre and a half, but turn it often in the mean time; then with a spoon take off the fat and fill it with Claret wine, and slice six Onyons, and a handful of Capers or broom buds, half a dozen of hard Letice sliced, three spoonfuls of wine-vinegar and as much verjuyce, and then set it a boyling with these things in it till it be tender, and serve it up with brown Bread and Sippets fryed with butter, but be sure there be not too much fat in it when you serve it.

MODERN VERSION
POT ROAST

(Serves 6)

4 pounds beef, rump or chuck
garlic

> *pepper and salt*
> *flour*
> *2 cups canned beef consommé or water*
> *1 onion, sliced*
> *2 stalks celery, sliced*
> *bay leaf*
> *red wine*
> *2 tablespoons butter*

Rub the beef with garlic and sprinkle with pepper and salt.

Roll in flour.

In a heavy pot melt a piece of beef suet and brown the meat well on all sides.

Add the consommé or 2 cups water, the onion, celery, bay leaf and red wine.

Simmer for 3 hours.

Do not boil!

Thicken the gravy with the butter and 2 tablespoons flour creamed together.

Serve with hot buttered noodles.

1663

TO MAKE A STEAK PIE, WITH A FRENCH PUDDING IN THE PIE

Season your steaks with pepper and nutmegs, and let it stand an hour in a tray, then take a piece of the leanest of a Leg of Mutton, and mince it small with Suet, and a few sweet herbs, tops of yong time, a branch of Penniroyal, two or three of red sage, grated bread, yolks of eggs, sweet Cream, Raisins of the Sun; work all together like a pudding with your hand stiff, and roul them around like balls, and put them into the steaks in a deep coffin, with a piece of sweet Butter; sprinkle a little Verjuyce on it, bake it, then cut it up, and roul sage leaves and fry them, and stick them upright in the walls, and serve your Pie without a cover, with the juyce of an Orange or Limon.

 MODERN VERSION

BEEF STEW WITH LAMB QUENELLES

(Serves 6)

Preheat oven to 375° F.

> 3 pounds lean sirloin steak
> 1 small piece beef suet
> ¼ cup flour
> 2 teaspoons granulated sugar
> 2 tablespoons melted butter
> 4 cans beef broth
> 2 small bay leaves
> ½ teaspoon thyme
> ¼ teaspoon powdered dried mint leaves
> ¼ teaspoon powdered sage
> ½ pound raw lean lamb steak run through a
>   meat grinder twice
> 2 egg yolks
> 1 whole egg
> 1 cup Pepperidge Farm Stuffing
> 2 scraped carrots, cut in 1-inch pieces
> 1½ dozen peeled white onions
> 1 cup milk
> ¼ teaspoon oregano
> ¼ teaspoon nutmeg
> pinch of sage
> ¼ cup seedless raisins, cut in two
> salt and pepper to taste
> strained juice of 1 lemon
> 1 tablespoon chopped parsley

ADMIRAL THE HON
JOHN BENBOW

Cut the beef into 1½-inch squares, discarding all the fat and white connecting tissue.

Wipe dry on paper toweling.

Render a piece of suet over low heat in a large frying pan until you have 4 tablespoons melted fat.

Discard the remaining piece of suet and add the meat.

Brown carefully on all sides.

In the meantime heat 3 cans beef broth in a separate pan.

Sprinkle the meat with the sugar, stir for a minute or two, then sprinkle with the flour.

Stir and add gradually the hot broth.

When it has thickened, transfer the whole to a casserole containing the melted butter.

Add the bay leaves, thyme, mint leaves, ¼ teaspoon sage and a very little salt and pepper to taste.

Also at this time add the carrots.

Cover the casserole and place in a preheated 375° F. oven to bake slowly for about 2 hours, or until tender.

Cook separately 1½ dozen little white onions until just tender.

Drain and add to the stew when it is done.

In the meantime make some lamb quenelles (a form of dumpling) in the following manner:

Run the Pepperidge Farm Stuffing through the meat grinder, using the medium blade, or roll to fine crumbs with a roller.

Stir in the milk.

Add the oregano, nutmeg and pinch of sage.

Set aside, covered with waxed paper.

To the stuffing add the raisins and the ground lamb.

Stir well, adding one at a time the egg yolks, followed by the whole egg.

When smooth and well mixed, heat in a shallow pan 1 can beef bouillon diluted with 1 can water.

When it comes to the boiling point, reduce the heat.

With 2 teaspoons, form the quenelles mixture into oval-shaped balls and slip them into the bouillon, being careful not to crowd them.

Cook for about 10 minutes, turning them over once during the process.

Place the quenelles on top of the hot stew (from which you should have skimmed off any excess fat), sprinkle with parsley and lemon juice and serve at once.

1663
TO BAKE RED DEER

Parboil it, and then sauce it in vinegar, then lard it very thick, and season it with pepper, ginger, and nutmeg, put it into a deep pie with good store of sweet butter and let it bake, when it is baked, take a pint of Hippocras, half a pound of sweet butter, two or three Nutmegs, a little Vinegar, pour it into the Pie in the Oven and let it lie and soak an hour, then take it out, and when it is cold stop the vent hole.

[*354*]

MODERN VERSION
VENISON TARTS
(Serves 6)

Plain Pastry with Butter (p. 154)
3 pounds venison steak, cut 1½ inches thick
2 large onions
1½ cups red Burgundy wine
½ cup beef bouillon
¼ cup olive oil
1 cup wine vinegar
1 teaspoon salt
½ teaspoon coarsely ground pepper
1½ teaspoons nutmeg
1½ teaspoons ginger
¼ pound butter plus 2 tablespoons
2 tablespoons flour
1 tablespoon chopped parsley
1 egg yolk
2 tablespoons cream

Place the venison steak in a large casserole.

Surround it with 2 large onions, peeled and sliced fine.

Mix together the wine vinegar, 1 cup red Burgundy wine, the olive oil, salt, pepper, 1 teaspoon nutmeg and 1 teaspoon ginger.

Pour over the venison steak, cover and place in the refrigerator at noon the day before the party.

Turn the steak over occasionally and leave it in the refrigerator to marinate until noon the next day.

At this time remove the dish from the refrigerator and let it stand at room temperature until you are ready to start cooking it.

Preheat the oven to 450° F.

Mix 1 recipe of plain pastry and line a rectangular baking dish 6 by 10 by 2 inches, managing to make a heavy rolled edge, prettily crimped.

Paint the edge with the egg yolk beaten with the cream.

Prick thoroughly all over to prevent bubbles forming.

Bake for 18 to 20 minutes, or until lightly browned.

Remove from the oven.

Increase the temperature of the oven to 500° F.

Remove the steak from the marinade and place it on a plate.

Sponge it well on both sides with paper toweling.

Strain the marinade, discard the onions and wash the casserole.

Place the steak back in the casserole, dot with ¼ pound butter, place in the very hot oven for 15 minutes, basting with the butter, then reduce the heat to 350° F.

Heat together ½ cup red Burgundy wine and ½ cup beef bouillon; pour over the steak, cover the dish and cook gently for another 30 minutes, basting occasionally.

Ladle off most of the juice and let it stand for a few minutes, then skim off the fat.

Cream together 2 tablespoons butter and the flour.

Stir this into the hot juice, bring to a boil, stir in ¼ cup of the marinade, add ½ teaspoon nutmeg, ½ teaspoon ginger and salt to taste.

Simmer until thickened, and keep warm over hot water.

Place the pastry shell back in the oven to heat through while you cut the steak crosswise in thin slices.

Lay these neatly in the hot shell, pour the hot sauce over all, sprinkle with chopped parsley and send to the table to be cut and served, giving each person a generous piece of the crust.

Serve with this a purée of chestnuts; red cabbage; and the same good red Burgundy wine used in the recipe.

1663
TO MAKE A CAKE THE WAY OF THE ROYAL PRINCESS, THE LADY ELIZABETH, DAUGHTER TO KING CHARLES THE FIRST

Take half a peck of Flower, half a pint of rose-water, a pint of Ale yeast, a pint of Cream, boil it, a pound and a half of butter, six Eggs (leave out the whites), four pound of Currans, one half pound of sugar, one Nutmeg, and a little Salt, work it very well, and let it stand half an hour by the fire, and then work it again, and then make it up, and let it stand an hour and a half in the Oven; let not your Oven be too hot.

This sounds like good old Kugelhupf to me!

MODERN VERSION
KUGELHUPF
(Makes 1 cake)

Preheat oven to 350° F.

½ cup milk
½ cup sugar
½ teaspoon salt
¼ cup (½ stick) margarine or butter
¼ cup very warm water
1 package or cake yeast,
    dry or compressed
2 eggs, beaten
2 cups unsifted flour
2 tablespoons bread crumbs
14–16 whole blanched almonds
½ cup seedless raisins
½ teaspoon grated lemon peel
¼ teaspoon nutmeg

Scald the milk; stir in the sugar, salt and margarine or butter.
Cool to lukewarm.
Measure the very warm water into a bowl.
Sprinkle or crumble in the yeast; stir until dissolved.
Stir in the lukewarm milk mixture.
Add the beaten eggs and flour.
Beat vigorously for about 5 minutes.
Cover; let rise in a warm place, free from draft, until doubled
in bulk, about 1½ hours.
Sprinkle the fine bread crumbs over the sides and bottom of a
well-greased 1½-quart casserole or fancy mold.
Arrange the almonds on bottom.
Stir the batter down.
Beat thoroughly.
Stir in the raisins and grated lemon peel.
Pour into the casserole or mold.

Let rise in a warm place, free from draft, until doubled in bulk, about 1 hour.

Bake in a moderate oven (350° F.) for about 50 minutes.

1663
TO MAKE CAKES

Take a pound of sugar finely beaten, four yolks of Eggs, two whites, one half pound of Butter washt in Rose-Water, six spoon-fuls of sweet Cream warmed, one pound of Currans well pickt, as much flower as will make it up, mingle them well together, make them into Cakes, bake them in an Oven; almost as hot as for Manchet half an hour will bake them.

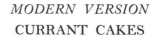

MODERN VERSION
CURRANT CAKES
(Makes 12 cakes)

Preheat oven to 350° F.

> *½ cup fine powdered sugar*
> *1 egg yolk*
> *1 egg white*
> *½ bar sweet butter*
> *2 teaspoons rosewater*
> *2 tablespoons heavy cream*
> *1 cup flour*
> *1 cup currants*

Wash the currants and dry on a paper towel.

Butter 12 muffin tins copiously and dust with flour.

Cream the butter until soft and light and add gradually the powdered sugar.

Add the unbeaten egg yolk and beat vigorously.

Measure out 1 cup flour and sprinkle a spoonful or two over the currants.

Add the rest gradually to the butter-egg-sugar mixture, moistening it with the rosewater and heavy cream.

When well mixed, add the floured currants and mix well.

Beat the egg white until stiff but not dry, and fold it carefully into the batter.

Place in the buttered and floured muffin tins, distributing it equally.

Place in a preheated 350° F. oven and bake until they test done in the center, or for about 30 minutes.

1663
TO MAKE A BANBURY CAKE

Take a peck of pure Wheat-flower, six pound of currans, half a pound of Sugar, two pound of Butter, half an ounce of Cloves and Mace, a pint and a half of Ale yeast, and a little Rose-water; then boil as much new milk as will serve to knead it, and when it is almost cold, put into it as much Sack as will thicken it, and so work it all together before a fire, pulling it two or three times in pieces, after make it up.

MODERN VERSION
BANBURY TARTS
(Makes 2 dozen)

Preheat oven to 450° F.

Plain Pastry (p. 153)
1 cup currants, washed and dried
½ cup mixed candied fruits
4 tablespoons sweet butter
grated rind of 1 lemon
strained juice of ½ lemon
1 teaspoon cinnamon
½ teaspoon nutmeg
¼ cup powdered sugar
½ teaspoon rosewater
1 egg, lightly beaten
¼ cup cream
confectioner's sugar

Mix the full quantity of plain pastry.
Chill while you make the filling.

Wash the currants and dry well on paper toweling.

Chop fine the mixed candied fruits.

Cream the butter into the powdered sugar.

Stir in the cinnamon, nutmeg, rosewater, lemon rind and lemon juice.

Add the currants and candied fruits, mix well, and last of all stir in the lightly beaten egg.

Roll out half of the pastry at a time, and manage to cut out of it 1 dozen 3¼-inch circles.

Repeat the process with the remainder of pastry, making 2 dozen circles in all.

You will have to gather up the bits in both cases and roll them out in order to make so many.

Have ready two cookie sheets.

Place in the center of each circle about 1 teaspoon of the fruit filling, using all of it.

Dip your finger in cold water and moisten the edge of each circle, folding it over so as to cover the filling and make a half-circle.

Press the cut edges together firmly.

Dip a fork in flour and crimp the cut edges.

Prick with a wide-pronged fork, being careful not to prick through the bottom.

Place on cookie sheets and chill for 5 or 10 minutes in the refrigerator.

Brush the surface of each with a little cream, place in a pre-heated 450° F. oven and bake until a delicate brown, or for about 20 to 25 minutes.

Sprinkle copiously with confectioner's sugar and serve while still warm.

For a richer dessert, double the amount of filling and serve half of it, well heated, on top of the pastries.

1663
TO MAKE PRINCE BISCUITS

Take a pound of searced Sugar, and a pound of find flower, eight eggs with two of the reddest yolks taken out, and so heat together one whole hour, then take your Coffins, and indoice them over with Butter very thin, then to it put an ounce of Anniseeds fine dusted, and when you are ready to fill your Coffins, put in the mixture and so bake it in an oven as hot as for Manchet.

MODERN VERSION
ANISEED CAKES
(Makes 2 dozen)

Preheat oven to 400° F.

>*2 eggs*
>*5 extra egg yolks*
>*1 cup sifted pastry or cake flour*
>*1 teaspoon baking powder*
>*1 teaspoon vanilla*
>*½ cup granulated sugar*
>*confectioner's sugar*
>*1 tablespoon aniseeds*

Put the whole eggs and the extra yolks into the top of a large double boiler.

Have ready 1 cup sifted pastry or cake flour sifted again with the baking powder.

Add the granulated sugar to the eggs and beat with a rotary beater just long enough to mix.

Place the pan over boiling water and continue beating until the mixture feels lukewarm.

Remove from the bottom of the double boiler and continue beating until the mixture will stick to a finger without dropping off when the finger is inserted and withdrawn.

Flavor with the vanilla.

Fold in ¼ of the sifted flour at a time, using a large spoon.

Last of all, fold in the aniseeds.

Place in 2 dozen muffin tins, lightly brushed with melted butter.

Place in preheated 400°–425° F. oven and bake until lightly browned, or for about 8 minutes.

Remove from the pans at once and place on cake racks to cool.

Sprinkle with confectioner's sugar before serving.

1663
TO MAKE FINE PIES AFTER THE FRENCH FASHION

Take a pound and half of Veal, two pound of suet, two pound of great Raisins—stoned, half a pound of Prunes, as much of Currans, six dates, two Nutmegs, a spoonful of Pepper, an ounce of Sugar, an ounce of Carowayes, a Saucer of Verjuyce, and as much Rosewater, this will make three fair Pies; with two quarts of flour, three yolks of Eggs, and half a pound of Butter.

MODERN VERSION
MINCEMEAT PIE

See my Mincemeat recipe on page 160.

1663
TO MAKE FINE PAN-CAKES FRYED WITHOUT BUTTER OR LARD

Take a pint of cream, and six new laid eggs, beat them very well together, put in a quarter of a pound of Sugar, and one Nutmeg or a little beaten Mace (which you please) and so much flour as will thicken almost as much as ordinarily Pancake batter; your pan must be heated reasonably hot and wiped with a clean cloth, this done put in your Batter as thick or thin as you please.

Not many changes to be made here.

MODERN VERSION
PANCAKES
(Makes 24 large pancakes)

6 eggs
2 cups cream
¼ pound sugar

¼ teaspoon powdered nutmeg
3 cups flour
3 teaspoons baking powder
1 teaspoon salt
2 ounces butter, melted

Beat the eggs and sugar and nutmeg together.
Add the cream and stir well.
Sift together the flour, baking powder and salt into a bowl.
Add the liquid to the flour, mixing well.
Add the melted butter.
Bake on a hot buttered griddle.

1663
TO MAKE TOASTS OR POOR KNIGHTS

Cut two peny Loaves in round slices, and dip them in half a pint of Cream or cold water, then lay them abroad in a Dish, and beat three Eggs and grated Nutmegs, and Sugar, beat them with the Cream, then take your frying Pan and melt some butter in it, and wet one side of your Toasts and lay them in on the wet side, then pour in the rest upon them, and so fry them; send them in with Rose-water, butter and sugar.

MODERN VERSION
FRENCH TOAST

slices of white bread or raisin bread
2 eggs
½ teaspoon salt
2 tablespoons sugar
½ cup milk
½ cup cream
dash nutmeg

Beat the eggs, add the other ingredients, except bread, mix well and strain into a shallow dish.
Dip slices of bread in the mixture, turning to coat both sides.
Cook on a hot buttered griddle or frying pan until golden brown on both sides.

[363]

Turn carefully with a pancake turner.

Serve with marmalade which has been heated and liquefied.

1663
TO MAKE A QUAKING PUDDING

Take a pint and somewhat more of thick cream, ten eggs, put the whites of three, beat them very well with two spoonfuls of Rose-Water, mingle with your cream three spoonfuls of fine flour, mingle it so well, that there be no lumps in it, put it altogether and season it according to your tast. Butter a Cloth very well, and let it be thick that it may not run out, and let it boyle for half an hour as fast as you can, then take it up and make Sauce with Butter, Rosewater and Sugar and serve it up.

You may stick some blanched Almonds upon it if you please.

MODERN VERSION
BAVARIAN CREAM PUDDING
(Serves 6)

Preheat oven to 350° F.

> *2 cups heavy cream*
> *2 tablespoons arrowroot flour*
> *6 egg yolks*
> *2 egg whites*
> *2 tablespoons granulated sugar*
> *1 teaspoon rosewater*
> *1 teaspoon vanilla*
> *1 tablespoon butter*
> *¼ cup blanched almonds (optional)*

Butter copiously a 1-quart ovenproof baking dish.

Mix together in a little bowl the arrowroot flour and granulated sugar.

Add a small quantity of heavy cream and stir until smooth and free from lumps.

Beat together the egg yolks and whites, and stir into them the remainder of the cream and the arrowroot-sugar-cream mixture.

Flavor with the vanilla and rosewater.

Mix well and strain into the buttered dish.

Place the dish in a shallow pan of hot water, cover the dish and bake until just set through, or for about 1 hour.

Cool slightly while you make the sauce.

Sauce

6 tablespoons granulated sugar
6 tablespoons sweet butter
3 tablespoons Madeira wine
1 tablespoon rosewater

Melt the butter in the top of a small double boiler, over boiling water.

Stir in the granulated sugar and Madeira wine.

Flavor with the rosewater.

Run a knife carefully around the edge of the pudding and turn out into a shallow dessert dish.

Pour the hot sauce over all.

Garnish with blanched almonds, if you so desire (we didn't), and serve at once.

1663
TO MAKE A DEVONSHIRE WHITE-POT

Take a pint of cream and strain four eggs into it, and put a little salt and a little sliced Nutmeg, and season it with Sugar somewhat sweet; then take almost a penny Loaf of fine bread sliced very thin, and put it into a dish that will hold it, the cream and the Eggs being put to it; then take a handful of Raisins of the Sun being boiled, and a little sweet Butter, so bake it.

MODERN VERSION
BREAD PUDDING
(Serves 6)

Preheat oven to 350° F.

8 slices white bread

¼ pound butter
½ cup seedless raisins
2 teaspoons cinnamon
4 whole eggs
3 cups milk
1 teaspoon vanilla or lemon extract
⅔ cup granulated sugar
cream to pour on

Wash the seedless raisins and soak in warm water until plump, about 10 minutes.

Drain and pat dry.

Remove crusts from 8 slices white bread ½ inch thick.

Butter copiously and cut each into 4 squares.

Butter lightly a rectangular baking dish, 10 by 6 by 1½ inches.

Place 16 squares of bread in the bottom of the dish.

Sprinkle with 1 teaspoon cinnamon and the raisins.

Cover with another layer of buttered bread, and sprinkle with 1 teaspoon cinnamon.

Beat the eggs.

Heat the milk with the granulated sugar in the top of a double boiler, over boiling water.

Add to the eggs.

Flavor with the vanilla or lemon extract.

Strain over the bread.

Place the dish in a shallow pan of hot water and bake until set through like custard and lightly browned on top, or 30 to 40 minutes.

Serve hot with a pitcher of heavy cream.

1663
TO MAKE A SWEET SMELL

Take the Maste of a sweet Apple tree, being gathered betwixt the two Lady dayes, and put to it a quart of Damask Rose-water, and dry it in a dish in an Oven; wet it drying two or three times with Rose-water, then put to it an ounce of Benjamin, an ounce of Storax Calamintae; these Gums being beaten to powder, with a few leaves of Roses, then you may put what cost of Smells you will bestow, as much Civet or Ambergreese, and beat it all together in a Pomander or a Bracelet.

Maste is the resin which exudes from some trees and has a resinous flavor.

1663
TO WRITE LETTERS OF SECRETS THAT THEY CANNOT BE READ WITHOUT THE DIRECTIONS FOLLOWING

Take fine Allum, beat it small, and put a reasonable quantity of it into water, then write with the said water.

The work cannot be read, but by steeping your paper into fair running water.

You may likewise write with Vinegar, or the juice of Limon or Onion; if you would read the same, you must hold it before the fire.

1663
KING EDWARDS PERFUME

Take twelve spoonfuls of right red Rose water, the weight of six pence in fine powder of sugar, and boil it on hot Embers and Coals softly, and the house will smell as though it were full of Roses; but you must burn the sweet Cipress wood before, to take away the gross air.

1663
QUEEN ELIZABETHS PERFUME

Take eight spoonfuls of Compound water, the weight of two pence in fine powder of sugar, and boil it on hot Embers and Coals softly, and half an ounce of sweet Majoram dried in the sun, the weight of two pence of the powder of Benjamin. This Perfume is very sweet and good for the time.

[367]

1663
DR. KINGS WAY TO MAKE MEAD

Take five quarts and a pint of Water, and warm it, then put one quart of Honey to every gallon of Liquor, one Lemon, and a quarter of an ounce of Nutmegs; it must boil till the scum rise black, that you will have it quickly ready to drink, squeeze into it a Limon when you turn it. It must be cold before you turn it up.

d'un verd plus brun, & d'une
odeur beaucoup moins agréa-
ble que le *cha* du Japon, auſſi
la teinture de ce Thé eſt-elle
plus verte & beaucoup moins
plaiſante, en ſorte même que
l'infuſion du plus commun, a
un goût qui approche en quel-
que ſorte de celle du ſené.
A tout prendre, il y a nean-
moins aſſés de rapport entre
l'arbriſſeau qui produit le *cha*
du Japon, & celuy qui fournit
le Thé de la Chine, pour s'en
faire une idée ſuffiſante par
l'inſpection de la figure qui eſt
à la page qui ſuit.

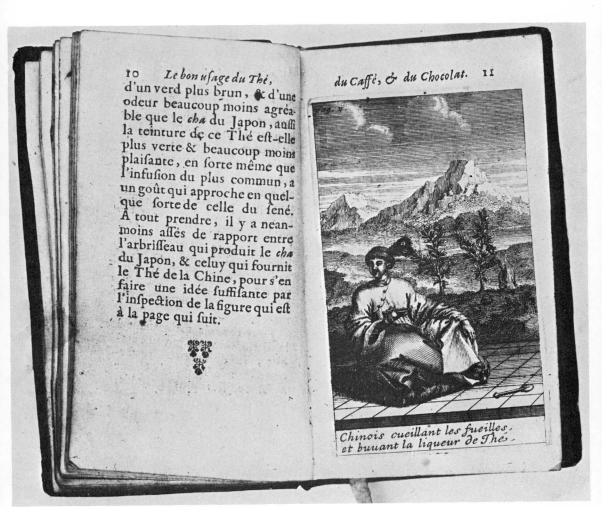

Chinois cueillant les fueilles,
et buuant la liqueur de Thé.

LE BON USAGE
DU THE'
DU CAFFE'
ET
DU CHOCOLAT
POUR LA PRESERVATION
& pour la guerison des
Maladies.

Par M.r de BLEGNY, Conseiller, Medecin
Artiste ordinaire du Roy & de Monsieur, & preposé par ordre de sa Majesté,
à la Recherche & Verification des nou-
velles découvertes de Medecine.

A PARIS,
Chez ESTIENNE MICHALLET, ruë
S. Jacques, à l'Image S. Paul.

M. DC. LXXXVII.
Avec Approbation & Privilege du Roy.

1687

THE GOOD USE

OF TEA

OF COFFEE

AND

OF CHOCOLATE

FOR PRESERVATION

AND FOR THE CURE OF

SICKNESSES

By Monsieur de Blegny

Councillor, Doctor, Artist ordinary of the King and Monsieur and proposed by the order of His Majesty, for the Research and Verification of the new Discoveries of Medicine

at Paris
with the approval and privilege
of the King
1687

Here is a book which takes the drinking of these beverages as a mighty important performance.

Nowadays we drop a tea bag into water (all too often just hot water—not even boiling), but this chap would curl up and die at such behavior.

TEA

The name *tea* is given to a dried leaf from the Orient and also to the infusion of this leaf, which is an agreeable drink with the addition of sugar or cardamom.

Japanese tea was called *cha* and was clear yellowish green and of an odor so sweet it resembled violets and was often called "flowers of *cha*." It was considered better than the best tea of China.

Pure "flowers of *cha*" cost as much as 500 francs per pound in 1687 ($100?), but the price of mixed or blended tea was 10 to 80 francs per pound.

China tea had larger leaves of a brownish green and an odor less agreeable than the Japanese.

The best tea is the small delicate leaf which can be seen opening to its original form in the hot water and, after the proper time, gives to the water a clear yellow-greenish color. On the contrary, poor tea comes from the large thick leaves and has little odor, bitter taste and rusty color.

Tea leaves must be kept in an air-tight box and not kept too long.

The mistress of the household used to keep the tea locked in tea caddies, and she alone made the tea—by covering the proper amount of tea leaves with fresh boiling water, covering the teapot and letting the infusion stand "for one third of a quarter of an hour," during which time the tea leaves settled on the bottom of the teapot and the tea infusion was tenderly poured off into the cups. When this was properly done, no strainer was necessary.

Tea must be drunk immediately after brewing and never —Heaven forbid!—reheated.

The amount of tea to water depends upon one's taste and upon the strength of the particular kind of tea being used.

One speaks also of smoking tea like tobacco in a pipe which "fortifies the brain."

The good M. de Blegny was convinced that drinking good tea was a cure for all sorts of maladies—upset stomach,

[*372*]

indigestion, headache, brain fever, catarrh and "all indis-
positions following debauchery." He said "nothing was more
rare in China and Japan than people tormented by gout and
gallstones, or apoplexie, epilepsie, or paralysis"!

COFFEE

He was very fussy about his coffee. The coffee beans had
to be just the right shade of pale gray before roasting, and he
had to be sure they were not mixed with dried peas.

The roasting was done on a fire of coal in a basin of "cui-
vre étame" or earthenware and stirred continually with an
iron instrument until just the right color—half burned—
then cooled and powdered. But this was a tricky business,
and "in all of Cairo there were only two men who had the
secret of roasting coffee without losing the volatile qualities."

Those who searched for the secret invented a roaster
which turned on a spit, but little did they know that the brass
roaster they used was all wrong! There were holes in the
roasters, and out went the volatile oils.

But our friend himself invented one with two cylinders,
one inside the other, and he seemed to think he had the
answer!

But beware of the merchant who sells powdered coffee!
Our friend M. de Blegny says it might not be only coffee but
a mixture! He always smelled it, but "it is impossible for me
to clearly explain how it should smell—all depends on delicacy and long experience which can establish a certain
knowledge of odor, color, too little or too much roasted, but
the best thing is to be sure of your merchant or do it yourself."

And if you do it yourself, "use only a coffee mill found at
the Quincallers; don't let the coffee fall onto a plate, exposing
it to the air, but only into a leather bag tied to the coffee mill"
or pound the beans in a mortar.

"And then, too, the coffee merchants grind the coffee and
put it in a paper bag. What a sin! It should be only in a

leather bag with double seams and well closed up."

And why not! In 1687, 100 pounds of coffee cost 40 to 60 pounds ($300).

After all the preamble, we will now make the coffee his way (which is quite like our way today!):

1. Don't put the ground coffee into the coffee pot until the water is boiling—never make coffee with cold water.

2. Prevent the froth of the boiling coffee from spilling over by keeping the cover on the pot and shaking it from one moment to the other to preserve the subtle volatile oils.

3. Only boil it for "the third part of a quarter of an hour," for too much boiling forces the volatile parts to escape.

4. In one word, "he who wants to go to the last refinement should prefer instead of a fire of wood or coal, an alcohol flame in a silver burner which is so light that a traveler can carry it in his pocket with his coffee pot, his coffee, his cup, his sugar and his alcohol."

Our coffee friend even put in a picture "to favor the persons in the provinces who have never seen one, not only assembled but in separate pieces."

He liked English pots better than French pots because "the metal was finer."

Half an ounce of coffee was "enough for six cups," according to M. de Blegny. This is very little coffee, but we must remember that coffee was very expensive. A dash of cold water when the coffee is done will settle the grounds. Some voluptuous people sweetened with essence of amber, cinnamon or cardamom instead of sugar.

The first cup of coffee in Europe was made and presented to Louis XIV at Versailles in 1664.

Cardamom in Coffee

In each demitasse of hot coffee put 6 cardamom seeds. This adds a delicious aroma and spicy flavor.

CHOCOLATE

After the discovery of the New World, chocolate was brought to Europe by the Spaniards. Cocoa found in Guatemala was the base, and it was mixed with sugar.

Indian Formula

To make a usable chocolate for the European taste, it was necessary to remove some of the oil from cocoa, and the oil was used medicinally and as a cosmetic.

In 1684 M. Bochot wrote that "well-prepared chocolate is such a noble confection it is indeed nectar and Ambrosia, the real food of the Gods, and merits better to be considered divine than the mushrooms of the Emperor Claudius."

PART FIVE

IRELAND

IN 1953 my husband and I made our first visit to Ireland to do some salmon fishing and to search for a church in County Carlow where we knew a Rudkin ancestor was buried.

One warm sunny day, rather rare in Ireland, we drove out from Dublin, with map in hand, and found what we were looking for. The Cathedral of St. Laserian turned out to be a lovely relic of the past, part of it dating from the twelfth century, and, sure enough, in the floor of the nave, just where we had been told to look (by a genealogically minded Rudkin cousin), we saw the green marble tombstone of the first Henry Rudkin, who went from England to Ireland in the seventeenth century, founded the Anglo-Irish branch of the family and died in 1726 at the age of 101 years.

Delighted with our discovery, we then wandered around the churchyard. Here and there, among the knee-high weedy grass and nettles, the old tombstones marked the resting places of those long since departed from this vale of tears.

We spied the family name on one stone, but the letters were dimmed with moss and black with age. We gathered handfuls of grass and scrubbed and rubbed until we could read the words:

Sacred to the Memory of
Anne Rudkin

Beloved Wife of Gilbert Pickering Rudkin This stone was erected in order to perpetuate the virtues of the best of

wives, the fondest of parents. Her life was short and not unchequered by pain and affliction but she bore with Christian resignation the dispensations of Heaven and knowing that this earth was not her place, she sought her abode above all sublunary things

1818   Age 38 years

She must have been a darling. Her husband and children, who loved her dearly, would have been happy, I feel sure, if they could have foreseen the future. They never knew that one day, almost a century and a half later, there would stand a kinsman of theirs, reading those words. And they never knew that the name Gilbert Pickering Rudkin would survive right into the present generation of our family.

C'est la vie.

There was nothing much left of the original family house, but we knew that one of the sons had built another house in 1704 and that Rudkins had lived in it for 150 years until the famine year of 1855, when one branch of the family left for the United States. The place had then passed to another family, who had owned it for the following ninety years.

This old house had never been spoiled. It was a simple square manor house, by no means an Irish castle or Georgian mansion, and over the stream below the path to the house was a moss-covered ancient stone bridge with a Rudkin family crest roughly carved into the keystone of the arch.

We were told the old place was going to be sold. What did we do? One guess! We bought it—the house, the stone bridge and 150 acres. More of the original land was added later, and now we are farming the ancestral acres.

Restoring the house and finding old furniture for it in Dublin was a great pleasure. The ancient garden walls have been repaired and the lovely old garden is replanted. We go there every summer, and on quiet evenings, when I sit on the garden steps in the long Irish twilight, watching the slope of Mount Leinster change color under the cloud shadows, I like to think that perhaps the spirits of one or two long-departed ancestors may come back in the moonlight now and then and smile happily to see Rudkins there again.

There's a tale of one girl of the house whose marriage portion from her father was "gold sovereigns equal to the weight of herself in a pair of lead shoes." Another one ran off with the man her father had forbidden her to see, and her marriage portion was "naught but the gold of her hair and the green riding habit she wore when she left the old house forever."

Life in Ireland has none of the rush and tension of American life, but we are always busy there. I find we need lots of good eating, for most of the time we are outdoors. There is always farming to see to, walking over our mountain farm to count the lambs, checking the haying on the valley farm, going to race meets and country fairs, or to cattle markets to buy and/or sell, or following the hounds on a damp, cold March day, which works up an appetite. And then, because of the mild climate, gardens flourish, so there's always gardening to do.

When we were looking for a gardener, one man was recommended to us in these words: "He has a bit of trouble with his heart betimes, but he's a tasty man for a garden." Do you suppose he tasted the delphiniums and roses?

One of our farm neighbors told me, "Oh, you could grow anything on your place. There's a terrible lot of good dirt there."

A year after we bought the place, we went over early in March, when the weather is cold and windy. We had no sooner arrived than a large cocktail party was given by friends to introduce us to our neighbors, all of whom have fairly large land holdings for raising cattle and sheep or Irish hunters or racers as well as crops.

We learned quickly that most Irish houses are heated only by open fireplaces—so you are warm only in front of the fire. But hearts are warm, and invitations galore poured in to us.

I remember the first dinner party we went to. The cocktails in the cold drawing room were strong enough to make up for the lack of steam heat. The drawing room was lovely in the soft light of candles and the glow from the flaming logs and sea coal on the hearth.

The dining room, with red velvet curtains drawn over the windows, polished firebrasses gleaming in the firelight, a huge bowl of daffodils on the old mahogany dining table, which was set in full regalia, the maid in a neat starched cap and apron and dark brown uniform and the houseboy in a starched white coat looked as if we were back in the eighteenth century.

Dinner consisted of grapefruit, tomato soup, roast chicken with bread sauce and brown gravy, roast potatoes and mashed potatoes (always two kinds), sprouting broccoli (which grows there all winter long), baked tomatoes (hothouse), prunes wrapped in bacon and cooked with the chicken.

As always at an Irish dinner party, there were three desserts—vanilla ice cream, a chocolate mousse covered with whipped cream and chopped nuts, and fruit salad with maraschino liqueur and thick cream poured on.

Sherry was served with the grapefruit, a Rhine wine with the chicken and champagne with dessert.

Coffee and liqueurs were served in the drawing room, and entertainment was supplied by my collection of stereo slides of American scenes. These were enthusiastically received, for no one had ever seen stereo slides before.

The hospitality of the Irish is legendary and, as always, at the end of the evening invitations were issued to the newcomers for all sorts of activities—lunches and dinners and fishing and race meets.

When I give dinner parties there, I try not to be too American, but we do have one problem, and that is to get properly hung beef suited to American taste.

We discovered that steers are butchered on Monday and by Thursday the meat is sold. We took the matter up by consultation with the butcher in our small country town.

In Ireland one approaches a problem by circuitous ways. The weather is always a good starter, followed by talk of business in general, politics and gossip. Finally the receiving end of the line realizes that something specific is coming up.

"Why don't you hang the beef here to tenderize it?"

"Oh, we do, sir, for three days."

"But it's hung for three weeks in the United States."

"Glory be to heaven, sir, it would shrink fifteen per cent, and who'd be paying for that?"

"Well, I'll tell you what you do—I'll buy that rib roast there today and pay you for it, and you hang it and let it shrink for me for three weeks."

So now we get well-hung beef, although I'm sure the consensus in the village is that those crazy Americans like over-ripe beef.

As for a thick, tender Porterhouse steak, I have never seen one in Ireland—a minute steak is the best you can do in the hotels. Our butcher will hang a loin of beef for us and cut it into thick steaks, but we have to stand over him while he cuts it, for he says, "Sir, that's not a steak—that thick it's surely a roast of beef."

Salmon is plentiful in the Irish areas, and fishing starts in February in the south and continues through August northward up the west coast. According to gossip, "Sure, but if ye do but drop a pin and a bit of a fly's wing into an Irish river, you'll be killing a fish in five minutes." Well, I've yet to see that happen, but we have had some fine salmon fishing.

A good fresh salmon dinner in February and March, when the fish are running, is always a treat. The whole salmon is boiled and served hot with a Hollandaise sauce, boiled potatoes and vegetables, usually peas put up by the cook last summer.

An invitation to tea in Ireland is no small matter of a simple cup of tea and a biscuit! You sit down at the table in the dining room and the usual everyday tea starts with slices of brown Irish soda bread and slices of homemade white bread lavishly buttered, a pot or two of jam for the bread, hot crusty scones, a plate of cookies, a "sponge sandwich" cake (two layers of sponge cake, jam between and sugar sprinkled on top) and a chocolate cake with thick, creamy, chocolate icing—or warm gingerbread full of currants. Cups of hot tea all around three or four times and you'll last till suppertime.

Or perhaps there'll be those marvelous potato cakes you eat with a knife and fork, dripping with butter and honey, or cold thick pancakes buttered and sprinkled with brown sugar.

Of course if it's a special tea party, there'll be bowls of raspberries or strawberries with whipped cream—fresh fruit if in season or "bottled" fruit done up in the house and kept in the cool larder.

The family cooking in Ireland is quite similar to cooking in England and America. We all grow our own vegetables and fruits, and the gardens yield everything from artichokes to sea kale.

We have fine strawberries, raspberries, black currants, apples and pears. Some people have greenhouses, or glass houses, for delectable peaches, early strawberries and tomatoes, which cannot be grown outdoors because of the cool summer weather.

For some strange reason, the Irish, like the English, finish with a savory after the sweet—a bit of toasted cheese, or an oyster wrapped in bacon and broiled, or a bit of toast spread with anchovy paste. This, they say, is to clear the palate for the port. Cheese is usually good old Stilton, ripe and strong.

An Irish breakfast is a real meal. In our house we stick to the simple American style for weekdays, but on Sundays we go all out. Early in the morning the maids go off on their bicycles to church, and leave breakfast all fixed for us. On the sideboard is a large electric hotplate, and there sit covered dishes of broiled kidneys and bacon, scrambled eggs piled on toast slices, or broiled sausages and fried slices of tomato. Sometimes we have a kedgeree—boiled rice and flaked fresh boiled salmon in equal quantities, tossed in hot butter, with chopped hard-boiled eggs mixed in. Pitchers of fruit juice are ready and the loaf of homemade bread or Barmbrack is on the breadboard ready to be sliced and popped into the toaster. Coffee and tea are kept hot over candle burners.

All our bread is baked at home except Barmbrack, a yeast bread thick with raisins and currants and cherries and cinnamon, which is bought once a week at the village bake shop, to be toasted for Sunday breakfast.

[*384*]

Our cook is a good baker and is proud of her prizes at the county fairs. Her half-whole-meal-and-half-white-yeast bread is wonderfully good, and her soda bread is perfect.

Scones always appear at teatime and Sally Lunn or yeast rolls are made frequently.

I've always been intrigued by what is called a potato ring. This is a silver ring beautifully cut out or engraved, usually eight to nine inches in diameter and five or six inches high. They say that the country people boiled their potatoes in the skins, wrapped them in a cloth and served them in a plain wooden bowl, but the gentry added elegance to their wooden bowls by placing the bowls of potatoes on top of these silver rings. They seem to be collector's pieces today and with glass liners make attractive flower holders. But why not use them again for serving potatoes?

Colcannon is a good Irish potato dish—half hot mashed potatoes and half hot cooked chopped green cabbage or kale, well salted, with chopped cooked onion added.

What we call dessert is called the sweet in Ireland. Dessert means only fresh fruit.

A proper dinner for guests in Ireland would be:

Appetizer	Grapefruit or melon.
Soup	Clear strong consommé. Sherry served with this.
Fish	Lobster, cold with mayonnaise or hot such as Thermidor or lobster Newburg. White wine, French or German, served with this.
Meat	Roast chicken, or
	Roast duck, or
	Fillet of beef. Claret or Burgundy served with this.
	Vegetables in season.
Sweet	Mousse, chocolate or mocha, and/or
	Meringues, whipped cream, and/or
	Ice cream and/or
	Fruit salad with fresh cream.

Savory	Cheese on toast.
	Anchovy paste on toast.
	Oyster wrapped in bacon and fried.

Table is cleared and only port glasses are left.

A plate and fruit knife and fork are placed before each guest.

Dessert	Fresh fruit—preferably hothouse (your own).
	Vintage port—the decanter is passed once around clockwise; then the ladies, after one glass of port, leave the dining room, and the gentlemen continue.

No smoking until after the port.

Coffee—for gentlemen at the table, for ladies in the drawing room.

Summer activities include frequent country fairs and horse shows, so picnics are the rule of the day all summer, rain or shine. Since it rains often, one just goes ahead anyway because it clears up off-again, on-again all day. But you always go to a picnic with a raincoat tucked in the car.

We like Thermos bottles of hot clear consommé laced with sherry, as well as lots of tea and coffee, plus a bottle or two of wine.

Picnics mean hot meat pasties or shrimp pasties, cold beefsteak-and-kidney pie cut in wedges, sausage rolls, broiled chicken in handy pieces to eat from the hand, fried country ham between split scones, all kinds of sandwiches, hard-boiled eggs, cakes and cookies.

Lots of good fish and fine shellfish are available in Dublin and the coast cities. There's nothing more delicious than lunch at the Russell Hotel in Dublin with Dublin bay prawns for a first course.

They are served as a prawn cocktail, cut into small pieces

and accompanied by a lovely, very unusual mayonnaise sauce, or served in the shell with the head and tails on, so that you pull out the prawn to dip into mayonnaise. But, oh dear, I don't like the beady black eyes looking at me, so I have the prawns taken out of the shell in one piece and served on a flat plate, about a dozen of them, with mayonnaise on the side, and they are heavenly good—sweet and tender as butter.

The excellent restaurant at Shannon Airport makes a specialty of fish. It has haddock, kippers, white fish, codfish, brill, scallops from the Aran Islands, lobster and shrimps and Galway oysters. Irish kippers are lightly smoked and sold quite fresh. Plaice is a great favorite and always available. Irish sole is wonderful, as good as any English sole. Herrings, fresh and salted, are abundant.

Fishing off the Hook near Waterford on the Irish Sea, I saw two hundred mackerel caught by one man in about five hours.

Meals at the good Dublin hotels and restaurants are really superb. The Russell Hotel, Jammet's Restaurant, the Shelburne and the Hibernian are all tops.

The Russell does a fine salmon coulibiac and crêpes de fruits de mer, thin pancakes rolled around a filling of creamed scallops, lobster and fish.

Smoked trout, salmon cold or hot or smoked to perfection, and marvelous Irish sole grilled perfectly, laved with melted butter and dressed with a few capers. Lobster Thermidor or plain broiled lobster, scampi, sole Véronique with white grapes and the kind of sauce you soak up with a piece of bread—it's so good you can't resist.

Broiled and roast chickens, grilled minute steaks, wonderful escalope of veal, kidneys cooked in Madeira wine, sweetbreads braised with celery, Limerick hams and bacon, and grouse and game in season.

Vegetables are about like ours—spinach, plain or creamed, peas, cauliflower, carrots, tomatoes, onions, mushrooms, asparagus and sea kale.

Desserts in the good hotels are mostly pastries of the French type, soufflés, crêpes Suzette, meringues, fresh fruit salad, ice cream.

When we sail for home from Cobh, we drive down early and lunch at the Imperial Hotel in Cork. There you can find a good à la carte menu with smoked salmon, oysters, lobster cocktail, excellent soups, the famous Irish sole cooked in half a dozen different ways, good chicken dishes and good mixed grills and steaks. A complete à la carte dinner would be about 25 shillings ($3.50) and the table d'hôte dinner 14 shillings and sixpence (about $2.00).

Their table d'hôte lunch is very good. For 8 shillings ($1.14) you have clear or cream soup, a choice of a fish dish, or roast leg of pork, or stewed steak and onions, or cold ham or cold roast beef with salad, cabbage or carrots, potatoes, pear tart, or tapioca pudding, or sherry trifle with cream or ice cream.

Outside of Dublin, Cork, Limerick and a few other towns, the restaurant and hotel food is very plain. You'll get thin soup, fried fish without any sauce, nine times out of ten a cabbage of some kind, or tinned peas and two kinds of potatoes, or boiled lamb with a tasteless white sauce, or roast lamb with a mint sauce tasting of vinegar, or steak and kidney pie, and a pudding—almost anywhere it will be exactly this.

Each year there seem to be more lovely private homes to stay in as paying guests. The Irish Tourist Bureau will give you a list. Then you will enjoy fine home cooking in charming houses with delightful hostesses.

But I have yet to find corned beef and cabbage on any menu, either in a hotel, restaurant or private house, although elsewhere it seems to be considered the Irish national dish.

Frozen foods are becoming popular all through the country, in small towns as well as large—frozen chickens and fillets of fish, frozen vegetables and strawberries and raspberries can be purchased.

Bacon is a staple dish in the farmhouses. A good piece

of boiled bacon and greens—cabbage, kale or turnip tops—
with boiled potatoes is often on the table.

To fry, there are two kinds of bacon—rashers (lean
bacon) or streaky (lean and fat), either smoked or "green"
(not smoked).

Sausages are not very spicy.

Pig's head is boiled and served hot or cold.

Boiled pig's feet are known as crubeens.

Fresh pork is used in many ways.

Lamb is used a great deal. A good Irish stew is made from
the neck and shoulder end. Leg of lamb is boiled with caper
sauce or roasted. Chops are cut rather thin, dipped in egg
and fine bread crumbs and fried.

The well-known Irish Coffee is seldom served in private
houses, but is a great favorite in hotels and restaurants.
Looked on as the tourists' drink, it is very popular in the
United States too, and I serve it frequently.

In making it you are supposed to use only Irish whisky or
liqueur. My favorite Irish Coffee is made with Irish Mist,
Ireland's legendary liqueur. According to tradition, this is
a cordial based on whisky and heather honey; whatever it is,
it's delicious.

Irish Mist recipes have wonderful names tacked onto
them—Velvet Mist, Fancy Free, Murphy's Dream and Hibernian Mist.

The popular drinks in the small taverns or "pubs" are porter, Guinness' stout and Irish beers. Irish whisky—Pow-
ers', Jamieson's, Tullamore Dew—is taken plain, no ice, no
water!

A good stiff drink on a bitter cold, wet day, when the farm-
ers have been standing about outdoors all morning in the
midst of hundreds of cattle and sheep at a cattle market, is
Port and Brandy—half and half in generous measure. That
warms them up in a hurry!

FARM SOUP WITH BOILED POTATOES
(Serves 6–8)

2 pounds boiling beef
3 quarts water
½ cup split peas (quick-cooking kind)
½ cup barley
1 onion, sliced fine
1 leek, sliced fine
1 carrot, sliced fine
1 turnip, sliced fine
1 stalk celery, cut fine
½ head cabbage

Put everything into a pot except the cabbage.

Simmer for 3 hours.

In the meantime, shred the cabbage fine and add to the soup for the last ½ hour.

Boil the potatoes separately, drain well and shake over the heat to dry out.

Serve the soup in bowls over the hot boiled potatoes.

THIN KIDNEY SOUP
(Serves 6)

1 beef kidney
1 onion, chopped
pepper and salt
6 cups water
2 potatoes, diced

Wash and skin the kidney, remove the white center part.

Soak the kidney in cold salted water for 1 hour.

Drain and cut into thin, small pieces.

Cover the sliced kidney with boiling water, cook for 5 minute: and drain off the water.

Add 6 cups fresh water to the kidney.

Add the onion, potatoes, salt and pepper, and simmer for 1 hour.

[*390*]

THICK KIDNEY SOUP
(Serves 6)

1 beef kidney
6 cups water
1 onion
1 carrot
1 potato
2 stalks celery
4 tablespoons butter
4 tablespoons flour
salt and pepper
thyme
¼ cup red wine

Wash and skin the kidney, discarding the white center part.
Soak the kidney for 1 hour in cold salted water.
Drain and slice the kidney into small thin pieces.
Slice the onion, carrot, celery and potato.
Melt the butter and cook the chopped vegetables 5 minutes.
Add the sliced kidney, sprinkle with the flour and cook a few minutes until the flour is absorbed. Add the water and simmer until the kidney is very tender, about 1 hour.
Remove the meat and chop very fine or put through a food chopper.
Put the soup and vegetables in the blender and mix till smooth, or force through a strainer to make a purée.
Add the chopped kidney and reheat.
Season well with salt, pepper and a good pinch of thyme.
Add the red wine just before serving.

Irish Soda Bread is the popular brown bread in Irish country homes, although sliced white bread now appears in gay waxed-paper wrappers in Dublin and other towns.

The whole-wheat flour is stone ground, and baking soda, cream of tartar and sour milk are used to lighten it.

Every farmer's wife had to make butter almost every day, for it was one of the main cash crops. There was always buttermilk from the churning, and it was the family drink and handy for the baking.

The soda is alkali and the cream of tartar acid. When they are mixed with sour milk or buttermilk, gas is formed and the heat of the oven makes the gas bubbles expand in a way similar to the action of yeast.

Sometimes soda bread is made of all whole wheat and sometimes with part whole wheat and part white.

Sweet milk can be soured by taking two tablespoons of milk out of a full cup and substituting two tablespoons of vinegar or lemon juice. Let this mixture stand about ten minutes before you use it.

BASIC WHOLE-MEAL IRISH SODA BREAD

(Makes 1 large loaf)

Preheat oven to 400° F.

> *½ cup sifted white flour*
> *1½ cups whole wheat flour—not sifted*
> *1 teaspoon salt*
> *1 teaspoon baking soda*
> *½ teaspoon cream of tartar*
> *1 teaspoon granulated sugar*
> *¾ cup sour milk or buttermilk*

In a bowl mix together all the dry ingredients by stirring and tossing with a spoon or fork. Make a hole in the center, pour in the sour milk or buttermilk and mix together to a dough. If a little too dry, add a bit more milk so that you have a nice pliable dough.

Knead about ten times; form into a circular loaf; cut a deep cross on the top surface and bake for 50 minutes to one hour in a 400 degree oven.

This bread is best served the day it is baked as it is apt to dry out rather quickly. However, it can be sliced and toasted on the second day.

MAGGIE MURPHY'S POT OVEN BREAD

Down yonder in one of our big fields is a lovely mysterious ruin of an old house and grist mill—moss-covered stone walls, roof fallen in over a perfectly arched stone doorway—and at one end of this relic of the past is a tiny two-room cottage that was once the miller's cottage. There, almost fourscore years ago, Maggie Murphy first saw the light of day, and there she will live out all the days that are left to her.

Spry as a cricket, she bicycles the five miles into the village once a week and peddles back (uphill most of the way) with whole-wheat flour among her purchases.

She cooks over an open hearth fire and mixes her soda bread just as I gave you the recipe, but she has no oven—just a three-legged iron pot oven. She sets this right in the red-hot coals on her hearth, rubs it inside with a bit of fat pork, drops her cake of whole-wheat dough into it, puts on the cover and then shovels some of the red coals onto the cover. Heat top and bottom she then has, and the bread bakes for an hour while she sits by the hearth, from time to time turning the handle on her wheel bellows—which makes a draft of air come up through the tiny hole under the coals, bringing them to life with a golden glow.

At just the right minute she brushes the hot coals off the cover, lowers the crane to catch the handle of the pot and swings it out away from the fire.

Out comes a perfectly baked, crusty loaf, fragrant and golden "and good enough for the likes of me," says my dear friend Maggie Murphy.

WHITE SODA BREAD

(Makes 1 loaf)

Preheat oven to 450° F.

>1 pound white flour
>1 teaspoon salt
>1 teaspoon sugar
>2 teaspoons baking soda
>1 cup buttermilk or sour milk (about)

Sift the dry ingredients several times through your fingers.

Add the milk gradually, mixing well.

Have the dough not too dry.

Turn it out onto a floured bread board and knead lightly just a few times.

Shape into a round flat loaf and cut a deep cross from side to side.

Bake on a flat pan in a hot oven (450° F.) for 45 minutes.

RAISIN SODA BREAD

(Makes 1 loaf)

Preheat oven to 450° F.
Use the White Soda Bread dough recipe (p. 393) and add

> *½ cup sugar*
> *1 beaten egg*
> *4 tablespoons butter, melted*
> *½ cup seedless raisins (or more),*
> *if you like raisins*

GRIDDLE BREAD

Mix the White Soda Bread dough (p. 393).
Roll it out to about ¾ inch thick.
Cut in pieces any size you want and bake on a hot greased griddle for about 10 minutes on each side.
Eat while hot, with butter and honey on it.

PAN-FRIED SODA BREAD

Soda bread should be eaten the day it is made, for it dries out very quickly.
But when you have some left over, use it with bacon and eggs.
Fry some bacon and remove the bacon to drain off.
Into the hot bacon fat put slices of the soda bread and brown them on both sides.
Serve with a fried egg on top and the bacon on the side.

BARMBRACK

(Makes 2 loaves)

Preheat oven to 375° F.

> *¾ cup milk*
> *½ cup sugar*
> *1½ teaspoons salt*
> *¼ cup margarine or butter*
> *3 packages or cakes yeast,*

> *dry or compressed*
> ½ *cup very warm water*
> 2 *eggs, beaten*
> 5 *cups sifted flour (about)*
> *grated rind of 1 lemon*
> 1¼ *cups golden seedless raisins*
> ⅓ *cup chopped mixed candied fruits*

Scald the milk.

Stir in the sugar, salt and margarine or butter.

Cool to lukewarm.

Sprinkle or crumble the yeast into the very warm water in a large bowl.

Stir until dissolved.

Add the lukewarm milk mixture, beaten eggs and 3 cups flour.

Beat on the medium speed of the mixer for 2 minutes (or 300 vigorous strokes by hand).

Stir in the lemon rind and enough remaining flour to make a soft dough.

Turn the dough out onto a lightly floured board.

Knead until smooth and elastic.

Place in a greased bowl; brush the top with soft shortening.

Cover.

Let rise in a warm place, free from draft, for about 40 minutes.

Punch down and turn out onto a lightly floured board.

Knead in the raisins and mixed candied fruit.

Divide in half.

Shape into loaves.

Place in 2 greased loaf pans, 9 by 5 by 3 inches.

Cover.

Let rise in a warm place, free from draft, until doubled in bulk, about 50 minutes.

Bake in a moderate oven (375° F.) for 30 to 35 minutes.

BUTTERMILK PANCAKES

(Makes 3 or 4 dozen pancakes, depending on size)

> 4 *cups sifted white flour*
> 4 *ounces butter*

½ *teaspoon baking soda*
½ *teaspoon cream of tartar*
2 *tablespoons sugar*
1 *teaspoon salt*
2 *beaten eggs*
3 *cups buttermilk or sour milk (about)*

Sift the dry ingredients together.

Rub in the butter with the tips of your fingers.

Add the eggs and just enough milk to make a thin batter.

Cook on a hot greased griddle by dropping from a tablespoon to make small cakes.

Turn when the top is covered with bubbles.

Serve hot with butter and brown syrup.

In the back of one of my old Irish cookbooks I found a hand-written recipe for scones cooked in hot ashes and served with rashers and eggs (bacon and eggs).

It reminded me of the baked potatoes we used to cook when I was a child. We put unpeeled potatoes right into the hot coal or wood embers, and when they were cooked we peeled away the black scorched skin. Sprinkled with salt and eaten piping hot out of our little hot hands, those potatoes were different from any other I ever ate.

Maybe the hot ashes impart something extra, but it would be fun to try this ash-cake recipe on your charcoal broiler someday.

You could wrap the scones in aluminum foil or even try a cabbage leaf!

This is the recipe just as I found it in the book.

ASH CAKES TO EAT WITH RASHERS AND EGGS

The meal was just scalded with boiling salted water.

It was then made into a dough rolled out thin, and cut into little scones.

A bed was made on the hearth by raking away the spark-sprinkled ashes.

Each scone was rolled in a cabbage leaf, placed in the bed of hot ashes and hot ashes were then piled on top of them and left for half an hour.

When they were lifted out of the scorched leaves and eaten with rasher gravy they had a sweet nutty flavor.

CORNMEAL CAKES

(Makes 1 dozen)

Preheat oven to 375° F.

> *1 cup cornmeal, white or yellow*
> *   (stone-ground cornmeal has best flavor)*
> *½ teaspoon salt*
> *1 cup boiling water*
> *3 tablespoons melted butter*

Add the cornmeal and salt to the boiling water and mix just till smooth.

Add the melted butter and mix well.

Drop by spoonfuls on a flat buttered baking sheet and flatten out with a wet spatula.

Bake in a moderate oven (375° F.) until browned, about 20 minutes.

Another way

Put the baking sheet with the cornmeal cakes on it on the grid of your charcoal fire.

Turn once when the underside is brown, but don't press down —leave them just as they are.

Another way

Have ready 5-inch squares of buttered aluminum foil.

In the center of each square drop a tablespoon or two of the cornmeal mix.

Fold the aluminum, carefully sealing all edges.

Place right over the hot coals on your grill and cook about 15 minutes, turning every 5 minutes.

The time depends on the heat of your fire—better test one first.

Unwrap and serve hot.

CORNMEAL CAKES OR SCONES WITH
BACON GRAVY AND FRIED EGGS

Cook some bacon and remove from the pan.

To the bacon fat in the frying pan, add 1 tablespoon flour and cook until blended with the fat.

Add 1 cup milk and bring to a boil and cook, stirring constantly, until smooth.

On the plate with the bacon and eggs put a split cornmeal scone and pour the gravy over the scone.

A good ham should never be boiled, but simmered in water just under the boiling point.

The Irish country hams are still slow cured and well smoked. They are not too fat and have an excellent flavor and texture.

Your butcher in the United States can get you an old-fashioned dry-cure smoked ham if you ask him to order it for you. A good size is about fifteen pounds.

IRISH COUNTRY HAM

Put the ham to soak in the morning well covered with cold water, and leave it overnight (change the water once).

Next morning, drain and scrub well.

Put in a large pot and cover with fresh cold water with 1 cup sugar, 12 cloves and 2 large onions.

Simmer, do not boil, 18 to 20 minutes per pound (or about 5 hours for a 15-pound ham).

If using a meat thermometer, insert in the top of the ham so the thermometer can be seen above the surface of the water and simmer until it reads 170°.

If to be served hot, let cool slightly in the cooking water, then remove from the water and peel off the skin.

Sprinkle the fat surface with fine browned bread crumbs and a little brown sugar.

Serve sliced thin with hot Raisin Sauce (p. 26).

If to be used as cold ham, let cool thoroughly in the water in which it was cooked. When cool, remove from the water and peel off the skin.

Sprinkle with browned bread crumbs and a little brown sugar.

BEEF AND KIDNEY PIE
(Serves 6)

Preheat oven to 350° F.

> *Plain Pastry (p. 153)*
> *2 pounds round steak or flank steak*
> *4 lamb kidneys or 2 veal kidneys*
> *2 onions, sliced*
> *¼ pound butter or margarine*
> *2 cups boiling water or beef consommé*
> *2 tablespoons flour*
> *salt and pepper*
> *1 bay leaf*

Cut the meat into cubes.

Wash the kidneys, remove the skin and white core and cut in quarters or small pieces.

In a heavy saucepan or oven casserole, melt the butter and brown the onions slightly.

Toss the meat and kidneys in the flour till coated all over.

Brown the meat in the hot fat, stirring constantly.

Add the liquid, salt, pepper and bay leaf.

Cover tightly.

Simmer until tender, about 1½ hours.

Stir from time to time as the gravy thickens.

Put in a shallow ovenproof casserole.

Cover with a pastry crust (p. 153) or a biscuit crust (p. 55), rolled thin.

Make a hole in the center of the crust.

Bake in a 350° F. oven for about 30 minutes until the crust is well browned.

BOILED BEEF

(Serves 8)

4-pound piece fresh brisket of beef
½ cup barley
2 onions, sliced
1 stalk celery
few sprigs parsley
pepper and salt
1 bay leaf

In a deep saucepan, barely cover the meat with boiling water.
Add the barley, simmer for 1 hour.
Add the onions, celery, parsley, pepper, salt and bay leaf.
Simmer for 2 hours more.
Thicken the sauce by putting ½ cup cold water in a small jar
with a screw top, then put ½ cup flour on top of the water, put
the top on the jar and shake vigorously.
Add to the boiling liquid, stirring constantly.

STUFFED PORK FILLETS

(Serves 6)

2 fresh pork fillets (or tenderloin)
stuffing
½ cup chicken broth or water
salt and pepper to taste
pinch oregano

Split the fillets carefully without cutting through.
Lay one out flat and cover with Bread Stuffing (p. 29) or
Potato Stuffing (p. 31).
Lay the other on top and fasten the sides together with skewers
or sew together.
Dip in flour.
Brown in hot fat in a frying pan.
Add ½ cup chicken broth or water.
Cover the pan and cook on low heat for 1 hour.
Add more liquid if necessary.
Remove from the pan and keep hot.

For gravy, add a little boiling water to the pan, salt and pepper and a pinch of oregano.

Boil up and pour over the fillets.

IRISH STEW

shoulder and neck of lamb with most of the fat cut off
potatoes
carrots
celery
onions
ham, minced
salt and pepper
pinch thyme

For every pound of meat, use 1 pound potatoes, 1 onion, 1 carrot, 1 stalk celery, 1 teaspoon minced ham and 1 cup water.

Have the butcher bone a shoulder and neck of lamb and cut into small pieces, trimming off surplus fat.

In a deep saucepan, put a layer of meat and a layer of sliced potatoes and some of the vegetables and seasonings and a little of the minced ham.

Repeat in layers and add just enough water to cover.

Cover tightly and simmer for 2½ hours.

If necessary, add a little more water as it cooks.

The potatoes will thicken the broth.

It is a good idea to make this the day before, cool it and leave in the refrigerator overnight.

Fat will rise to the top to be removed.

Reheat carefully and serve very hot with crisp rolls.

SHEPHERD'S PIE

Preheat oven to 400° F.

> *leftover roast of lamb or beef*
> *salt and pepper*
> *mashed potatoes*
> *cooked carrots*
> *cooked peas*
> *2 onions*

gravy or canned chicken broth
plenty of butter

Put the meat through a chopper, using the medium blade.
Sprinkle with salt and pepper to taste.
Place in a shallow baking dish.
Add a layer of carrots, peas and the onions thinly sliced, and enough gravy or canned broth to moisten.
Cover with mashed potatoes about ½ inch to 1 inch thick, dot over with plenty of butter, and bake in a medium hot oven (400° F.) until the potatoes are nicely browned, or about ½ hour.

PICKLED BEEF

(Serves 6–8)

6 pounds corned brisket of beef
4 slices smoked bacon
2 onions
1 carrot
handful of parsley, celery tops, thyme
6 cloves
6 allspice

Put the beef and bacon in a saucepan, add the seasonings, and just cover with cold water.
Bring just to the boiling point and simmer for 4 hours.
Cool in the water and then put on a platter, cover with another platter with a weight on it and leave until well pressed.
Use the water for soup stock.

LAMB KIDNEYS

(Serves 6)

1 dozen lamb kidneys (or 6 veal kidneys may be used)
2 tablespoons shallots or onions
1 cup sliced mushrooms
¼ cup diced green pepper
½ cup butter

½ *cup brandy*
1 *cup chicken bouillon*
3 *tablespoons flour*
½ *teaspoon salt*
freshly ground black pepper
3 *cups hot cooked rice*
½ *cup chopped parsley*

Split the kidneys and cut into ½-inch slices.

Sauté the shallots, mushrooms and green peppers in butter for 5 minutes.

Add the kidneys and simmer for 5 minutes, stirring once or twice.

Heat the brandy, light and pour over the kidney mixture.

When the flame dies, stir in the bouillon.

Cover and simmer for 10 minutes.

Stir in the flour mixed with salt and pepper and ¼ cup water, and cook until thickened, stirring constantly.

Serve over rice mixed with parsley.

CURRIED EGGS AND SHRIMP

Preheat oven to 400° F.

Allow 1 hard-boiled egg per person.

Slice the eggs into a flat buttered pie pan.

Cover with freshly cooked shrimp, four per portion.

Cover with hot Curried Cream Sauce (below) and place in a hot oven (400° F.) for 20 minutes.

Serve with hot dry boiled rice and Chutney (p. 184).

CURRIED CREAM SAUCE

To each cup of Cream Sauce (p. 34) add about 1 teaspoon curry powder mixed into 3 tablespoons cream.

EGGS IN CHEESE SAUCE

Allow 1½ to 2 hard-boiled eggs per person.

Slice the eggs into a buttered pie pan and cover with a rich Cheese Sauce (p. 35).

Sprinkle the top surface with finely grated cheese and place under the broiler until hot and bubbly.

OLD WIVES' SOD
(Serves 3–4)

Why it is called this no one knows!

Preheat oven to 375° F.

> *6 eggs*
> *1 cup milk*
> *pepper and salt*
> *butter*
> *stale cornbread or stale muffins (enough*
> *to cover the top of a baking dish)*

Beat the eggs well, add the milk, pepper and salt.

Butter a shallow ovenproof dish and pour in the egg mixture.

Break up the stale cornbread or muffins into small pieces and sprinkle on top.

Sprinkle melted butter over all and bake in a moderate oven (375° F.) for 20 minutes.

EGG PIE
(Serves 6)

Preheat oven to 450° F.

> *Plain Pastry (p. 153)*
> *6 eggs*
> *salt and pepper*
> *1 tablespoon chopped parsley*
> *1 teaspoon chopped mint*
> *crumbled cooked crisp bacon*

Line a 9-inch pie pan with pastry.

Break the whole eggs into the pie pan, sprinkle with the seasonings and crumbled bacon.

Roll a pastry top to fit, and prick all over.

Bake in a hot oven (450° F.) until browned (about 30 minutes).

BAKED EGGS

(Serves 6)

Preheat oven to 350° F.

> *6 eggs*
> *milk or cream*
> *¼ cup grated cheese (Parmesan or Cheddar)*
> *salt and pepper*
> *chopped parsley*

Put ½ inch milk or cream into a shallow 9-inch baking dish or pie pan.

Break the whole eggs into the pan, one at a time.

Season with salt and pepper and sprinkle with the cheese.

Bake at 350° F. for 10 minutes.

Sprinkle with chopped parsley and serve immediately.

BOILED SALMON

(Serves 12–18)

Salmon was once so plentiful in Ireland that the charter for indentured servants forbade the serving of salmon to them more than three times a week. Today fresh salmon in Dublin costs $2.50 a pound! When you can get it!

For a whole 10- to 14-pound salmon, you really need a fish boiler with a rack in it.

Make a bouillon of

> *4 quarts water*
> *¼ cup vinegar or lemon juice*
> *3 tablespoons salt*
> *1 bay leaf*
> *3 cloves*
> *6 peppercorns*
> *parsley*
> *2 onions*
> *3 stalks celery*

Let this boil for 15 minutes.

Clean and scale the salmon and remove the head and tail.

Wrap in clean cheesecloth and tie securely.

Place in the boiling bouillon, reduce the heat and simmer for 8 minutes per pound.

With the rack in the fish boiler you can easily lift the salmon out of the bouillon, untie the cheesecloth and gently roll the fish onto a large platter.

Garnish with hard-boiled eggs, sliced cucumbers and parsley and serve with a Hollandaise Sauce (below), fresh peas and tiny boiled new potatoes.

HOLLANDAISE SAUCE

(Serves 3–4)

This is really very easy, very quick and foolproof to make if you follow just one direction—don't let the top of the double boiler touch the boiling water underneath. Very little heat is needed, and overcooking will curdle the sauce.

> ¼ *pound butter (1 stick)*
> 2 *egg yolks*
> ¼ *teaspoon salt*
> 1 *tablespoon lemon juice*

Divide the stick of butter into three pieces.

In the top of a double boiler, put the egg yolks, salt, lemon juice and 1 piece butter.

Stir together with a small wooden spoon.

Place the top over the boiling water in the bottom of the boiler, but do not let it touch the water.

Stir constantly until the butter melts.

Add the second piece of butter, stir until melted.

Add the third piece of butter, stir until melted.

Give a couple stirs more until nice and thick, and you are done. This should take about 2 minutes.

Remove the top from the bottom of the boiler, cover and set aside to use.

FISH ROLL

(Serves 4)

Preheat oven to 375° F.

> *1 pound boiled codfish or haddock*
> *2 cups mashed potatoes*
> *2 eggs, well beaten*
> *pepper and salt to taste*
> *browned bread crumbs*
> *melted butter*

Remove all skin and bones from the cooked fish and break the fish into flakes.

Mix the beaten eggs with the potatoes and mix the flaked fish into the potatoes.

Shape into a roll and sprinkle with browned bread crumbs and melted butter.

Place in a well-buttered pan and bake for ½ hour at 375° F.

Serve with Hard-boiled Egg Sauce (p. 152) or Cheese Sauce (p. 35).

SALMON KEDGEREE

(Serves 3–4)

> *1 to 1½ cups flaked boiled salmon*
> *1 to 1½ cups cooked rice*
> *2 hard-boiled eggs, chopped*
> *salt and pepper*
> *2 ounces melted butter*
> *chopped parsley*

In the top of a double boiler, melt the butter over boiling water.

Add the flaked fish and the cooked rice, tossing together lightly with a fork.

Add the chopped eggs, again tossing together lightly with a fork.

Add salt and pepper to taste.

Garnish with chopped parsley and serve.

SOLE VERONIQUE
(Serves 6)

Preheat oven to 350° F.

> *6 fillets of sole*
> *salt and pepper*
> *½ cup white wine*
> *1 cup cream sauce*
> *1 cup small white grapes (these can*
> *   now be bought in cans)*

Put the fillets of sole in a buttered flat ovenproof dish which you can use for serving.

Add salt and pepper to taste and pour the white wine over them.

Cover the pan with foil and bake for 15 minutes in a 350° F. oven.

Meanwhile, make the cream sauce: melt 2 tablespoons butter, add 2 tablespoons flour, cook for 3 minutes, add 1 cup milk and cook till thick, stirring constantly.

Pour off the juice from the fish and add to the cream sauce, mixing well.

Add half the grapes to the sauce.

Pour all this over the fish in the ovenproof dish and place under the broiler just long enough to brown the surface.

Place the rest of the grapes around the fish before serving.

SALMON KOLOUBIAKA (Russian Pirogue of Fish)
(Serves 6–8)

Preheat oven to 475° F.

> For the crust
> *½ cup heavy cream*
> *½ tablespoon sour cream*
> *1 egg*
> *1 teaspoon double-acting baking*
> *   powder*
> *6½ tablespoons butter*
> *1¼ cups sifted pastry flour*

For the filling

½ pound smoked salmon
1½ pounds fresh salmon
2 heaping tablespoons cut dill
1 tablespoon chopped parsley
2 hard-boiled eggs
½ cup long-grain rice
2 tablespoons sifted bread crumbs
salt and pepper to taste
9 tablespoons butter

For the sauce

¾ pound butter
2 teaspoons curry powder
strained juice of 1 lemon
2 tablespoons cut dill

Buy 1½ pounds fresh salmon cut in slices 1 inch thick, and ½ pound smoked salmon.

Prepare 2 heaping tablespoons finely cut dill and 1 tablespoon chopped parsley.

Hard-boil 2 eggs, plunge in cold water and remove shells.

Cook ½ cup long-grain rice in 1 cup water with ½ table-spoon butter, following directions on the box.

When done, stir in 2 tablespoons butter.

Have ready 2 tablespoons fine sifted bread crumbs.

Cut the smoked salmon in small pieces.

Melt 6 tablespoons butter in a frying pan, add the sliced fresh salmon and cook on moderate heat, 5 minutes on either side.

Set aside until cool enough to handle, at which time carefully strain off but save the buttery juice from the salmon.

Remove the skin from the salmon and cut the salmon apart, removing any bones you may encounter.

Now mix the dough for the crust.

Mix together ½ cup heavy cream and ½ tablespoon sour cream.

In a separate bowl, beat 1 egg with a rotary beater.

Add half of it to the cream and save the rest to be used for painting the Koloubiaka before baking.

Add 1 teaspoon double-acting baking powder to the cream-and-egg mixture and stir thoroughly.

Now add gradually 1¼ cups sifted pastry flour and mix until the dough is soft and even. Let cool for 20 minutes in the refrigerator.

Remove the dough from the refrigerator and work into it 6 tablespoons soft room-temperature butter, working it well with a spoon until smooth and evenly blended.

Refrigerate for another 20 minutes.

Butter a shallow rectangular jelly-roll tin with 1 teaspoon butter.

Sprinkle a pastry cloth or board generously with flour, and do likewise to a stocking-covered rolling pin.

Roll out the pastry into a rectangular form about 14 by 16 inches. Roll it up quickly onto the rolling pin and unroll it onto the tin, endeavoring to place it in the center, with about 3 inches overlap on either of the long sides.

Flour your hands if you have to handle it.

Now spread over the center the boiled buttered rice.

On top of this place a layer of sliced hard-boiled eggs, then the smoked salmon, followed by the cooked fresh salmon.

Pour over this the strained butter from the sautéed fish and sprinkle with 2 heaping tablespoons cut dill and 1 tablespoon parsley.

Sprinkle with a little salt and coarsely ground pepper.

Join the 2 sides of the overhanging dough and pinch it together to enclose the filling securely.

Close the short ends, rolling them up securely too.

Brush the entire surface with the remainder of the beaten egg.

Sprinkle with the sifted crumbs.

Place immediately in a hot oven and bake at 475° F. until lightly browned, or for about ½ hour; reduce heat to 350° F. and continue cooking another 15 minutes, or about 45 minutes in all.

Transfer to a hot serving platter with the aid of two pancake turners, and with a sharp knife cut in slices 1½ inches thick.

Serve at once on hot plates accompanied by a melted-butter curry-and-lemon sauce, made as follows:

Heat ¾ pound butter until hot and stir in 2 teaspoons curry powder, the strained juice of 1 lemon and 2 tablespoons cut dill.

Creamed onions are good with this dish and serve a well-chilled white wine.

FRIED HERRING

> *herrings*
> *flour*
> *salt and pepper*

Scrape off the scales, cut off the heads and fins and clean the herrings.

Dry well.

Dip in flour seasoned with salt and pepper.

Fry in hot fat in a frying pan till crisp and brown on both sides.

INDIVIDUAL LOBSTER MOUSSE

(Serves 8)

> *1 envelope plain gelatin*
> *1 cup cold water*
> *1 cup boiling water*
> *1 cup Mayonnaise*
> *1 cup cream, whipped stiff*
> *2 cups cooked lobster, chopped into small pieces,*
> *or 2 6-ounce cans lobster meat*

Soften the gelatin in cold water for 5 minutes.

Add the boiling water and stir to dissolve.

Put in the refrigerator until slightly thickened.

Mix together the mayonnaise and whipped cream.

Add to the gelatin and mix well.

Add the lobster meat.

Put into 8 individual glass dishes.

Leave in the refrigerator until firm.

Serve in the glass dishes, garnished with chopped parsley.

If you wish to unmold the mousse, double the amount of gelatin.

INDIVIDUAL CRAB MOUSSE

Follow the recipe for Lobster Mousse (above), substituting crab flakes for the lobster in the same quantity.

SMOKED SALMON

On each individual serving plate put wafer-thin slices of smoked Irish salmon, with a few capers, a little chopped hard-boiled egg and a little very finely chopped white onion.

Serve with a wedge of lemon and a pepper grinder for lots of freshly ground pepper.

Thin slices of buttered brown soda bread must be served with this.

SMOKED TROUT

With smoked trout, serve an Unfrozen Sauce of Whipped Sweet Cream and White Horseradish (p. 151).

KIPPERS—IRISH STYLE

Eat this for breakfast with brown bread and butter.

Cover the kippers with boiling water for 5 minutes and then drain well.

Place on a flat buttered pan and cook in a 450° F. oven for 10 minutes.

CREAMED LOBSTER

(Serves 2)

4 tablespoons butter
1 minced shallot
2 tablespoons flour
¾ cup cream
4 tablespoons Irish whisky
1 pound fresh lobster meat cut in small pieces or
*   1 pound canned lobster, carefully separated into pieces*

Melt the butter, add the shallot and cook until tender.
Add the flour, cook and stir for 3 minutes.
Remove from the heat.
Add the cream slowly, stirring constantly.
Return to the heat and cook until thick, stirring constantly.
Add the Irish whisky.
Add the lobster and cook until heated through.
Serve with dry hot boiled rice.

SEA KALE

Sea kale is a vegetable that resembles both asparagus and celery. It is very delicate in flavor and is in season in Ireland and England in the early spring. The plants are started outdoors in August and left through the winter. They can successfully be forced in boxes or flats in a cool cellar by bringing the plants in from the garden in mid-February for use in a month's time.

Put sea kale into boiling salted water and cook till tender, approximately 15 minutes.
Drain well and pour over melted butter with salt and pepper.

CAULIFLOWER FRITTERS

1 head cauliflower
fat for frying (375° F.) in a deep kettle

For the batter

1 cup flour
½ teaspoon salt
dash pepper
⅔ cup milk
1 egg, beaten

Boil the cauliflower until tender, cool and break into sections.
Prepare the batter by mixing the flour with salt and pepper.
Add the milk, mixing until smooth.
Add the beaten egg.
Dip the cauliflower sections into the batter and fry.
Have fat at 375° F.
Dip a spoon into the hot fat and then pick up the pieces of coated cauliflower on the spoon and slide them into the hot fat.
Cook only a few pieces at a time for 3 to 5 minutes until golden brown.
Remove from the fat with a slotted spoon and drain well on paper.
They should be crisp and dry when served.

BAKED POTATO

Preheat oven to 450° F.
Scrub large baking potatoes and bake in a hot oven until tender, about 1 hour.
Split the skin across the top and squeeze the hot potato slightly to open it up.
Sprinkle with salt, put a good piece of sweet butter in the opening and cover with buttermilk.

Champ is smooth mashed potatoes, well seasoned with salt and pepper and various kinds of cooked vegetables mixed in.

Irish champ was always made with a beetle, which is just an old-fashioned wooden potato masher.

A lot of pounding was done to make sure there were no lumps, but today we put the boiled potatoes through a ricer or whip them up with a kitchen mixer.

Children used to sing an old song:

[*414*]

There was an old woman
who lived in a lamp.
She had no room
to beetle her champ.

Champ is used as a main country dish, piled on hot plates
with a hole in the center filled with melted butter. Each forkful
is dipped in the butter first.
A jug of buttermilk is the classic accompaniment for champ.

CHAMP WITH ONIONS

Chop fine 2 or 3 white onions, cook in butter till golden brown.
Mix into hot mashed potatoes.

CHAMP WITH CABBAGE

Shred some cabbage fine, put into a frying pan with a lump of
butter, cover the pan closely and cook about 10 minutes, shaking the pan every few minutes or stirring occasionally.
Mix into hot mashed potatoes.

CHAMP WITH PEAS

Add hot cooked peas to hot mashed potatoes.
You can mash the peas too, if you like, or mix them in whole.

CHAMP WITH CHIVES

Chop a cupful of chives and add to hot mashed potatoes.

POTATO CAKES

1 pound mashed potatoes
1 cup flour
1 teaspoon salt
4 tablespoons butter, melted
1 beaten egg
1 teaspoon baking powder

Add the salt, melted butter and beaten egg to the mashed potato.

Sift the baking powder and flour together.

Mix in as much of the flour as is needed to make a soft dough.

Roll out or pat out to ½ inch thickness.

Fry on a hot griddle or buttered frying pan until light brown.

Eat hot with melted butter and honey.

JERUSALEM ARTICHOKES AU GRATIN
(Serves 4–6)

Preheat oven to 375° F.

1 pound artichokes
2 tablespoons butter
2 tablespoons flour
1 cup milk
salt and pepper
grated cheese, Parmesan or Cheddar
crumbs, buttered

Scrub and peel the artichokes.

Cut in half and cook in boiling, salted water for 25 minutes, or until tender.

Drain well and put into a shallow ovenproof dish.

Make a cream sauce with the butter, flour, milk, salt and pepper.

Pour the sauce over the artichokes.

Sprinkle with cheese and crumbs.

Bake in a 375° F. oven for 30 minutes until browned.

MUSHROOMS
(Serves 4–6)

1 pound mushrooms
½ cup chicken broth
4 tablespoons butter
¼ teaspoon lemon juice
salt and pepper

Wash, peel and stem the mushrooms.

[*416*]

Put into a pan with the butter, chicken broth, lemon juice, salt and pepper.

Cook, covered tightly, for 5 minutes.

Remove the cover and cook till the broth evaporates.

CARROTS

(Serves 4)

> *1 pound carrots*
> *4 tablespoons butter*
> *¼ teaspoon lemon juice*
> *½ cup chicken broth or beef consommé*
> *¼ teaspoon sugar*

Scrub and peel the carrots and cut into thin slices.

Put in a saucepan with the other ingredients.

Bring to a boil and cover the pan.

Simmer ½ hour or less, until the liquid evaporates.

Serve with chopped parsley.

BRAISED CARROTS

(Serves 4–6)

Preheat oven to 325° F.

> *1 pound tiny young carrots about 3 inches long*
> *4 tablespoons butter*
> *1 cup beef stock or beef consommé*
> *1 teaspoon flour*

Scrub and scrape the baby carrots and leave whole.

Cut off the tops and root end.

Melt the butter and fry the carrots slowly until brown.

Sprinkle with the flour and cook for a few minutes more, stirring.

Place in an ovenproof shallow dish.

Pour on the beef stock and bake slowly for 1 hour in a 325° F. oven.

STUFFED CUCUMBERS
(Serves 4–6)

Preheat oven to 350° F.

3 large cucumbers
1 cup fine bread crumbs
1 teaspoon chopped parsley
4 tablespoons melted butter
1 cup chopped cooked meat—ham, beef or lamb
a little gravy or stock
salt and pepper
oregano or any herb flavoring you like
a little grated onion
2 tablespoons ketchup

Cut the cucumbers into 3-inch pieces and remove half the skin in alternate strips.

Remove the centers carefully, not breaking the pieces.

Parboil the cucumbers for 5 minutes.

Drain well and cool.

Mix all the other ingredients to make a moist stuffing.

Put the cucumbers in a buttered, shallow ovenproof dish and pack the centers with the stuffing.

Cover the pan with aluminum foil, bake at 350° F. for about 15 minutes.

Uncover for the last 5 minutes.

Serve with Tomato Sauce (p. 37).

PEACH MIST MELBA

For each portion:

On a bed of vanilla ice cream, place a fine fresh ripe peach which has been peeled and sprinkled with sugar (or use a canned ripe peach).

Cover with Sabayon Sauce (p. 178).

SURPRISE ICE CREAM

Make a fine fruit salad of fresh fruit—thin-sliced ripe pears, peaches, apples, orange sections and any other fresh fruit or berries. (If you use bananas, add them at the last minute to keep them from turning brown.)

To each cup of fruit add 2 tablespoons liqueur—maraschino or Irish Mist—and let stand in the refrigerator for 1 hour.

For each portion:

Place a good amount of the fruit salad in the bottom of an individual sherbet glass and cover with half orange ice and half vanilla ice cream.

Garnish with whipped cream.

SUMMER PUDDING

(Serves 4)

slices of buttered white bread without crust
1 pound raspberries
½ pound red currants
sugar

Line a buttered 2-quart bowl with slices of white bread, crusts removed.

Remove the currants from their stems.

Simmer the raspberries and currants, with sugar to taste, for ten minutes.

Add no water, and stir often.

Pour the stewed fruit into the bread-lined bowl, cover with more slices of buttered bread and leave in the refrigerator for 24 hours.

Turn out upside down and serve with Boiled Custard (p. 54).

GINGER BAVARIAN CREAM

(Serves 4–6)

1 cup preserved ginger, cut fine
1 envelope plain gelatin
2 tablespoons cold water
1 cup milk
2 egg whites
4 egg yolks

½ cup granulated sugar
2 cups heavy cream
4 tablespoons ginger syrup

Prepare the finely cut preserved ginger (the kind that comes packed in a syrup).

Soak the gelatin in the cold water.

Make a custard of the milk and egg yolks, sweetened with the granulated sugar.

Cook over boiling water until thickened, stirring constantly.

Add the gelatin and stir until dissolved, removing the pan from the heat.

Cool and chill in the refrigerator until it begins to jell, at which time beat well with a rotary beater.

Next fold in 1 cup heavy cream beaten until stiff and the whites of 2 eggs likewise beaten until stiff but not dry.

Last of all, fold in ½ cup finely cut ginger (minus syrup).

Pour into a 1½-quart mold and chill for several hours.

When ready to serve, turn out onto a pretty platter and surround with the remaining ½ cup cut ginger, to which you have added 4 tablespoons of the ginger syrup.

Serve with this a pitcher of heavy cream—not beaten, however.

COFFEE BAVARIAN CREAM
(Serves 6–8)

2 envelopes plain gelatin
2¼ cups water
½ cup coffee (drip grind)
4 eggs
1 cup milk
½ cup granulated sugar
2 cups heavy cream

Moisten the coffee with 2 cups cold water.

Bring to a boil and simmer about 5 minutes.

Line a fine strainer with cheesecloth and strain the hot coffee into a little pan.

This should give you 1 cup of very strong coffee.

Soak the gelatin in ¼ cup cold water for 5 minutes.

Bring the coffee to a boil, remove from the fire and add the gelatin.

Stir until completely melted.

Heat the milk with the sugar in the top of a double boiler, over boiling water.

Beat the egg yolks well, add some of the hot milk gradually to the yolks, then stir this into the remainder of the hot milk.

Cook, stirring constantly, until thickened or for a minute or two, then stir it into the coffee and gelatin.

Next add the heavy cream.

Cool, then refrigerate until it is about to become stiff, or for about ¾ hour.

Beat with a rotary beater for 5 minutes.

Fold in the egg whites, beaten until stiff.

When the whites have completely disappeared and the mixture is smooth, pour into a 2-quart mold, rinsed in cold water.

Cover and refrigerate until set stiff, or for about 2 to 3 hours.

When ready to serve, run a knife around the edge of mold and turn out onto a serving dish, and serve, with or without slightly beaten heavy cream.

SABAYON SAUCE FOR SOUFFLES

> *1 cup white wine*
> *juice of ½ lemon*
> *½ cup sugar*
> *2 eggs*
> *2 tablespoons corn flour*
> *½ cup whipped cream*
> *¼ cup Irish Mist liqueur*

In the top of a double boiler, mix together all the ingredients except the cream and the Irish Mist.

Cook over boiling water, but without the bottom of the top section touching the water, and whip constantly with a wire whisk until thick.

Remove from the boiling water and gently fold in the whipped cream and Irish Mist liqueur.

SWEET YORKSHIRE PUDDING

Although we think of Yorkshire pudding as an accompanying dish for roast beef, it is much used as a sweet dessert in country homes. Serve it hot and crisp with melted butter and syrup poured over, and you can even dress it up with a dash of good thick fresh cream on top of the whole thing.

Preheat oven to 450° F.

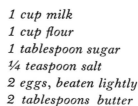

> 1 cup milk
> 1 cup flour
> 1 tablespoon sugar
> ¼ teaspoon salt
> 2 eggs, beaten lightly
> 2 tablespoons butter

Mix together the flour, salt and sugar.

Add the milk to make a smooth paste.

Add the eggs and beat with an egg beater or in an electric mixer for 2 minutes.

Prepare 2 bread pans 9 x 4 x 3 inches by putting in each one 2 tablespoons of butter.

But before you start beating the batter, put the pans into the hot oven so the butter will melt *but not burn* and then pour the batter into the piping-hot pans.

Batter should be only about ½ inch deep.

Bake at 450° F. for 25 minutes or until puffed up and golden brown.

Turn out of the pans, cut into squares and serve hot with maple syrup and cream poured on each piece.

BANANA DESSERT

> *sliced bananas*
> *whipped cream*
> *sugar*
> *shaved sweet milk chocolate*

In a glass serving bowl put sliced bananas, dusted with sugar.

Pour whipped cream over the top.

Cover the cream with a thin layer of finely shaved sweet chocolate.

Prepare just before serving so the bananas won't turn brown.

BLACK CURRANT TART
(Serves 6)

Preheat oven to 450° F.

> *Plain Pastry for a 2-crust pie (p. 153)*
> *egg white*
> *stewed black currants*
> *¾ cup sugar*
> *cream*
> *2 tablespoons minute tapioca*

Line a 9-inch pie pan with pastry.
Brush the pastry with beaten egg white.
Fill the pan with stewed black currants.
Sprinkle the tapioca and sugar over the berries.
Put on the top crust, prick well and bake in 450° F. oven for 15 minutes, then reduce heat to 350° for 30 minutes more.
Use aluminum foil under the pan because this is a very juicy pie.
Serve with thick fresh cream to pour over.

BRAMBLE DEEP-DISH PIE
(Serves 6)

In early September everyone goes to pick the wild blackberries, called brambles, which grow in high hedges along the country lanes. They make delicious deep-dish pies.

Preheat oven to 450° F.

> *Plain Pastry (p. 153)*
> *blackberries, about a quart*
> *¾ cup sugar*
> *½ teaspoon salt*
> *cinnamon*
> *2 tablespoons tapioca*
> *cream*

In a shallow baking dish put the cleaned washed berries, 2 inches deep.

Mix together the sugar, cinnamon, salt and tapioca.

Sprinkle over the berries.

Put a pastry top on the dish and prick well.

Bake in a 450° F. oven for 15 minutes, then at 400° for 30 minutes more.

Serve with thick fresh cream to pour on.

PEAR AND ORANGE SALAD

(Serves 6)

Peel and cut in half 3 ripe pears.

Remove the seeds.

Cook gently in medium syrup (1 cup sugar to 1 cup water) until tender.

Cool and slice.

(Sliced canned pears may be used.)

Peel and prepare 2 oranges in sections, removing any pits.

Arrange the sliced pears and orange sections and orange juice in a deep dish.

To the syrup in which the pears were cooked (or to the syrup from the canned pears), add 4 tablespoons Irish Mist liqueur and pour into the dish.

Chill thoroughly for several hours before serving.

FRUIT SALAD

peeled and sliced ripe pears
peeled and sliced ripe apples
peeled and sliced ripe peaches
peeled and sliced ripe bananas
peeled and sliced ripe oranges
fresh berries in season

Sprinkle the fruit with sugar to taste, and flavor with a few tablespoons maraschino liqueur.

Serve with thick fresh cream to pour on.

Don't prepare until the last possible minute so the fruit slices will look fresh and bright.

IRISH COFFEE

Irish Coffee can be made with Irish whisky or American Bour-bon whisky.

For each person:

In a stemmed goblet put 1 level teaspoon fine granulated sugar.

Fill the glass ¾ full with very hot coffee.

Stir quickly to dissolve the sugar.

Add 1 ounce of your preferred whisky or liqueur and stir once.

Top off with heavy thick cream poured on over the top of an upside-down spoon held just over the top of the coffee so the cream floats on the surface about ½ inch thick.

Do not stir!

The true flavor comes only by drinking the hot coffee through the cold thick cream.

EPILOGUE

I haven't really come to the end, for the more I searched into my memories and experiences, the more it seemed to me that I could go on forever and fill more pages—but enough is enough!

I still have a great many plans for the future. The whole world is coming closer together all the time, and there is so much to do that is new and exciting.

Just the other day I met a friend who had been off on a long trip. "For goodness sake!" he said. "What are you doing with Pepperidge products in Hong Kong! I was coming along a street there and saw some people staring in a store window, and there was a display of your products." That didn't seem a bit strange to me, for the Pepperidge Farm name is encountered now from Iceland to South Africa.

We have started moving out into far parts, and perhaps I shall keep looking for more recipes for the next book. ("Heaven forbid!" says my husband.)

INDEX

Entries in *italics* refer to Part Four, *Cooking from Antique Cookbooks*